HOUSES IN MOTION

THE GENESIS, HISTORY AND DEVELOPMENT OF THE PORTABLE BUILDING

Second Edition

Robert Kronenburg

To Lisa

*House in motion was an integral component of our
house service industry.* Buckminster Fuller

*I'm walking a line. I'm visiting houses in motion.
I'm walking a line. Just barely enough to be living.*
David Byrne

HOUSES IN MOTION

THE GENESIS, HISTORY AND DEVELOPMENT OF THE PORTABLE BUILDING

Second Edition

Robert Kronenburg

WILEY-ACADEMY

Acknowledgements

My interest in portable architecture began when I was a student of architecture and I was fortunate enough to win, with two colleagues, an RIBA sponsored competition for a mobile public information centre. Our design was built and I think we all learnt a lot from it. For myself, the excitement of seeing an urban space take on a new meaning because of the architectural presence created by a transient object has lingered. I have been involved in the creation of temporary and transient architecture since then; however, it is only in the last five years that I have been able to carry out the concentrated research that forms the basis of this book. In that time I have met many architects, engineers, designers and researchers who have shown interest and provided help and advice and I would like to thank them all. Though they may not share the opinions expressed in the book, which are my own, I owe special thanks to: Dr Rob MacDonald, who was one of the three who won the competition and is now my much respected colleague and always a good source of encouragement and advice; Dr Paul Oliver, editor of the *World Encyclopedia of Vernacular Architecture*, whose advice to me when preparing pieces for that book has proven as valuable for this; Michael Spens for his support in the publication of the first edition of this book; and Maggie Toy for the second.

Robert Kronenburg

The author and publishers would like to thank those who have kindly permitted the use of images in the illustration of this book. Attempts have been made to locate all the sources of illustrations to obtain full reproduction rights, but in the very few instances where this process has failed to find the copyright holder, apologies are offered.

Abbeville Press (8); Academy (134, 135, 136), courtesy of Lebbeus Woods (133, 151, 152); Appicella Associates (198, 199, 200); Author (1, 3, 9, 10, 12, 12a, 13, 16, 17, 19, 20, 21, 23, 24, 31, 36, 62, 65, 73, 86, 97, 99, 116, 132, 154, 156, 164, 165, 166, 167, 168, 169, 171a, 171b, 172, 173, 178, 181, 183, 184, 184a, 187, 188, 191, 213); Archigram © Reproduced with kind permission of Birkhäuser Verlag AG, Basle from the 1991 reprint edition (137, 138, 139, 140, 141); Aluminium Federation (81); *Architectural Design* (57); Architectural Press (74 above); photograph by Skyfotos Ltd, Ashford Airport, Hythe, Kent (71); Architectural Record (50, 96); *Architectural Review* (79); Tadao Ando (84); photograph by Yoshio Shiratori (82); Barrie and Jenkins, diagram by Paul Verity (14); Benthem and Crouwel, Architekten (111); © Bibliothèque Nationale de France (40); Bodleian Library, Oxford (190); British Aluminium Company (128); The British Library, London (41, 42, 44, 45, 47, 64); Buckminster Fuller Institute © 1960 (49, 51, 52, 53); © 1967 Allegra Fuller Snyder (56) courtesy; Buckminster Fuller Institute, Santa Barbara. For more information about the work of Buckminster Fuller contact: The Buckminster Fuller Institute, 2040 Alameda Padre Serra, Suite 224, Santa Barbara, CA 93103, USA +1-805-962-0022; *Building Design* (103); Buro Happold (192); Butterworth Architecture (113 below); California Historical Society, San Francisco (125); Cannobio, Milan (90); CargoLifter AG (34a); Chancellor Press, London (26); Chicago Art Institute (35); Crosby Lockwood Staples (27, 33, 34); photograph by Alo Zanetta Foto-grafica (118); Editions du Moniteur, courtesy of the Jean Villiers Collection (38, 39); EP Dutton and Co (153); Sue Ellis (129); ESCO, Tokyo (102); Eyre Methuen (32); Festo KG (207, 208, 209, 210, 211); Dr F Fisher (107, 108); Fleetway Publications (54); Mark Fisher (121); Mark Fisher and Jonathan Park (122); Margaret Fitzgibbon (37); FTL Architects, New York (120); FTL Happold Design and Engineering Studio (194, 195); Future Systems (145, 146, 147, 148, 149, 150, 186); Garrat Corporation (75, 76); Nicholas Grimshaw and Partners, photograph by Jo Reid and John Peck, London (117, 117a); Richard Horden (110); David Hutton, Barrier Reef Holdings Ltd, Australia (105); Imperial War Museum, London, photographs by Terence Fowler (68, 69); Institution of Civil Engineers (67, 70, 72); Institution of Royal Engineers, UK (63, 74 below); Kansas State Historical Society (11, 91); Lanchart Industries (92); Landesbildstelle Berlin (189); Maki and Associates (205, 206); Keith Mallory and Arvid Ottar (66); photograph courtesy of Andrew Reid/Martin Pawley, London (80); Martin Marietta Astronautics Group, Denver (160); Meyer Shipbuilding Works (31a); Mitsui Engineering and Shipbuilding Co Ltd, Tokyo (102a); Jean-Paul Morel and Partners (196, 197); Musée des Arts et Traditions Populaires, Paris (180); NASA (157, 158, 160a, 161, 163); National Automotive History Collection, Detroit Public Library (93); National Partitions and Interiors Inc, Florida (88); National Recreation Vehicles (174, 177); Ohio Historical Society (78); Office for Mobile Design (201, 202, 203, 204); Oosterhuis.nl (212); Frei Otto (58, 59, 61); OXFAM (126); Oxford University Press (95, 100); P&O Cruises, London (175); Pall Mall Press, photograph courtesy of Bayer Chemicals, Germany (127); Peterson Industries Inc, Kansas (98); Renzo Piano Building Workshop, photographs by Berengo Gardin (109, 112, 113 top, 114, 115, 119, 182); Riken Yamamoto and Field Shop (179); Cedric Price (142, 143, 144); *Progressive Architecture* (101, 104); The British Architectural Library, RIBA, London (46); ROFI Industrier AS, Norway (130); Aldo Rossi (83, 85); Rubb Building Co (89); Shelter Publications Inc (18, 55); *The Shipbuilder*, Patrick Stephens Ltd (25, 29, 30); TEPE Prefabricated Building Industries and Trade Co, Inc, Ankara, Turkey (131); Texas A&M University (162); UNDHA (124); Victoria and Albert Collection, courtesy of the Board of Trustees (48); Dr Fritz Vollrath, Oxford University (28); Wernick Buildings (185).

Cover: AT&T Global Olympic Village, Atlanta, USA by FTL Happold Design and Building Engineering; *Back cover*: Prototype recyclable portable fabric skyscraper by FTL Happold Design and Building Engineering; *Page 2*: Takashima-Cho Gate by Riken Yamamoto and Field Shop, 1989

First edition published in 1995.
Second edition first published in Great Britain in 2002 by
WILEY-ACADEMY
A division of JOHN WILEY & SONS
Baffins Lane, Chichester, West Sussex PO19 1UD

ISBN: 0-470-84331-4

Printed and bound in the UK
by TJ International Ltd, Padstow, Cornwall

Contents

FOREWORD

When *Houses in Motion* was first published in 1995, for me it seemed like a culmination of many years' work, initially as a practitioner designing and constructing mostly conventional buildings (though two were genuinely portable) and subsequently as a researcher attempting to pull together the strands of something complex, holistic, and to me at least, new. Of course, it turned out to be just the start. Since then, there have been two conferences, two exhibitions, further books, journal essays and consultancy. I am gratified to have been kept so busy, but I realise it is not because of me, but because of the subject.

Portable architecture is an area of design that grasps the imagination; it is a field that is expanding and which is gaining in relevance. In the past six years I have perceived a marked increase in the number and quality of portable buildings that are being built. The range of purposes for which they are being provided is wide and though some are still uniquely experimental or prototypical, many more are now being commissioned by clients and organisations that are setting aside a more conservative approach to their problem in order to find a solution that will be more successful. As it has at other times in history, portable building is re-entering the architectural mainstream.

If there is an increase in the number of the innovative buildings being designed and built it is a reflection of what is happening in the construction industry as a whole. New technology is revolutionising all aspects of the manufactured world and we can confidently predict that information technology, automation, intelligent building systems, and new materials will bring significant changes to the way that buildings are made and operated in the next decade. The way we inhabit the world is also in flux – lifestyle, working patterns and ecological issues are fundamentally altering the way we use buildings and the role that they play in society and in shaping the world's environment. It is therefore not surprising that a building type that seems to respond to change rather than resist it seems to possess a new relevance.

The first edition of *Houses in Motion* was intended to be an exploration of the portable building as an architecturally distinct genre – reviewing its beginnings and the more recent history that has influenced the design of contemporary examples. With this second edition I have set out to update this material and correct some important omissions without changing unduly the scope of the book. Much new material has come to my attention in the intervening years, and information which is crucial to the story of portable architecture has been added. However, I have purposely not included detailed information which is available elsewhere, either in my own work or in the work of others who are now adding valuable new perspectives to the field. The new final chapter to this edition explores how the changes described above are affecting the design of portable architecture, and the role it might have in influencing the form and construction of all architecture in the future.

Robert Kronenburg
University of Liverpool
August 2001

FOREWORD TO THE FIRST EDITION

In the 1970s, before the start of the school term in September, a large part of the nation's classroom accommodation was relocated. Temporary buildings were dismantled and reassembled and moved as components or complete units. These moving buildings were a familiar sight as they trundled across the countryside in a gigantic game of musical chairs. Temporary buildings or 'huts' remain a permanent part of all educational organisations, despite all efforts to eradicate them. They represent an estate within an estate and a county like Hampshire has had in excess of 1,000, though thankfully, now only 600. These portable buildings have always been reviled and one wonders why a more satisfactory answer has not been found to solve the fluctuations in pupil numbers or demographic trends. Over several decades some 15 per cent of educational space was categorised as temporary even though many of these buildings represented permanent accommodation (some have been in service for over 40 years). Each education authority can still parade a whole range of broadly similar proprietary types such as Medway or HORSA huts.

Can the current state of portable buildings used in this context be an indication of something more fundamental? There is seldom evidence of enlightened thinking or an elegant solution in this field. The educational hut seems as much a stereotype as system building was in the 1960s. Most portable buildings fall short of their primary purpose of being easily relocatable and suffer the worst characteristics of permanent buildings. Is this impoverishment of thinking caused by political expediency, a lack of forward planning or administrative and design incompetence, or does this whole issue reveal an inherent prejudice against portable buildings: that they are an unfortunate and undesirable necessity that somehow must be tolerated without any understanding of their potential? The mistaken assumption in this process is that the ephemeral solution must be *de facto*, cheap. If account is taken of land investment, infrastructure, caretaking, security risk, maintenance, environmental damage and the overall waste of surplus places, one realises the cost of the building is only a small part of this whole dynamic process. I have touched on only one aspect of the use of portable buildings, but even in this narrow context, the subject is far reaching for those involved in building management.

Robert Kronenburg applies considerable scholarship to an issue that has for too long been ignored, neglected or abused. I have tried to demonstrate the scale of this involvement in just one area that affects us all; however, the use of temporary buildings is not always the consequence of such a premeditated contingency. They are seldom preplanned or anticipated, or their implications fully understood. An impoverished culture has been created as a result of cheap politics and mean vision. With more imagination, innovation, better management and design, that tradition could be transformed. A genuine portable building culture is indispensable given the dynamic challenges of the twenty-first century. This book spells out a worthy aspiration and a relevant and needed focus.

Colin Stansfield-Smith

Robert Kronenburg, Ph.D., RIBA, is an architect and senior lecturer at the University of Liverpool, School of Architecture and Building Engineering, United Kingdom. His books include Portable Architecture, FTL: Softness Movement and Light, *and* Spirit of the Machine. *His research has been supported by the Building Centre Trust, London, the Graham Foundation, Chicago, the US Fulbright commission, St. John's College, Oxford University, and the Leverhulme Trust. He curated* Portable Architecture *at the Royal Institute of British Architects, London, the touring event* Spontaneous Construction, *and he is a member of the curatorial team of the Vitra Museum's international exhibition* Living in Motion.

INTRODUCTION

The Cultural Importance of Portable Architecture

The kinetic object has an innate potency that has persisted throughout human design history. Power, speed, intelligence, beauty, can all be conveyed in the vehicles which have always expressed significant technological advances in the most visible way. When these moving objects possess other functions associated with the rituals and circumstances of dwelling, commerce and industry, this significance is reinforced and in some cases reinvented. Yet moving buildings are amongst the earliest artifacts created by man, predating vehicles, and have a persisting relevance that enables a Bedouin tent to exist in the same world as a 90,000 ton aircraft carrier which is a moving home to 5,500 people.

1

The usual perception of temporary architecture is, however, of impermanent, transient, low-quality building, neither tuned to its purpose nor appropriate to its site. Yet there is no more profound indication of the need for study of the current state of design and manufacture of portable and demountable buildings than the images displayed in the media each time a major disaster occurs and the resultant homeless are seen sheltered in inadequate, makeshift accommodation.

2

In the developed world, commercially manufactured demountable buildings are already used in many diverse locations – in commerce, industry, education, health care, housing, and the military. Yet the varied products used in these roles, though considerably more sophisticated in materials and construction, seem to have evolved through an *ad hoc* design process. They appear to be made with little more care than that used by the refugee, who has to rapidly erect the best shelter he can manage in the shortest time with the minimum of materials. Very few demountable buildings have been designed for a dedicated user with that user's specific requirements in mind. Indeed, very few make much use of knowledge from designs that have gone before and the sometimes more advanced technology available in other unrelated applications.

This book examines the genesis, history and development of portable, demountable and relocatable architecture; makes an assessment of contemporary examples by designers, builders, and manufacturers; and explores the products of unrelated industries where the possibility of technology transferred to this area of design has yet to be assessed. Inherent in this study is the necessity not only to explore the physical manifestations of the type but to also examine the underlying philosophical, cultural and social issues that have shaped their creation. It is in this area that the relationship between architectural form and suitability to purpose can be effectively gauged, and the lessons drawn applied to future design work.

A Definition of the Movable Building

The architectural forms studied here are those that have a strictly ephemeral nature – that are movable in some form, and are designed specifically for deployment in different situations and/or locations. Though some possess characteristics from more than one category, temporary building systems can be simply divided into three specific types, listed below:

Portable buildings are those that are transported whole and intact. Sometimes they include the method for transport within their own structure (wheels, hull) and can be towed or carried – a few can be described as self-powered. However, the dividing line between building and vehicle then becomes blurred.

Relocatable buildings are those that are transported in parts but are assembled at the site almost instantly into usable built form. These are almost always carried but in a few limited cases may have part of their transportation system incorporated into their structure. The main advantage of this type is that it can provide space almost as quickly as the portable building without restriction in size imposed by transportation.

1 Mobile home in transport, Kansas, 1994;
2 A 4.26 m diameter GRP igloo, by Cohos, De Lasalle and Evany, Calgary, Alberta, 1967

3

4

5

Demountable buildings are those that are transported in a number of parts for assembly on site. They are much more flexible in size and layout and can usually be transported in a relatively compact space. They have some of the limitations that site operations bring to a conventional building and, depending on the size, complexity, and ingenuity of the system, are not as instantly available.

These building types can be further divided into deployment categories: module, flat pack, tensile, pneumatic and combined system. The study has examined buildings of this nature from all sources: vernacular and traditional architecture, the building industry, architectural design, product design, transportation and vehicle production. Prefabricated and pre-manufactured building systems have also been examined but only in reference to how their production techniques might impact on the field of transportable buildings. These definitions can effectively be applied to all movable buildings from the first prehistoric shelter to the International Space Station, and from the simplest portable temporary grass thatched dwelling to a large, technologically ambitious demountable exhibition building.

Within these general classifications there is, however, a wide range of variations in size, form and function. Relatively small portable and demountable buildings are commonplace objects that form part of the background of our urban and rural environments. Sometimes sympathetic, they are more usually an unwelcome intrusion that exemplifies the unconsidered approach habitually taken in their design and siting. On occasion a temporary building is called upon to fulfil a function that relates to an individual's organisational or social image, purpose or ambition. In this case, if an enlightened approach is taken to the design, a reusable building can result rather than one which is wastefully abandoned. The Crystal Palace (the 1851 Great Exhibition building by Sir Joseph Paxton) and more recently the British Pavilion at Expo 1992, a building by Nicholas Grimshaw and Partners and influenced by Paxton, are both buildings of an ephemeral and reusable nature that also express a strong cultural and technological statement. These two happen to be exhibition buildings and yet there is hardly any field of human activity which requires enclosed structures that does not utilise movable buildings in some form – the portable building can be found in all spheres of human activity. Yet it is only in a small percentage of these cases that the building has been designed specifically for that purpose. This can be seen as a result of one advantage of the type: flexibility and diversity of purpose. Yet it is also certainly one of the reasons portable buildings are not generally recognised as an area of relevant architectural concern.

The definition of the portable building is therefore not a straightforward task. It is in some way linked with the definition of *architecture* in comparison to *building*. Like all inhabitable constructions, these structures must perform the functions of environmental modification and lend themselves adequately to the purpose of the activities carried out within their enclosure. But if they are also to express in their appearance and disposition the physical manifestation of their creators' ambitions, then the building type must be called *architecture*. In some examples this is already the case, and in others it ought to be. A further ambition of those who wish to understand the nature of temporary architecture is therefore to make the distinction between *portable building* and *portable architecture* and to make the case for the relevance and importance of the latter in shaping our current and future built environment.

Human Understanding of Ephemeral Architecture

Movable buildings are a valuable, if comparatively unrecognised, component of the built environment. It has already been stated that they fulfil many roles in many different areas of life and work; it must also be acknowledged that many of these functions could not be carried out in any other way. This functional aspect of their existence is, however, a problem in that the design of these buildings is seen to be a direct solution for a specific task as opposed to a considered response to a series of complex issues. It is reasonable to assess the current perceived status of most contemporary movable buildings as that of convenient tools rather than architecture. For this reason they are created without the cultural and artistic components that are generally attached to even the most functional building

3, 4, 5 'Architecture on the Move'- a mobile exhibition for the RIBA, Liverpool, 1979. Robert Kronenburg, Graham Haworth and Rob MacDonald. The design, based on a 10 ton truck, emphasised the transformation from vehicle to building

designs. In fact, most contemporary movable buildings are created without any significant professional design input whatsoever, the physical result of which is a poor quality product, further degrading their status. Furthermore, there is confusion regarding the temporary nature of these buildings amongst many users and, surprisingly, many manufacturers as well. Disposable products are naturally manufactured in the most economic way as they have only a limited life. However, portable buildings, though temporary in location, are not temporary in use. Their portability is precisely what makes them non-disposable. The fact that they can be reused means that they can be an efficient use of materials and resources and should therefore be designed with care – high quality products tuned to a specific need if not a specific location. The problem of poorly designed and manufactured portable buildings does not go away; it moves somewhere else.

There is no such confusion amongst those who build and use vernacular examples of movable buildings. These peoples express a sophisticated awareness of the essential characteristics of a sense of place and the importance of home as a concept. They perceive their buildings as an essential component in the generation and continuation of those ideas. For these reasons, vernacular architecture is an important resource in the study of the potential of movable buildings, another being the finely tuned response that these buildings bring to often harsh and extreme climates using the minimum of materials in the lightest structural form.

The study of vernacular movable buildings may also help in our understanding of the development of permanent architectural forms. Ephemeral architecture was without doubt man's first form of building. Although examples are generally not present in architectural history books, archaeologists have found sufficient clues to the nature of these artifacts to enable us to understand the essential role they played in the survival of man as a species. Human beings require shelter in order to survive the extremes of the world's climate. When existence is based on a transient lifestyle, as it was for the first humans, the ability to create a portable or temporary shelter is one of the most important man-made factors for their survival. By modifications to the basic shelter, greater comfort and improved serviceability could be incorporated into the building. As man developed the knowledge to engage in agriculture and thereafter establish permanent settlements, the earliest of these buildings undoubtedly became the precursors for permanent structures. The arch and the vault can both be traced back to precedents in temporary architecture.

The nature of nomadic and migratory peoples' relationship with the lands they inhabit can also be examined in order to develop our understanding of one of the crucial factors in creating new environments: the creation of a sense of place. These peoples have an intimate understanding of their place in the landscape which extends to the relationships between their buildings and even to the layout of the interior spaces. Sophisticated and symbolic patterns have been developed

6

7

6 Pick-up truck camper module complete with berths, food preparation and hygiene facilities;
7 An illustration from *The Book of Ser Marco Polo* by Sir Henry Yule, 1871, showing a thirteenth century Tartar encampment with yurts

11

8

9

which aid in the spatial understanding that seems to be an essential factor in human existence. In some societies only the simplest or most ephemeral sign is necessary for people to determine the conceptual image that shapes a range of complex emotions, such as understanding, remembering and belonging. It is not unreasonable to suppose that this comprehension of the physical environment, which brings about universally understood emotions, could provide simple, clearly interpreted clues to human understanding of what makes a sense of place in the built environment. These more readily understood ideas could provide lessons for architects who endeavour to create meaningful public spaces and buildings for a complex society, and dwellings that are appropriate to an individual's concept of home. In essence, these examples show it is possible to create with the most temporary of structures, the most ephemeral of buildings, the most transient of impressions in the landscape (both rural and urban), an architectural identity without architecture.

Portable buildings also have a unique place in the human understanding of the nature of object and place as they can be artifacts that cross cultural and symbolic boundaries. It is normal for even the most land-bound individual to admire the grace and beauty of a sailing ship; its purpose is evident in its shape and form. Yet the structural principles of pneumatics, tension and compressive systems are part of architectural design as well as the fact that this vehicle also contains the function of a dwelling which adds to the romance and excitement conjured in the mind and heart of its admirer. The visual form of transport: ships, cars, trains, aircraft and spacecraft, have all been used by architects to add a specific image to a building, even though the inherent message for a static structure must ultimately be sterile. Truly mobile buildings contain the essence of this romance in their purpose. Therefore they have the additional potential to make use of an extra creative dimension to that of the permanent structure.

The Value of Portable Architecture

Though philosophical design issues are significant, there are also great pragmatic opportunities in the exploration of portable architecture. Movable buildings should be percieved as an important part of all building, and therefore their impact is as complex and significant as that of architecture in general. There are some specific areas where the contribution of moving buildings is especially important: the environmental impact of building; technological development in the construction industry; the provision of shelter after disaster.

It has already been stated that, in general, the potential of the portable building has not been fully explored by industry. Surprisingly, this is not because there has been a lack of interest by the design professions. Since the Second World War there have been many experiments in areas related to the idea of portability in architectural design: for example, prefabrication. This method of construction, which incorporates many types of materials in a multitude of building types, has become one of the options explored by architects and designers when assessing the alternatives for building a project. However, the concept of significant movable components within buildings has been realised, yet not broadly implemented. Buildings are generally completely demolished to make place for new ones, with very little of the old fabric being capable of reuse. In the automotive industry the concept of the recyclable car is now established and in many western countries is controlled by legislation. This includes not just the basic construction materials but entire component assemblies and body shells as well. In a world that is becoming more aware of the limitation of natural resources, the requirement to recycle all the products we manufacture is inevitable. The natural resources of the planet need to be carefully conserved if they are to survive, yet they must be used if they are to retain their meaning. The need for buildings that have minimal and, in many cases, temporary impact on these environments is obvious. What seems to be less clear is that these buildings should have a similar level of care and attention paid to their design as is given to the control of the environment in which they are located.

The complexity of contemporary existence is manifest in every component of life and work. This complexity reveals itself in an ever-changing society that makes new and different requirements continuously. Each generation develops

8 Zep Diner, vehicle imagery in a static structure;
9 'Metamorphosis of the City Lot', project for a demountable structure that would act as a catalyst for the regeneration of vacant sites, David Meis, Kansas State University, 1994

new artifacts appropriate to its level of cultural and technological awareness. Buildings have been and should still be an important part of this legacy. An understanding and knowledge of the fine buildings of the past is an important part of the maintenance of civilisation. However, the requirements of the future need to be understood as well. One of the features of technological innovation in the twentieth century has been that of technology transfer. This involves the utilisation of advances in science and industry in other areas, sometimes quite remote from those in which they were developed. Some scientific fields have resulted in significant 'spin-offs' that have had dramatic repercussions in the way technology and ultimately society has developed. Some fields of industry have become finely tuned to the possibilities of technology transfer – the building industry, with some specific exceptions, has not been one of these. The possibility of utilising advances in materials and construction techniques from the vehicle manufacturing industries alone in the creation of portable buildings is both obvious and exciting. Furthermore, because the portable building must be lightweight in nature and able to cope with the dynamic stress of movement it is well placed to take particular advantage of advances in structural development and materials in other industries. Modular construction techniques which are particularly suitable for demountable buildings can take advantage of factory-based manufacturing methods. Portable building design therefore has the potential to serve the building industry as a whole in the development and application of advanced constructional technology.

All these reasons provide compelling arguments for the study of the current state of movable buildings; however, there is another cause that is perhaps unique in terms of impact. All buildings help to provide adequate levels of comfort and security for their occupants. However, only portable buildings, because of their dynamic nature, have the ability to play an active role in saving lives. Disaster relief activities are an obvious role for the portable building. The lack of shelter in a post-disaster situation can lead to loss of life from exposure and disease that can be in excess of that caused by the disaster itself. It is essential that people caught in these situations are helped within a very short period, 48 hours or less, if that help is to be effective. Temporary shelter which is reusable is a core requirement in this area but equally important, and more so in the long term, is an appropriate level of facilities for medical, administrative, and rebuilding centres, which can be deployed immediately and help nurture such activities during the reconstruction period. There is no doubt that well designed, appropriately used and deployable disaster relief facilities can save lives. However, the vast majority of movable structures used when disasters occur are products developed for a completely different range of circumstances and functions rather than fine-tuned specific responses to a particular problem.

The search for appropriate solutions in this area is therefore of great importance. A greater understanding of the nature of transient architecture could result in a new ecologically aware design strategy – the design of buildings that 'tread lightly on the earth' and still convey the sense of identity and community that is necessary for an established, responsible society.

10

10 The British Pavilion, Seville, Expo '92 by Nicholas Grimshaw and Partners – detail of the end walls made by a yacht sail maker; solar panels on roof

11

CHAPTER I
PREHISTORIC AND TRADITIONAL PORTABLE BUILDINGS

In the history of architecture, the early dwellings of prehistoric societies are largely ignored. Architectural history begins with the examination of significant, usually stone, buildings which have functions with a mystical or sacred background. The reason for this is no doubt related to the availability of relevant, easily examinable remains and in some cases largely intact structures. But there is also the possibility that most historians believe that 'non-pedigreed' architecture (as it is called by Bernard Rudofsky) has had no bearing on the mainstream development of the subject: 'Although the dismissal of the early stages [in architectural history] can be explained, though not excused, by the scarcity of architectural monuments, the discriminative approach of the historian is mostly due to his parochialism'.[1] Claude Lévi-Strauss, in his influential work, *Structural Anthropology*, first published in 1958, described an unnatural division between anthropology and history that had led to unnecessary confusion about the importance of man's early history.

In recent years this 'confusion' has become less easy to understand as archaeologists, equipped with better techniques and more advanced technology (for example carbon dating can accurately date artifacts up to 50,000 years old within a few decades), have been able to make more accurate findings and complete our understanding of early peoples' day-to-day existence. Though it is difficult to separate chronologically the confused, overlaid activities which took place at complex sites, experience has enabled much greater detail to emerge from research into early human settlements. Contemporary architectural historians now have a far greater source of archaeological information than was available to those in the past, even if they may still choose to ignore it.[2]

Eight to five million years ago our human ancestors evolved from the apes in the continent we now call Africa. About two million years ago the first tools began to be made: simple chipped pebbles like those found in the site at Olduvai Gorge, Tanzania, East Africa.[3] These early hominids were adapted to life in a tropical climate and probably had little need of shelter beyond the use of a convenient cave. Around one and a half million years ago the first full scale Ice Age occurred. This significant change in climate probably 'favoured the development of man as a species encouraging human intelligence as a tool of survival'.[4] In order to survive the Ice Age humans had to develop further their ability to make tools and clothing, and to organise their daily existence. This meant searching for an increasingly scarce food supply, locating or creating shelter and defining temporary and permanent settlements. These new requirements provided the reasons whereby early hominids spread from the original African homeland into Asia and Europe. The fundamental pattern of existence for prehistoric man was as hunter-gatherer, living off wild edible plants and fruits, but becoming increasingly dependent on the flesh of the wild animals which his abilities with tools enabled him to catch, slay and prepare for food.

The site at Bilzingsleben in Germany has yielded much information about the early Europeans.[5] It was occupied by a group of hunter-gatherers from 700,000 to 120,000 years ago. They lived primarily by big-game hunting: the remains of Rhinoceros are most common, but nearby vegetation also contained nuts and berries, wild honey and resin, and a river and marshland contained fish and birds. As well as sustenance, the animals were also valued for the raw manufacturing materials they offered. Beavers were caught for their fur, and the bones of the larger animals used for tools and for props for the first primitive shelters which were covered with their skins. At Grotte du Lazaret near Nice in France a mid-Pleistocene (150,000 years old) excavation:

> revealed the traces of a large hut built against the cave's east wall, 11 metres long and up to 3.5 metres wide. Its edge is marked by a scatter of stones some of

11 Plains Indian Tipi. Part of the covering, in this case canvas although skins were used originally, is pulled back to reveal the interior

12

which are thought to have supported upright posts, while animal hides probably completed the shelter ... [This is] characteristic of hunter-gatherer societies, where groups consisting of only a few individuals moved from camp to camp in an annual cycle.[6]

Homo Sapiens emerged about 100,000 years ago and by 30,000 years ago our species had spread throughout the habitable regions of the world; however, it was only as recently as 10,000 years ago that humankind became a 'widespread successful species'.[7] The remains of the Upper Palaeolithic period (35,000 to 12,000 years ago) show a marked increase in the number, size and complexity of sites, with larger dwellings, huts and tents and the beginnings of signs of permanent settlement. The timber buildings of a village of hunter-gatherers have been found preserved in peat on the banks of the Chinchihuapi Creek in Southern Chile dating from 13,000 years ago. These buildings consisted of rectangular wooden frames 3 to 4.5 metres across, clad in Mastodon skins (a type of extinct elephant), remains of which were still attached to the poles. Each hut had a fireplace and there was also a much larger structure with the remains of plants and herbs derived both from local origin, and from surprisingly large distances. All the signs present indicate an organised community with established manufacturing and storage areas.[8]

The people who lived at the site in Pincevent in the Seine Valley, Northern France about 10,000 years ago lived in 4.5 by 3 metre 'portable tents constructed of wooden poles with animal skins lashed to them'.[9] This site was occupied seasonally, between midsummer and midwinter, as the hunters followed their prey, a pattern of existence that was common to human existence worldwide. Finds in the Tehuacán Valley, Mexico, show the hunter-gatherers moved between the valley floor and the uplands depending on the season and would even disband or reunite depending on conditions.[10] From 10,000 years ago, a gradual shift in this community's organisation has been charted which reveals the change to a fully agricultural pattern of existence, and the establishment of permanent dwellings.

It is from this period that formal architectural history dates, with the establishment of permanent communities, occupied year round on a continuous basis, and revealing the inhabitants' ability to invest time and energy in permanent, substantial structures. However, it is clear that for many thousands of years before this man led a transient lifestyle – for a much longer period than that of a primarily settled existence. Although his very first dwellings were, as with his food, provided from the natural resource in the form of a cave or a tree, the first manufactured shelter was undoubtedly temporary. Initially made from easily available materials and then discarded when a move became necessary, these developed into part of his expanding kit of portable tools. The ability to move from territory to territory was an essential factor in the early humans' survival of the first major Ice Age and those that then followed at regular intervals.[11] In these travels he needed to be able to find food regularly and be able to rely on shelter. To these early people this shelter therefore demonstrated the qualities of life preservation, as with their tools, weapons, and clothing. Without such items they would certainly have perished.

12 Reconstruction of 10,000 year old tent structures from remains found at Pincevent, Northern France

The detail of these essential artifacts appears ill defined because of the transient nature of the materials from which they were made. It is only by freak chances that traces of the physical objects have survived for us to examine today: 'the anonymous non-architecture of primitive cultures ... was not built to last; it was not built to testify to official history of an era'.[12]

Prehistoric architecture was generally functional and personal, and has proved ephemeral – it does not bear a message of formal cultural aspirations – perhaps this is why it has not been of interest to architectural historians. As has been discovered by anthropologists, there is a valuable research resource available for the investigation of these dwelling systems in the legacy of those who live on in the unchanged pattern of their ancestors. Furthermore, much of the technology developed by our ancestors is invested with the ingenuity and inherent understanding of the environment which they possessed and used in coming to such appropriate and long-lasting solutions with limited resources. These finely adjusted and innately appropriate forms present lessons for those who seek to solve related problems today, often based in similar environments and addressing comparable logistical and constructional issues.

12a

Traditional Architecture

Though agriculture and the pastoral life have led to enormous changes in the pattern of life for the majority of mankind, a number of societies have retained the nomadic existence as part of their culture, some by necessity, some by choice. A few have even changed to a travelling existence after many centuries in stable, permanent communities, resulting in complete and dramatic changes in their lifestyle and the design of their artifacts, most significantly in their buildings.

These patterns of life which still occur in numerous locations around the world (though under constant threat from various sociological, economic and environmental factors) can be examined in order to provide information on the very earliest form of dwellings devised by man.[13] Indeed, their great success as building types that have managed to survive largely unchanged for thousands of years makes them worthy of examination in order to find patterns of knowledge applicable to problems which are current in the minds of designers today. Paul Oliver in his book, *Shelter in Africa*, summarises and refutes the common attitude of the casual observer when commenting on the tents of the Arabised Berber nomads of Southern Morocco, the Tekna: 'A structure which may be dismissed somewhat summarily because of its apparent simplicity is seen to have a degree of refinement which custom, use and necessity have determined'.[14] Barry Biermann in his essay on Zulu dwellings, also in *Shelter in Africa*; states:

> Assessed by contemporary standards of excellence in architecture, considered as absolutes and not relative to any preconceptions, the Zulu hut stands in the forefront of architectural efficiency, constructional economy and exploitation of the nature of the material. The Zulu hut has achieved more in its own right than the latest advances of contemporary architecture. Any human endeavour, no matter how humble, that has attained perfection in its own field, is a rare enough phenomenon to merit due acclaim.[15]

Nomadic peoples have no permanent geographical base, though they do generally range within a defined territory, often associating specific parts of that territory with certain times of the year. This may be linked with climate, as in the herding tribes of North Africa, or linked with the migration or availability of their prey, as in the case of hunters. These societies generally have no more possessions than those they carry with them, objects which may be shared amongst the group or individually owned. Because everything must be transported, very little is there which is not required for survival, though this does not mean that dwellings and possessions are not without comfort and beauty. The relationship with the territory is more profound than in permanent settlements as the nomad not only passes through the land but lives off it and must be receptive to its nuances. This has a significant effect on the form and construction of their buildings. These forms are diverse and vary in detail dramatically; however, they can be roughly apportioned into two specific groups, demountable and portable, of which the former is far the larger due to the limited carrying ability of human beings and animals.

12a A Bedouin tent and a commercial exoskeleton structure at Expo '92, Seville

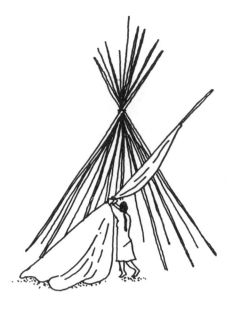

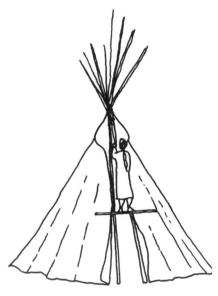

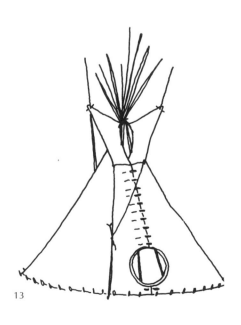

Although there are similarities in shape and, in some cases, construction between buildings found in different parts of the world, the division further than this into subgroups based on arbitrary observations is suspect. It is more appropriate to examine the main patterns of building on their own merit than to seek common factors that may lead to a supposed archetype. Enrico Guidoni states that this is essential in the understanding of primitive architecture:

> With regard to the constructed object, its use, and its significance in relation to all the societies in contact with it, every culture – every class – furnishes its own interpretation, attitude, associations and explanations of why it is what it is. Such interpretations are not merely *a posteriori*. They reflect a complex of attitudes toward architecture, which, as values only partially put into use, each culture develops for its own assimilation and transformation of architectural types and materials without necessarily implying a total mutation in the social context.[16]

Even though architectural forms may *appear* similar, the significance which the people who have developed those forms invest in them may be, and probably will be, totally unique. Building is just one physical manifestation of a culture and should be seen in relationship to all others, including social organisation and behaviour. These factors are so complex that apparently similar physical artifacts can result for quite different reasons and also be utilised and understood in quite different ways. Similarity in building form does not necessarily mean that it is the result of similar cultural viewpoints or social pressures.

However, to examine systematically the various forms of traditional demountable and portable architecture it is beneficial to order them in some way. A non-hierarchical observation of the main types shows that of the demountable forms the main types are the tipi of the North American Indian; the tent structures of the desert nomad based primarily in North Africa; and the yurt of Asia. These three building types form the bulk of all movable architecture; however, the portable forms such as the lightweight hut of equatorial Africa and the boat house of the Far East, though less widespread and more attuned to specific local circumstances, are also of interest.[17] In addition, there is a large range of diverse buildings which do not fit easily into either category but in specific cases should be examined because of the unique solutions found to answer a specific problem.

The Tipi

The first North American Palaeolithic inhabitants lived in groups that followed the herds of Mastodon, Mammoth, Ground Sloth, and forms of Bison that migrated seasonally. Between 12,000 and 6,000 years ago these groups became the first Native Americans that made up the great and diverse range of tribes that inhabited the continent before the arrival of the white man. As the importance of agriculture increased, the tribes developed a range of permanent building types. In the North, tribes such as the Mandans, the Minnetarees, the Mewoks and many others developed the Earth Lodge, a building constructed of substantial timbers covered with earth and turf. In the Southern, warmer climate, tribes built Adobe buildings rendered with clay.

With the introduction of the horse, many of these groups abandoned their lodges and farm plots and became buffalo hunters, following animal herds once again. This relatively abrupt transformation to a new way of life led to a building type that developed swiftly, though it was certainly based on traditional patterns.[18] Faegre describes the Great Plains in the mid-west of North America at this time, as 'a great design laboratory in which every conceivable variation of this simple conical tent existed'.[19]

Though varying greatly in size and complexity, the various tipi (from the Dakota word *tipi* meaning 'they dwell' or 'dwelling') designs follow a set pattern, that of a lightweight conical building with the cladding of animal skins spread around a framework of braced poles. The building is made and owned by the women of the tribe who are also responsible for its erection. In the sewing of the skins the women enlist the help of other females who are paid with food. In erection, the frame is established with a set number of main poles. Different tribes have characteristic patterns, for example the Sioux have a three-pole main frame, while the Blackfoot have a four-pole main frame. The main poles are supplemented by

13

subsidiary poles which are lashed at the top. Again, the pattern of the poles at the apex is distinctive to each tribe. The cover, which is made in a defined semicircular pattern, was generally made from buffalo skins (though when it became available, canvas was also used), twenty for a tipi of five metres diameter. The cover is large and heavy and is hoisted into place with a lifting pole, then pinned into place on the entrance side. The poles can be erected in five minutes and the cover attached in fifteen.

Though simple in form, the tipi has ingenious features which make it a comfortable dwelling. The building is set up at an angle, braced into the prevailing wind and it has a smoke flap which can be moved to avoid draughts and to ensure smoke from the fire is not blown back inside. Streamers on the tips of the poles indicate the wind direction. The interior is lined to a height of about 1.5 metres with a dew cloth which allows condensed moisture to run down outside the living area. This also provides some insulation and helps prevent draughts reaching the living area.

The organisation of the tipi is not simply based on pragmatic concerns, though; the symbolic significance also proves eminently practical. The shape of the dwelling had great emblematic importance. The Plains Indian believes: 'everything that the "Power" of the world does is in a circle, the sky, the earth, the stars. The tipis were made round like the nests of birds and arranged in a circle'.[20] It may also be significant that this shape is a great aerodynamic advantage in retaining stability in the substantial winds of the prairie.

The building is erected with reference to the rising and setting sun, with doorways facing the East, into the sun, and away from prevailing westerly winds. Even the poles might be set up in relation to the cardinal points. Internally there is a strict spatial organisation. The hearth is laid on axis with the entrance, though not central, as it is directly below the smoke vent. There is another sacred hearth to the rear, where burnt offerings are made. Gathered around this are the places for special objects and trophies. The left side of the tipi is occupied by the adults and the right side by the children. This strict organisation of the limited space is a common feature of transportable architecture – as time has passed, these arrangements have become ritualised. Equally, there is no doubt that they are based, at least in part, on the practicalities of living in a confined space which also has all its contents repeatedly disgorged.

The tipis were highly successful dwellings adapted by the inhabitants of an entire continent, though of many different nations. Groups such as the Cheyenne took part in great summer camps such as the Sun Dance where up to a thousand buildings gathered in a circle of concentric rows up to 1.6 kilometres in diameter. But these temporary cities did not last long: '... almost as soon as it began it was over. The Native Americans were forced into reservations and discouraged from living in the tipi – since it was a "pagan house"'.[21] Because of their conviction in

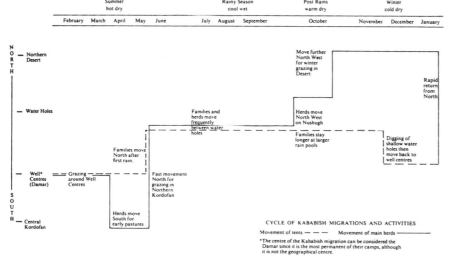

13 Tipi erection process (after Faegre); 14 Pattern of seasonal movement of the Kababish nomad by Paul Verity from 'Kababish Nomads of Northern Sudan'

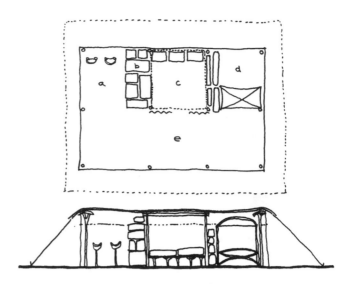

15

the power of the circle the 'Plains Indians believed they lost their powers when placed in square houses on reservations'.[22]

The tipi possesses the honour of being the only traditional structure to have been adopted in significant numbers by Western people seeking alternative lifestyles in their own personally constructed movable homes. It is also the only type to have been put into manufacture in its original recognisable form for sale in the West. There is little doubt that this is due to its simplicity and practicality and its ability to cope with a diverse range of environmental conditions, even today. It is probable that it also possesses significance for many modern tipi dwellers as a practical symbol of a people more in harmony with the environment which they inhabit.

The tipi is now once again used extensively by Native Americans as a temporary dwelling for the regular pow-wows and meetings that have formed the venue for the reassessment of their culture. It is a political symbol, as are the traditional crafts and rituals that continue to be revived as part of the general reestablishment of the Indian nations throughout North America.

The Tent

The tent is one of the earliest forms of architecture. Because it is still in active use today, it can be said to have survived longer than any other form of building. The tent form possesses great potency as a worldwide symbol of shelter regardless of

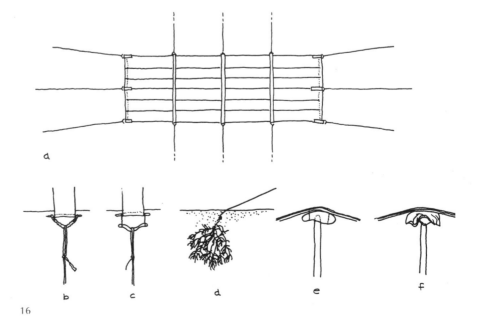

15 Kababish nomad tent layout (after Verity):
a) kitchen/store
b) storage containers
c) bed
d) women's area
e) public area
16 Bedouin nomad tent details (after Faegre):
a) tent roof plan
b) stay fastener with braided cord
c) stay fastener with bent stick
d) tent anchor with rope tied to buried bush
e) tent pole, *triga*, top with wooden spreader
f) rag spreader

16

20

cultural boundaries. 'In the vast desert area the tent of a nomad is the unique shelter for anybody coming across the wastes ... The tent ... is a relic of the symbolic nature of a shelter in the traditional sense'.[23] The tents of the nomadic peoples of North Africa have been developed over thousands of years. The climate and topography in which these people exist is harsh and extreme. The inhabitants, both human and animal, need to be responsive to their environment to survive, and the artifacts which have been made to aid with that survival must be completely dependable:

> The nomadic inhabitants of desert and semi-desert regions use tents of considerable diversity. They are always strictly functional with every detail of material and form meticulously worked out; they are lightweight, an excellent protection from the rigours of the climate, and practical as regards availability and use of material.[24]

The reason for the nomads' transitory lifestyle is based on their existence as herders: moving their flocks of goats and camels to fresh grazing, often over relatively short distances for periods of a few weeks, but seasonally over great distances to differing climates. For example, the Kababish nomads of Northern Sudan pasture in the South of the country in the summer and move North during the rainy season, using water holes as stopping-off points. They winter in the relatively warm desert then return to the South once more as summer brings the early pasture there.

The nomadic culture of these peoples is woven completely into their pattern of existence; the Bedouin traditionally pity the sedentary settlement dweller, believing his own existence is the only truly 'free' one. Nomads also feel that the safety of the tent is more profound than that of a permanent dwelling and in some cases when resettled to load-bearing buildings with solid roofs have preferred the shelter of the tent and relegated the house for use by the animals.

As in North America, there are a great number of different tribes amongst the nomads of North Africa. Each has its own distinct heritage and lineage and sometimes widely different social patterns; however, all have adopted the tent as their main form of shelter. The patterns of building of these structures vary in detail and scale, but they all have certain common factors inherent in their design. A transient culture requires lightweight and portable possessions: 'the nomadic way of life necessitates moving camp every two or three weeks, and probably more often; the Bedouin possesses nothing that cannot be moved by two people'. [25] The Bedouin are the 'nomads of the nomads'[26] and travel faster and farther than any others among those who use the black tent, so called because it is made of black goat hair, sometimes mixed with camel or sheep wool. They are called *Ahl el beit*, 'people of the tent', and they can travel up to 64 kilometres in a single day.[27] These people inhabit the Rub'al-Khali, the empty quarter of the Arabian desert, and have a culture that 'has evolved over thousands of years to meet harsh environmental conditions with minimal resources'.[28] The Bedouin call their tents *beit sha'r*, 'house of hair'.[29] The main fabric of the tent is woven in strips between 60 and 70 centimetres across and sewn together incorporating strengthening tapes that run crosswise to which tension fasteners are attached. This large, generally rectangular piece of fabric is spread out and the poles are erected inside, with a wooden shoe or rags to spread the load where it comes into contact with the cloth. The tent is tensioned and pegged, or in unsuitable ground conditions the guy ropes are fastened to a bush which is buried. The walls of the tent are suspended around the perimeter and the bases buried in sand or covered with rocks and bushes. These parts of the tent rot first, so the tent is constantly being renewed from the top portion, growing as the bottom disintegrates. Internally there are dividing curtains and specific areas set aside for certain purposes: cooking, sleeping (separated by sex), guest area. The decoration and pattern of the tents vary greatly, even within the same tribe, and though these are simple dwellings, they can be beautifully decorated both in the weaving of the fabric, the mats and cushions laid inside, but also in the essential elements that make up the structure of the dwelling, such as the fasteners and ties.

The tent construction possesses great flexibility in the way it is used. The walls of the tent can be raised to allow the passage of cooling winds, or be fully enclosed in a storm. The tent can be split into many compartments or left as a single large

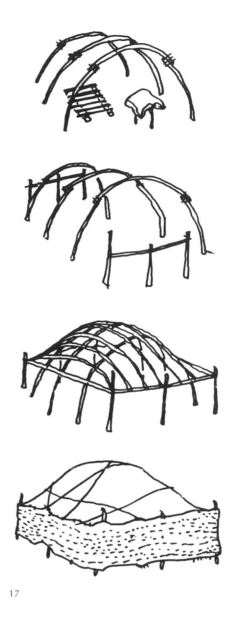

17

17 Erection procedure of a Tuareg mat tent

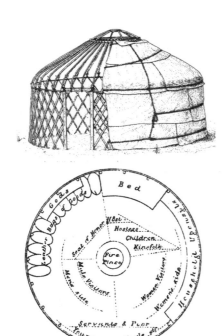

18

18 The Asian yurt. The sectional perspective shows the separate components used in the construction. The plan shows the precise layout of the interior space

space. The quality and size of a tent is an expression of its owner's wealth and importance; however, in all cases the women are responsible for its maintenance and erection. The tent is pitched facing East to Mecca or South so the back wall is to the North winds and the men's side is towards Mecca.

Many tent patterns are similar to that of the Bedouin, such as the Tekna of southwest Morocco; however, some have distinctive variations which it is worth noting.[30] Tents can be found in Tibet which have developed in a different manner to those in North Africa in that they are supported by an exoskeleton of poles and guys, providing the tension and stiffness for a much reduced internal pole assembly.

Some systems have developed in response to different materials such as that of the Tuareg, nomadic and semi-nomadic herders of the central and southern Sahara. These people use tents clad in either skins or mats. The mat-clad buildings have attributes of both the tent forms of North Africa and the yurts of Asia and are of special interest. The structure is formed from a series of bent poles which arch to form a barrel-vault type structure. This is coupled with a rectangular wall section made from more substantial wooden poles. Cords are wound in this structure for the insertion of more slender rods, giving the roof a complex dome-like shape. The structure is clad with the mats which are made from differing plants depending on their purpose: Dum palm plants externally and plant stems internally. Each of the components of this elaborate structure has its own name and, despite its complexity, can be fully erected in 30 minutes.[31] The frame of this tent has great strength and must be self-supporting as the skins and mats used for cladding have little tensile strength. The structure is related in form to the dome and it is probable that this earlier, temporary pattern played an important role in the development of the permanent architectural form. Torvald Faegre has noted the importance of early traditional building patterns in the development of established architectural form: 'it is clear that the tent reaches far into the past and provides us with a link to that past which has been lost in most sedentary dwellings'.[32] He goes on to quote a specific example related to the form shown by the Tuareg mat tent: 'The great masonry domes of both the East and the West can ultimately be traced back to the simple arched brick hut or tent'.[33]

The Yurt

The yurt is the standard transportable dwelling type of the Asian continent. It is used by tribes from Iran to Mongolia, and has a heritage that stretches back thousands of years. 'Construction has been standardised for centuries, for it would be difficult to improve or, indeed, vary this extremely lightweight structure, which is easy to set up, take down, and transport and is perfectly adaptable to both winter and summer conditions'.[34]

The Steppes of Central Asia were first occupied in the more temperate regions by agricultural communities over 7,000 years ago. By 3,000 years ago the great dry grassland areas were also occupied by specialised nomadic societies based on the horse. They lived by rearing herds of cattle and sheep, supplemented with some hunting. The artifacts of this society were more substantial than those found in North America and the desert and semi-desert regions of North Africa. Although seasonal movement between pasture grounds meant that all equipment was portable, the use of sophisticated horse-drawn wagons, even as early as 5,000 years ago, meant that this equipment could be transported. The inhabitants of the Steppes were fierce warriors, and this, coupled with their mobility, made them 'a redoubtable force, especially when united under a strong leader'.[35] The burial tombs of this period emphasise this fact as they contain valuable prizes taken in battle from wide areas of the ancient world: silks from China, and gold and bronze ornaments made by Greek craftsmen. Around 2,000 years ago, China, India and Europe all suffered devastating raids by these nomads, a taste of further, more extensive trouble once the 'strong leader', Ghengis Khan, arrived. He led the Mongols in long campaigns far into these countries. The Mongols, however, were not the only tribe to inhabit the Steppes and there were, and still are, many more peaceful peoples amongst them; for example the Turks, Kazakhs, Bashkirs, Altais, all of whom use the yurt.

Yurt or *yurta* is the Turkish word for dwelling but is also known as the *kherga* in Afghan, the *kabitka* in Russian, and the *ber* in Mongol. The building is of particular interest as it is so easily transportable yet appears, and indeed is, so solid. The walls of the building are one of its most interesting elements – trellises (called *khana*) made from strips of willow with swivelling joints, traditionally a rawhide link, that enable the panel to be contracted for transport and expanded for use. These are erected in a circular shape and a tension band is placed around the top and tied to the door frame which is quite conventional in pattern, but made of juniper wood for lightness. Three roof poles are inserted in a circular crown, which is the most complex part of the building 'kit'. This is held in place by two central poles while the rest of the roof poles are added. The Steppe dwellers make felt as a covering for the yurt, sometimes plain, sometimes decorated or coloured. Up to eight layers of felt are used to make a warm, weatherproof dwelling. Men make the wooden parts of the yurt but the women make the felt and are responsible for the erection and dismantling of the building, which takes about 30 minutes. It is transported by horses, sometimes on a cart by the wealthier owners, but more usually on *travois*, two wooden, trailing poles tied to the saddle to make a simple platform. In common with all travelling dwellings the inside of a yurt is set out in strict accordance with a set of conventions, transformed into rules: 'The interior plan of [a] ... yurt was firmly established by rules of etiquette. These rules were adhered to from Mongol to Tibet, by emperors in palaces to Tartars in their tents'.[36] The yurt is placed with the door facing South to allow the sun entering through the smoke hole to act as a sundial. The hearth is in the centre beneath this hole, to the West is the women's side, to the East is the guest's and the rear of the building is where the men may sit in the day and where the bed is made at night. The building may be ventilated by rolling up some of the felt from the sides. In summer the floor may simply be a layer of felt, and traditionally in winter this was covered with ten centimetres of dried grass as insulation and then further rugs laid on top. The yurt has many specific symbolic intentions incorporated into its form:

> To the Mongols, the roof is the sky, the hole in the roof is the Sun, the Eye of Heaven through which comes the Light. And when in the morning one pours an offering on the hearth fire, the vapours mix with the smoke and rise up to God. The hearth is a sacred area, the 'square of the earth', and the Asian five basic elements are contained therein: Earth on the floor, Wood in the frame enclosing the hearth, Fire in the hearth itself, Metal in the grate over the fire, and water in the Kettle on the grate.[37]

The yurt is a traditional building that evolved over centuries of use and still has potential ideas for today's designers. What modern alternative can be erected or dismantled in less than an hour and loaded on two camels, bullocks or yaks? Its structure is so strong that it can be lifted up and moved short distances as a pragmatic method of cleaning the building's site. The yurt is still firmly established as a practical economic building type as Mongols still live in them in substantial numbers (three quarters of the population), no doubt because a good yurt costs the average worker only two to three months' wages and provides reliable and *transportable* shelter.[38]

Portable Structures

Few examples of portable buildings exist in traditional architecture. This is due to the restriction in weight and bulk that can be carried by human beings or domesticated animals. No matter how sophisticated their application, materials form the limiting factor, for traditional buildings are universally manufactured from what is available locally without difficulty. In certain cases, however, some cultures have developed buildings that have a real, if limited, portability factor built into them that enables them to be relocated, complete, to an alternative site. The driving force in nomadic existence is survival; however, the reasons to move are sometimes more diverse and the distance of the move is quite short.

The yurt has limited portability. The Steppe Nomads' access to wagons can also be pressed into service for slightly longer moves than those required for cleaning,

19

20

19 Traditional houseboats in Srinigar, Kashmir; **20** A communal house in Sumatra, Indonesia that shows constructional and formal references to boat building

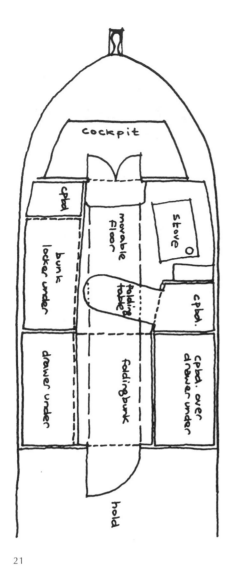

21

though this is an inefficient use of a vehicle capable of carrying a much greater weight, if less bulky.

The strength and quality of the Zulu hut, the Indlu, has previously been mentioned. This building is made of a woven thatch supported on a separate timber framework. These buildings were required to be portable as tradition decreed that if an inhabitant died, his dwelling was to be burnt. The remaining buildings of the community are then relocated whole to a new location, or if a suitable one is not available locally, the thatch is abandoned and the frames of the buildings transported to form the basis of the new village.[39] The reason for this dramatic move may at first appear superstitious; however, in a community with limited knowledge of medicine, the prophylactic relocation of an entire village is reasonable if it saves lives.

In Chad, the roofs of buildings are portable as they are prefabricated and then moved to the walls which have been erected on site. This also means that the roof becomes a separate commodity which can be removed to another building if required.

Boat 'Buildings'

Bernard Rudofsky reinforces the intimate relationship between boats and buildings in his review of the world's prototypical life raft:

the Ark was commissioned by the Lord Himself and built to His specifications. The question whether the Ark ought to be called a building or a nautical craft is redundant ... ships were not known as yet, since their existence would have defeated the very purpose of the Flood.[40]

The earliest manufactured form of transport available to man was water-borne. As distances travelled on boats became greater, the sailor made the transition to living on board his craft. In certain unusual circumstances the priority of the vehicular characteristics of the boat has been made subordinate to those of the living side. In some areas of the world the water can provide a better place to live: 'waterways are permanent, drains suffer no stoppage, a bath is available at all hours. The water acts as a cooling plant in the hot season'.[41] The Junk is an archetypal floating house that contains not only a place to live, but to work as well. In the giant floating cities of China and the Far East boats are sometimes moored to each other to present an endless floating platform.

Lanes are left at intervals of 20 or 30 boats to facilitate communication. This is very necessary, for the nautical 'commuter' returning from work may, as likely as not, find that his floating home has moved to another 'street'. No phase of life is unrepresented among this population. Kitchen boats supply hot food at a low rate. The barber calls in a small sampan which he rows himself, calling attention by ringing a bell. The river doctor also gives notice of his approach by beating a drum; and when his medicines prove of no avail, there are floating mortuaries.[42]

Kashmir houseboats are richly carved and decorated timber buildings of high quality, built to float so that they can be easily transported to their sites around Lake Dal near Srinigar. These are the ultimate in luxurious, though traditionally developed, floating buildings, and were adopted enthusiastically by the British Raj in the nineteenth century. The boats are made to a similar pattern by local craftsmen though each is extensively carved with unique decorations. The dwellings are moored along the shores of the lake, the main form of transport being by boat. They are serviced externally from separate kitchen boats, which use produce grown on great 'fields' that float on the lake's surface.

Boats play a significant part in many cultures, particularly those that survive by living off the sea. In these societies the boat can become more than an artifact or a tool, and may develop into a symbol. Some of the traditional buildings of these cultures exhibit the influence of boat manufacture in their construction – sometimes not simply a transfer of building techniques, but of image as well. On the Indonesian island of Sumatra the great timber communal dwellings, though in some cases many kilometres from water, show a direct influence from the ancient maritime traditions of the community. The inhabitants' ancestors arrived on the island in boats and the retention of this shape for their buildings is a symbolic link with their identity as a unified crew.

21 The layout of a nineteenth century English canal boat. The cabin contains many demountable and variable use elements to make the most of the small mobile space that the bargee and his family must inhabit

In Ceylon, the community's ceremonial boats are brought onto land when not in use, raised on posts in the centre of the village, then thatched with a temporary roof of palm leaves.

It is clear that such a boat stored in the middle of a village retains its importance in the eyes of the community. It is still the communal boat, symbolising the unity of the society, and retaining all the special powers it assumes when in ceremonial use. It is not difficult to understand its eventual influence on the design of buildings of symbolically related function and importance.[43]

Buildings/vehicles such as this are part of an interesting direct form of technology transfer that exists in societies where skills and knowledge are not separated between disciplines and therefore instantly available for use in diverse applications. The Aymara Indians of Bolivia, South America live at an elevation of 3,800 metres by fishing in lake Titicaca. Their boats are made from bundles of tutura reeds and their houses, though framed with a small number of supporting poles, are based on the same method of construction. The dwelling's keel-like form is a direct transfer from the design of the boat's hull. In the West, the influence of boat design on building construction is not so apparent – there are cases of boats being pressed into a second lease of life when they have become too fragile for a maritime role, but these are generally isolated and unconnected cases. Mediaeval timber buildings which were made using complex interlocking frames are said to have been influenced by the skills used to build boats made from the same materials. Although these buildings were at least partly prefabricated and have proved demountable when dismantled in recent times for relocation and preservation reasons, this was not a factor in their original design.

The inland waterways' canal boat is a Western example of a form of existence that made the transition from living ashore to living aboard, and developed specialised portable dwellings and social organisation. The canal system in Great Britain developed out of the natural waterways of the coastal areas which formed a convenient route for the transport of goods and materials. Before 1770, distances that the barges travelled were short and there were no cabins as the bargee could return home after work. In 1776 the Bridgewater canal was opened, followed in 1777 by the Trent and Mersey, and in 1789 England was crossed from West to East by the Thames and Severn canal. This interlinked network served to increase the duration of journeys up to 150 kilometres or more. The bargee and his family took on a transient existence, living in their boats on the water. The 1881 census shows that there were 40,000 men, women and children living and working on the inland waterways, of which 7,000 to 9,000 had no other dwelling but the cabin of their barge.[44] The cabin was small, 2.5 metres long by 2 metres wide by 1.5 metres high, and fully occupied with man, wife and children, and sometimes, if the children were young, a 'chap' to help. As many as nine people would occupy the space, though five to six was more common. The timber fittings were manufactured by the barge builder and followed an established pattern with a range of demountable and hinged panels to form sufficient bed space, folding screens to give a degree of privacy, and a range of storage compartments for food, clothes, utensils and other possessions. There was also a solid fuel stove for cooking and heating. Although the basic pattern of the cabin was set, the canal boat people invariably modified their space with intricate decorations that show a similarity to gypsy art, though the inspiration for the motifs, based on roses and castles, cannot be established with any degree of certainty. The people who lived on the canals developed their own culture and society, usually marrying within their group, leading them to be seen by the Victorians as a race apart. Robert Louis Stevenson took part in a journey on the inland waterways which he recounted in his book *An Inland Voyage*, and though his views can sometimes be observed to be excessively romantic, he keenly observed the pattern of life of this transient society. The families gathered by the canal side at the end of the day and then in the morning the 'impromptu hamlet would separate, house by house, to the four winds', the meeting place of boats the next evening being quite different.[45]

22

22 Mrs Jarley's caravan from Charles Dickens' *The Old Curiosity Shop*. Illustration by C Green, 1876

By the beginning of the twentieth century the canal-boat existence was in firm decline, unable to meet the competition of the railways which provided a much quicker and efficient service. Many of the inland waterways of Great Britain and Europe do still exist and are employed as a leisure resource, still utilising portable dwellings in the form of modern steel barges built specially for the tourist industry incorporating kitchens, dining/living rooms and bathrooms.

Wheeled Vehicles

Many forms of wheeled transport have been in use throughout Europe and Asia for centuries but the incorporation of a dwelling into the vehicle is a relatively recent invention. Though Herodotus described the Scythians as having no homes but their wagons, it is probable that they did not sleep in them but erected simple demountable dwellings for shelter and rest. The relatively affluent traveller was the first to incorporate a dwelling into a wheeled vehicle, simply because of the investment in resources: its manufacture and the use of beasts for drawing it. In the seventeenth century it was known that Cardinal Richelieu had a horse litter which contained a bedroom/study, and Napoleon's campaign coach, which contained cooking, eating, resting and working facilities, is well documented as it was brought to England for Madame Tussaud's exhibition in London.[46] Travelling sleeping carriages were developed in the eighteenth century for gentlemen engaged in the Grand Tour, but the first real caravans were developed by the travelling menagerie show operators at the beginning of the nineteenth century. The animals were contained in travelling cages which formed their place of habitation as well as exhibition, and the keepers, who originally would lodge wherever they could whilst on tour, developed simple mobile dwellings as a cheaper, more reliable, and more comfortable alternative.

It is often mistakenly assumed that the gypsy or Romany invented the caravan.[47] However, the traditional gypsy dwelling was a tent or a 'bender', a construction of bent twigs arched into a dome or simple barrel vault, then covered with blankets. These people adopted the caravan from the precedents created by others, the English gypsies being the first to do so about 1860. The gypsy society traditionally has as its base of existence the horse, which was bred, sold and kept to pull their vehicles. Romanies came originally from Eastern Europe and Asia and their language is based on Sanskrit. From generation to generation they have handed down a traditional skill as fabrictors, existing by mending and manufacturing everyday objects for the sedentary population.

In Ireland, the gypsies are called Tinkers and are said to have their own distinct history from the Romanies. There were nomadic *Tynkers* in Ireland more than 800 years ago.[48] These nomadic people are shunned and feared by the settled population, a feature which is as much a part of today's Tinkers' life as in the past, so their dwellings need to have special significance in terms of sense of place: 'A mobile home poses the need to find a way of creating an atmosphere of stability'.[49] Their timber dwellings were called *keir-vardo* in gypsy language, highly crafted and ingeniously designed to accommodate large families in a small space. Their floor height was about 1.2 metres, and to the roof they measured about 3.4 metres. Such a height made the vehicle unstable in high winds so special props were incorporated to steady it on uneven ground. The walls spread out to give about 1.5 metres in width and the roof was often curved in section with a raised central area to give added light and ventilation. Though cooking was generally done outside, there could be a stove inside for heating, as well as beds, cupboards and a larder. Modern gypsies still live in caravans and though based on commercially available touring vehicles they are often highly decorated, externally and internally, in a distinctive style that defines the identity and lineage of the occupant.

The caravans of the great cross-land trade routes between the West and the East developed a continuous tradition of moving habitation across the great plains and deserts. The dwellings used by these caravans were most often demountable tents, such as that already described. Vehicles were sometimes used to carry goods, though this was not generally the case as conditions made the use of pack animals faster and less prone to delay. However, many trade caravan traditions have persisted and been adapted to their circumstances of the present day. Even in the West, the truck driver has a vehicle specially designed to provide shelter over long journeys and a social system that relates to his mode of living. However, in the East, the caravanserai tradition is much stronger and the distances are greater. The conditions are also much more severe, with badly maintained and inadequate roads; the danger of being marooned far from civilisation in the event of a breakdown; and the very real threat of bandits. The day-to-day existence of these drivers is therefore still far from assured, and their vehicles still part of a craft tradition as their superstructure is largely handmade. In Pakistan, the truck drivers exist for long periods on the road. For security, they travel in groups by day, only stopping each evening at *addas*, caravanserais on the route. All the truck bodywork is hand built to the owners' requirements. The decorations are complex and symbolic and carried out by a craft artist, the *ustad*, with his apprentices. They are usually redone every six months. The cab interiors are also decorated using new and recycled materials. The trucks undoubtedly take on the symbolic potency of something more than a vehicle; they 'are at the crossroads of two cultures – the traditional and the technological – symbolised by their mobile shelter'.[50]

Inuit and Nootka Buildings

Human ingenuity is manifest in the range and diversity of traditional building types that have been created to meet specific problems of climate, topography, and subsistence patterns. In this study, only those that can be viewed as demountable or portable have been examined, yet there are many more types that for engineering skill, suitability to purpose and functionality deserve investigation. For example, two further dwelling types, whilst they do not strictly fall within the field of portable architecture, are worthy of explanation.

The Inuit, or Eskimos of North America and Greenland, occupy an extensive yet harsh and monotonous landscape: about 100,000 people inhabit 1,000,000 square miles. These people originate from about 12,000 years ago when their descendants migrated across the Bering land bridge from Central Asia, camping on beaches as they travelled in demountable skin-clad tents. These people developed an elaborate method of existence specifically adjusted to their Arctic habitat. Hunters tracked the caribou on their annual northward migration from winter to summer grazing, and the salmon on their mass migration upstream. They used tents of caribou or seal skin for these summer travels before taking up winter

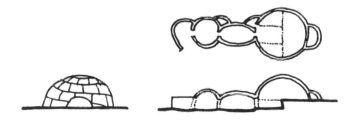

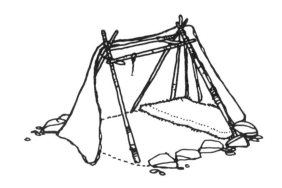

23 Igloo layout of the Canadian Eskimos and a skin-clad summer tent or *tupiq*

23

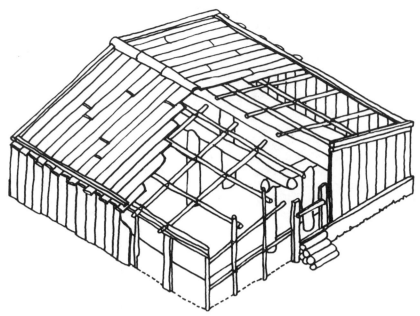

24

residence in permanent, semi-underground dwellings that had to be repaired and reinforced, or sometimes completely rebuilt each year.

The igloo (the term means 'house' of any type, a more precise term is *igluvizaq*, meaning 'snowhouse'), which is the replacement for these inadequate dwellings, is made from cut blocks of snow. Temporary shelters can be made in a short time after a day's travel. More permanent buildings are made new each year, situated together in community groups, not always in the same place as the year before. Although individual layouts may vary, the building is always manufactured in the same manner:

> To build an igloo, the hard-packed snow is cut into blacks with a knife of bone or ivory, and these are laid against one another in a spiral; the result is a cupola, whose keystone is inserted from the outside. The gaps are filled in with loose snow, and the interior may be covered with skin stretched on sinews so as to leave a circular chamber of cold air between the skins and the wall, a zone of insulation that makes it possible to heat the interior to temperature of 15 degrees centigrade (59 degrees Fahrenheit) without damaging the structure.[51]

In a way, the igloo *is* an example of portable architecture in that it is often built on the floating ice floes, which enables the Inuit to continue to hunt the seal and other marine animals that form an important part of their diet during the winter. The igloo is an example of an indigenous architecture perfectly tailored to its environment in that it uses the very conditions that make that environment difficult to survive in, to aid in the builder's survival. Other types of snowhouse are made in North America such as the *anegiuchak* with square walls and the *killegun* which surrounds a tent as an external insulating/windbreak structure.

The Nootka Indians of British Columbia in Canada, North America also lead a seasonal existence. In the winter they live by hunting inland and in the summer by fishing in the sea. Rather than build two sets of dwellings, one for each season in its separate location, or live in demountable or portable dwellings which move with them, they have devised an ingenious system that gives them continuity and comfort all year round. They build two permanent frameworks of exactly the same dimensions at the two sites. The planks of the roofs and walls are dismantled and transported on canoes from the inland sites along creeks and inlets to the seaside sites for the summer. This has practical and symbolic advantages.

The Nootka are highly gifted craftsmen who prepare the buildings and their decorations with great care. They invest substantial time in preparing spacious and richly decorated homes which can, in this way, be enjoyed in two locations.

24 Nootka house from Vancouver Island, British Columbia, Canada showing the separate transportable cladding planks and the permanent, main structural framework (after Guidoni)

The permanent structure also provides a symbol of ownership while the owner is living elsewhere. The Nootka houses are amongst the most substantial and permanent of traditional structures. Yet their creation is not only based upon significant transportable elements but also upon the careful use of resources which are allowed to continue living after providing the building materials.[52]

Traditional building patterns hold many lessons for contemporary designers – not simply in the forms they have adopted, but in the constructional methods employed to utilise often barely adequate materials to solve complex problems in a sophisticated manner. Not least of these lessons is the way in which the use of these materials has been free of harm to the environment. Modern civilisation is now remote from the implications of environmental damage in a way in which the traditional craftsman, manufacturing his own tools, artifacts and housing was and is not. If a craftsman destroys a tree he is aware that the tree will now not be available for his use in the future – he is aware that he must suffer the consequences of the damage he does. The architect who specifies a hardwood from a non-renewable resource many thousands of kilometres away is not aware of the nature of the environment he is changing. This remoteness from the problem is one of the important issues of contemporary design which must be overcome. The immediacy of the traditional builders' relationship between problem and solution has value not only in the forms they create and the techniques they have developed, but also in their approach to the utilisation of materials. The vernacular architecture of today and the immediate past is as important to us as the study of more conventional history, in that it provides lessons from which we may learn. It is not credible to assume that although technology has progressed, all our problems are now so different from those of the past. Architectural development is based on deeply established notions that remain constant despite the development of constructional processes. Though it is not sensible always to seek the solution to contemporary problems from historical examples, vernacular models can enhance our understanding of the issues of what makes appropriate architecture, as well as, sometimes, its form.

CHAPTER II
NON-ARCHITECTURAL PRECEDENTS

Traditional building patterns are in essence a response to the physical situation of the culture to which they belong. Paul Oliver's description of indigenous rural African buildings can, in the main, be attached to all primitive forms: 'In their construction, structure, performance, accommodation, serviceability, these are analysable buildings, relatively simple and satisfying the material needs of the community that uses them'.[1]

However, as has been described in the previous chapter, this is not to say that these buildings are without merit: 'In some examples of vernacular architecture they may meet demands in a precise and even sophisticated manner'.[2] Nevertheless, the merit of these structures can be understood as a result of pragmatic expediency and as a reaction to local spiritual and mythical lore.

The modern designer has, potentially, a much richer vein of inspiration and influence to draw upon. Much of this has been set by historical architectural precedent; however, the open-minded can also seek examples from less obvious sources – fields of design other than architecture and the inspiration of forms, patterns and structures found in nature. The opportunities of technology transfer are an important influence on the developed world's approach to demountable and portable building systems and will be examined in detail in later chapters; however, it is appropriate to examine first the historical basis and development of related systems associated with structures of a lightweight nature.

Natural Structures

Bionics is the study of natural systems as a resource for application into engineering systems. A simple example of the way a system in nature has been duplicated in engineering might be that of pneumatics. Tropism is movement as realised in plants, the most potent example of which is the Venus Flytrap which is haptotropic: responsive to touch. The Venus Flytrap moves by transferring fluid under osmotic pressure, a system of hydraulics utilisation which is related in principle to pneumatics, the movement of air under pressure to realise structural rigidity.

There is a common belief amongst naturalists that evolutionary progress in organisms tends towards increased effective use of resources and independence of the environment, an aspiration which is mirrored in engineering. Some engineers look on nature as a self-designing system that reacts to stress and produces counter-measures to resist it. This is borne out by the growth patterns of bones which not only show stress patterns in their make-up that relate directly to the loads applied to them, but also can repair themselves to counteract additional imposed stresses after fracture.[3] In plant life, studies have shown that stress stimulates cell growth and molecular change which increases strength without alteration of outward appearance.

Crystalline and organic structures have also proven an inspiration for man-made forms; the geodesic dome in particular is looked on as 'organic' in shape. Of interest is the fact that the shell of an egg was used as a model for the thickness of the concrete skin covering the first ever geodesic dome.[4] The six-sided cell combination is an extremely strong structural pattern, utilised by the honey bee in the manufacture of the hive but also seen in the make-up of plant and geological systems. Even the products manufactured by other natural creatures have the potential to inspire human built form.

> Man shares with a vast majority of animals and insects and birds the need for shelter of a kind. Burrowing, cocoon-making, nesting, spinning, weaving, fabricating shelter from mud and earth, twigs and straw, man must have witnessed in animals the reflection of his own need for protection from the elements and other creatures.[5]

Animals do in fact build dwellings, many of them temporary and portable. Our closest relatives, the primates, make significant structures that may relate in form

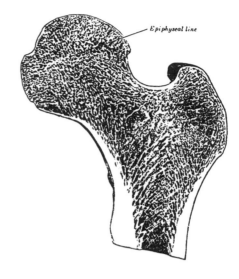

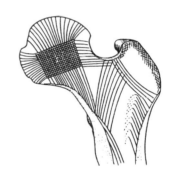

26

25 The *Olympic*, sister ship to the *Titanic* and the largest vessel in the world when it was launched in 1911; 26 Section through the human upper femur showing the cancelli, a network of plates and bars that forms the bone's structural pattern. From Henry Gray's *Anatomy*

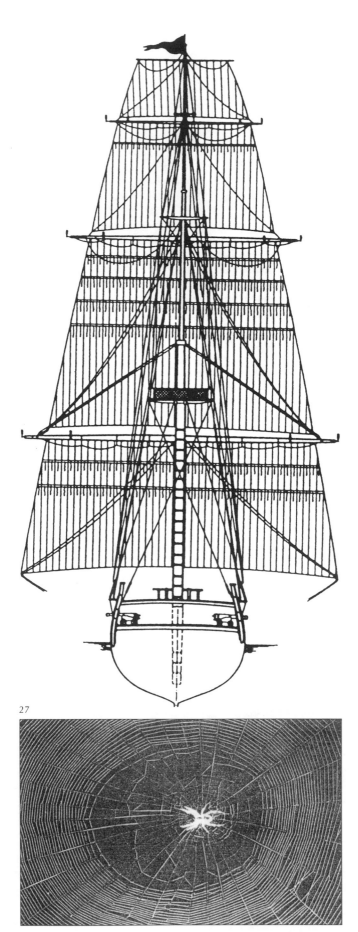

27

28

to man's first buildings. The gorilla will construct a simple overnight shelter in a tree or on the ground, sometimes with the structural requirement of making safe a sloping site. The rare primate, the Aye-Aye, makes a more complex structure that takes up to 24 hours to manufacture from interwoven twigs and branches, with a soft floor of shredded leaves.[6] Other mammals and birds are even more expert builders, and these have influenced the way man has built his dwellings; however:

> it is only man, on this planet, who has the capacity to design structures consciously for a particular purpose. It distinguishes man from all the other animals that he, instead of adapting to nature, has aimed at subduing the environment to his own purposes.[7]

The search for new materials and techniques or the improvement of those that already exist is crucial in the development of lightweight buildings technology, a factor common in the design of other portable products such as vehicles. The investigation of systems that occur in nature provides a valuable source for design inspiration. The method of flight evolved by birds was keenly examined by inventors in the hope of providing the key to human flight.[8] A different route to man's conquest of the air has been developed through the structure of the birds' bones, remarkable in terms of strength and lightness, which have formed a model for developing new patterns of lightweight man-made structures. Natural models were investigated extensively by Frei Otto in the development of tension structures – for example soap bubbles, used to observe the natural surface tension of liquids as an exploration of the relationship between form and efficiency.

The physical characteristics of some natural products in some cases have a far greater performance, weight for weight, than conventional man-made materials. For example, the thread spun by a spider has a strength to weight ratio many times in excess of our strongest steel. In an attempt to utilise this little understood yet commonly seen substance, scientists are now attempting to synthesise it.[9] Peter Rice's work for Ove Arup on the pavilion of the Future at Expo '92 in Seville, Spain used the same structural principle as a spider's web as it was designed to allow for deflections rather than resist them.

Maritime Precedents

Five and a half thousand years ago, mariners in Crete devised a method of harnessing the energy in the wind to propel their boats. By using sails made of skin (and later, cloth) they transferred the load applied by the wind down through a compression structure: the mast, aided and stiffened by tension structures; the rigging, to the hull of the boat. The sail itself uses differential pressure of the wind and is in effect a pneumatic structure. This remarkable and useful invention was developed dramatically over the ensuing centuries into a highly sophisticated, immensely strong and lightweight structure. The nineteenth century culmination of this development was the *Cutty Sark*, built in 1869. At 16 knots this ship could hoist 9,997 square metres of sail, which generated an effective strength of 2,250 horsepower. This development continues today, on a less impressive scale, using new materials and design techniques to create the super-efficient sailing yachts. Carbon fibre and epoxy resins are used in their construction and computer-aided design is employed to model their performance prior to building. The engineering skills of the manufacturers of world class sailing yachts are influencing architects because of their skill in the production of precision lightweight structures and fittings (see Chapter VII).

Engineering skills of a different kind led to the construction of the 'floating palaces' of the great transatlantic ocean liners, which dwarfed virtually all the buildings of their time. Le Corbusier stated in *Vers une Architecture*: 'our daring and masterly constructors of steamships produce palaces in comparison with which cathedrals are tiny things, and they throw them in the sea!'[10] The peak of Edwardian maritime engineering was in the construction of the triumvirate of great White Star Line transatlantic ocean liners of the Olympic class, the *Olympic*, the *Titanic*, and the *Britannic*. Although the Cunard Line's *Aquitania* (illustrated in Le Corbusier's book), launched three years after the *Olympic*, was 30 metres longer, it was the result of a race to devise a ship of greater tonnage and did not possess the same sensitivity in its design as the earlier class of ships which, 'if one word can describe the look ... it is classic; and, as with all classics, the keynote is simplicity'.[11]

27 *The Cutty Sark*, 1869; 28 Temporary animal architecture: the spider's web

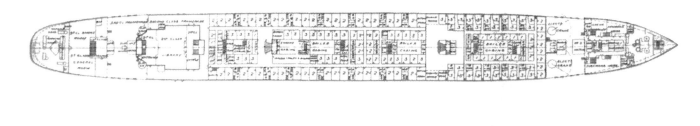

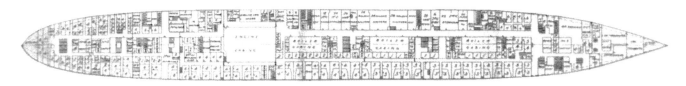

29

30

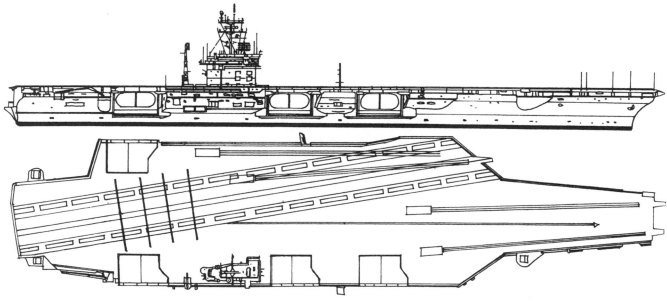

31

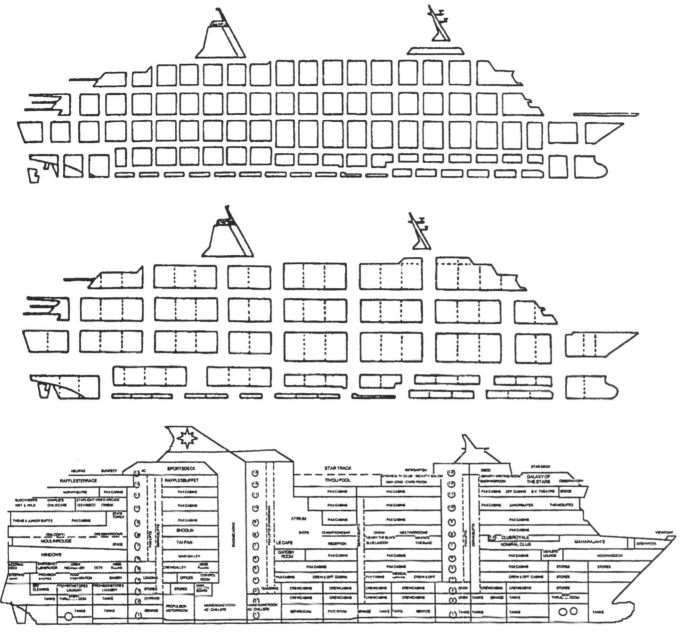

31a

The *Olympic* was the first of the three to be launched (1911) at Harland and
Wolff in Belfast and was designed by the yard's chief naval architect, Alexander
Carlisle.[12] At the time it was laid down, the shipyard employed 14,000 men, most
of whom were involved in the manufacture of this goliath, 259 metres long, 28
metres in the beam; it had a displacement of 60,000 tons and weighed 45,000
tons.

It was powered by reciprocating steam engines combined with a low pressure
steam turbine that developed 46,000 horsepower, allowing a top speed of 21
knots. The electrical system was powered by four dynamos generating 1,600 kilo-
watts and exceeded, 'in current capacity many large city central stations'.[13] The
ship could carry 2,440 passengers and 860 crew, 3,300 in total.

The machinery developed in the construction of the ship was also remarkable.
Two special slipways were built with a 6,000 ton removable gantry that enabled
the economical building of two ships at one time. The gantry carried eight travelling and revolving cranes capable of carrying up to 203.2 metric tons, as well as
the giant portable riveting machines. After the launch of the ship, its fitting-out

29 Plans of the White Star transatlantic ocean
liners *Olympic* and *Titanic* from *The Shipbuilder*,
1911; 30 Harland and Wolff gantry built for the
Olympic, *Titanic* and *Britannic* in their Belfast
yard; 31 *USS Nimitz*, CBN71 class aircraft carrier,
1972. It is 317m long, weighs 90,000 tons and is
home to 5,500 crew; 31a Modular construction
layout for the 3,900 berth *Super Star Leo*
constructed by the Meyer Shipbuilding Works,
Papenburg

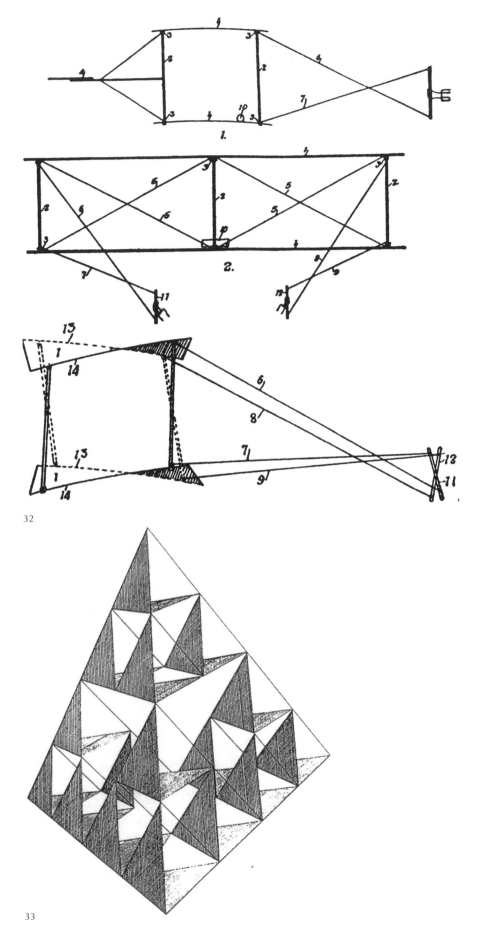

32 Patent drawing for the Wright brothers' kite-
glider of 1899; **33** Tetrahedron kite by Alexander
Graham Bell, 1903

was made possible by the use of a 200 ton floating crane capable of lifting 150 tons up to 45 metres high.

These ships were spectacular feats of engineering by any standards, but when viewed as examples of portable architecture, the achievement of their designers and builders can be seen in perspective. Maxtone-Graham describes them as objects that cross engineering boundaries in that they can be seen against the background of all human achievement: 'The *Titanic* and her two sisters rest securely in their apportioned niches in maritime history, among the marvels of their age and in no need for further deification within ours'.[14]

Contemporary passenger ships are built for leisure rather than transport and special techniques have evolved for faster, more economical construction. The *Super Star Leo*, launched by the Meyer works in Papenburg in 1998, is 268 metres long and 32 metres in the beam and carries 2,800 passengers and 1,100 crew. The ship was built utilising a modular system where compartments are made individually to high dimensional tolerances and then assembled by a large travelling crane within an enormous 300 × 60 metre construction hall.

The most impressive military maritime vehicles are the CBN71 Nimitz class aircraft carriers the *Nimitz*, *Dwight D Eisenhower*, *Carl Vinson*, and *Theodore Roosevelt*. The *USS Nimitz* is a nuclear powered ship launched in 1972 and commissioned in 1975; it displaces more than 90,000 tons, is 317 metres long, 41 metres in the beam and can travel at 33 knots. It has a range of over 1.75 million nautical kilometres.[15] Its sister ship, the *USS Theodore Roosevelt*, displaces 97,000 tons and carries 5,500 personnel, has a 4.5 acre flight deck and carries 75 aircraft, their fuel and ordnance. The ship has more than 4,000 compartments and three galleys that serve 186,000 meals a day. Even the largest buildings are dwarfed in comparison to these portable feats of engineering: 'An aircraft carrier of the Nimitz class has been said to be the most complex entity that mankind has ever put into one package in history.'[16] However, the ultimate floating city is *Voyager of the Seas*, the first of three Eagle class cruise ships to be launched by the Kvaerner Masa Shipyard in Finland. It weighs 143,000 tons and can carry 3,840 passengers and 1,180 crew. Its main engines generate 75.6 MW of power and it cost over $1 billion. On board are restaurants capable of serving 2,100 people at one time, a four deck 140 metre long shopping arcade, an art gallery, a revolving casino, an ice rink and a climbing wall!

Aviation

The ultimate in lightweight, man-made structures are those associated with aviation. The endeavour to make machines that can be supported by the pressure of the air has been an ambition for many centuries. Yet of all the fundamental artifacts that have come to shape the twentieth century the flying machine has had the shortest and most dramatic history. In the space of just 66 years man went from the first heavier-than-air flying machine to the first successful journey to another planet.

The Chinese played a fundamental role in the very early days of both heavier-than-air and lighter-than-air flight. The kite was invented in China over 2,000 years ago and kite flying has been a popular pastime there for centuries. Although the Chinese developed kites that were sufficiently large to carry a man, the further exploitation of lightweight structures did not take place until the Renaissance, when between 1503 and 1506 Leonardo da Vinci carried out an extensive series of investigations into the nature of air and birds' method of flight. Leonardo's experiments with ornithopters failed but he was successful in developing a practical parachute.[17] In the eighteenth century the first systematic practical experiments took place in England where Sir George Cayley developed the man-carrying glider. In the nineteenth century Otto Lilienthal brought an unprecedented level of scientific investigation to lightweight structures, although he was unsuccessful in creating a genuine flying machine. Orville and Wilbur Wright were a pair of inventors and bicycle mechanics from Dayton, Ohio, USA, who after a series of experiments based on Lilienthal's work synthesised their own ideas into the design

34

34a

for the first successful heavier-than-air flying machine in 1903. They based their structure on the simple box kite, a framework which gave rigidity through the arrangement of compressive struts and tension wires. The pattern they made successful was emulated for the first two decades of flight until material technology advanced sufficiently so that a wing could be made structurally stable by its internal structure alone. The structure of the biplane was sufficiently symbolic of lightweight efficiency for Le Corbusier to include it in his illustrations for *Vers une Architecture*, but he also saw in its design an appropriate solution to a well-understood problem: 'The airplane is the product of close selection'.[18]

A direct transition from structures associated with flight to those required in building construction was made by the American inventor, Alexander Graham Bell. He had worked on a long series of designs for box kites and devised a framework based on the tetrahedron. In 1903 he published his findings in which he stated: 'This [tetrahedral] form seemed to give maximum strength with the minimum of material'.[19] The tetrahedral shape was inherently stable and very strong. Bell made massive kites of up to 3,395 tetrahedrons and had ambitions to develop them into aircraft, although they lacked the aerodynamic form which by now the Wright brothers had deduced would produce a successful flying machine.

However, Bell did recognise the structural potential of his developments. In 1902 he built a lightweight temporary shelter for his livestock on his farm in Nova Scotia, North America, and in 1907, he designed and built a 24 metre-high tower using a 1.2 centimetre diameter iron pipe with iron connectors. This structure demonstrated the potential of what has come to be called the space frame, in that it took just ten days to erect and weighed only five tons.

The Chinese also invented the hot air balloon about 800 years ago. Once again this device was not developed as a serious vehicle until nearly 600 years later when the French Montgolfier brothers made the first man-carrying flights in Europe, beginning in 1783. Hot air balloons developed slowly through the nineteenth century and it was not until the discovery of manufacturable lighter-than-air gases such as hydrogen that a more controllable lighter-than-air flying machine became practical. The balloon is essentially a pneumatic envelope, the gas within the envelope exerting pressure to rise if it is in excess of the weight of its container and any load attached to it. The early development of the airship was by Count Ferdinand von Zeppelin, who gave his name to these innovative influential machines. By containing several gas bags within a single structure of aerodynamic shape and adding engines and propellers, the lighter-than-air flying machine became a practical proposition. The structure which contained the bags had to be lightweight and strong, and this part of airship construction is of as much significance in lightweight building development as the pneumatic principles incorporated in the gas bags. The most innovative designer in the field was the British inventor, Sir Barnes Wallis, who designed the R100 airship between 1924 and 1930. This aircraft's structure utilised geodesic principles to provide the lightest and most rigid framework possible.[20] Wallis went on to use geodesic principles in the design of the Wellington bomber which flew during the Second World War and had a remarkable reputation for holding together even after suffering substantial damage. The big flaw with the airships of this time was that the gas which was used, hydrogen, was extremely combustible. The famous and dramatic explosion of the *Hindenberg*, the world's largest airship, effectively sealed the fate of the type.[21]

The new generation of airships are filled with non-flammable helium. German company CargoLifter AG plan a fleet of lighter-than-air freighters beginning with the CL75 which was inflated for the first time in July 2001 with a gas volume equivalent to the *Graf Zeppelin*. The CL160 will be over 260 metres in length and carry a payload of 160 metric tons, lifted into place while the aircraft hovers 100 metres in the air. These latest airships use high-tech fabric skins instead of relatively heavy frames with just a keel below the gas bag to spread the load and contain the cargo bay, engines, fuel, and crew quarters.

34 The internal structure of a Zeppelin;
34a CargoLifter CL160 lighter-than-air freight carrier

The opportunities for technology transfer between different areas of research are vast. Many vehicle designs result from large and exhaustive research programmes and take advantage of the transfer of material, constructional and structural principles from sometimes quite remote industrial applications. The effective transference of the results of scientific investigation in diverse fields is an observable characteristic of dramatic periods in the history of technological development.[22]

CHAPTER III
THE AGE OF INVENTION: TECHNOLOGICAL CHANGE BEFORE 1900

The architectural development of lightweight temporary structures is driven by two forces: the need for such functions in a building, and the availability of suitable materials. Prior to the twentieth century the limited presence of these factors reduced the development of significant buildings of this type to a few notable examples. In earlier history, building types that required large open spaces were restricted to those that were used for substantial gatherings of the populace, generally for assembly at a performance. Even then, the necessity for a lightweight element in the building was restricted as the early centres of civilisation evolved in a generally equitable climate, the Mediterranean. With the development of industrial techniques came not only the capability for larger spans but the necessity in new building types and functions, and with the advent of the notion of technology as a benefactor, the ambition to use it to the fullest led to ambitious and innovative buildings which also had the purpose of portraying the achievements and power of their creators.

Auditoria and Theatres

Although the Greeks built special auditoria for performance, they were generally set in natural amphitheatres and their plays were so stylised as to require little in the way of demountable props or sets. The Roman amphitheatre was, however, a much more ambitious building, creating its own architectural type, independent of geographical location. The Colosseum in Rome was built between AD 70 and 82 and is described by Banister Fletcher as a:

> type unique among ancient buildings. The structural problems were engineering in character, and all the more so because the Romans built up the whole gigantic edifice without that extraneous support which the Greeks secured in theatre building, by scooping the auditorium out of the earth.[1]

The building could seat 50,000 spectators and was used for a wide variety of events, including the well-known gladiatorial combats. As well as battles between men and wild beasts the entire auditorium could be flooded for naval battles. The changing uses must have required substantial demountable structures, much of which can now only be guessed at. However, it is certain that the building featured a removable tension roof of canvas (called a velarium) suspended from 7.6 metre-high masts around the perimeter. This roof was 189 by 156 metres and erected by sailors who would have been familiar with this transferable technology.

Less audacious entertainment was popular all over Europe in mediaeval times, and though more limited in variety, the content was extensive. Mystery plays were populist parables that related to biblical stories but were a valid and attractive form of entertainment as well. Some plays had up to 80,000 lines and took 40 days to perform. The plays were acted in demountable theatres called 'mansiones': platforms or booths set up in the town market place, or sometimes in an existing building. Boxes or even galleries might be set up to one side to enable those with more prestige and more money to attend in comfort and safety. The mystery plays continued into the seventeenth century, but by that time the permanent theatre building was well established in Europe.

Other types of theatre performances became popular in the Renaissance and architects were sometimes asked to devise dramatic temporary transformations of existing buildings. Filippo Brunelleschi used many ingenious systems to manufacture scene changes and special effects for dramatic religious productions from 1439. These were on a grand scale and involved flying whole hosts of 'angels'. His work at S. Spirito in Florence in 1471 included the creation of a castle and a mountain and a kinetic device that allowed for the ascension of Christ into Heaven who 'seemed to rise on his own, and without any sort of wobbling went up to a great height'.[2]

35 Marco Marcola, a *Commedia dell'arte* in the Arena at Verona, 1772

36

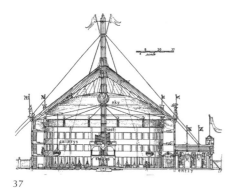

37

Paradoxically, many temporary stage sets of the Renaissance, created from painted scenes on timber frames, illustrated images of idealised cities, executed in correct renditions of the relatively recently rediscovered perspective.[3] Peruzzi designed many stage sets for Italian plays between 1513 and 1531. The work of this designer of demountable 'cities' was influential. Vasari praised his work on Calandria which was presented in Urbino in 1513 and repeated in Rome in 1518:

> One can hardly imagine how in such restricted space so many streets, so many palaces and so many strange temples, halls and cornices could be arranged. They were done so excellently that ... the square did not appear painted and small, but extraordinarily large ... Lighting was done cleverly too, so that it supported the effects of perspective.[4]

In sixteenth century Italy, floating pavilions called *teatri del mondo* were built to celebrate special occasions. They were generally circular in form, like a classical temple with a canopy supported by a perimeter row of columns. The top of the pavilion might support a group of musicians whilst on the lower stage a performance might take place, or perhaps form a platform for dignitaries to sit while other acts of the pageant were enacted.[5]

The Royal court has had a quality of spectacle and pageantry that is closely associated with the development of the theatre; in certain societies it has even formed one of the main venues for the development of such entertainment. The English Tudor monarchs of the early sixteenth century were particularly enthusiastic about performances, often taking part themselves, as well as funding the arrangements. The more permanent theatre buildings such as the Swan and the Globe, which were to establish the permanent nature of theatre building, had yet to be built, and the revels and pageants were generally held in existing permanent buildings. For diplomatic reasons, the Monarchy occasionally felt it necessary to hold gatherings when no suitable venue was available. This led to the design and erection of great temporary banqueting and entertainment halls by the royal revels office. Two such great meetings were held by Henry Tudor VIII in Northern France in 1520.[6] The first, held in June at Guisnes near Calais, was the largest and consisted of the erection of a large temporary 'palace', with apartments, kitchens and 122 entertainment halls, though it was of conventional form and materials. The second, built in Calais itself, used skills from shipbuilding to create a unique and evocative architectural form. The building was circular in plan, 37 metres diameter with 16 sides. Its structure consisted of a single 40 metre high central mast which supported a double skin roof: the outer, a weatherproof layer of canvas, the inner a decorated fabric painted to represent the sky. The perimeter of the building was made of timber boards 12 metres high, covered in canvas and then decorated. Around the internal perimeter was a continuous gallery structure with three upper floors, which in turn had three levels each so that those standing at the back could see over the heads of those in front. A stage was established around the mast at the centre and the Royal party sat at tables on the floor in the most prominent position. This flammable building was lit entirely with candles supported on great chandeliers and in the hands of statues; however, it was not fire that was to cause its downfall but the wind. The English Channel is well known for summer storms, and on 12 June 1520, shortly before the great banquet was to take place, the canvas roof and thereafter all the interior works of the building were destroyed. This building was remarkable in its use of a now familiar form, the conical tent, on such a large scale as to create an architectural image that was not only suitable for its function, but also expressed it so well.

The form and character of Henry VIII's 1520 banqueting house at Calais reflects a type of portable building that remains redolent with the excitement of performance to this day: the circus. Reference has already been made to the very first type of circus, the travelling menagerie (see Chapter I) but once this form of entertainment started to become a performance, it became necessary to develop a movable building that could shelter the performers and audience, as well as divide those who had paid from those who had not. Though the very first circus tents started to appear at the end of the eighteenth century, the metamorphosis to a travelling circus, with a recognisable 'big top' and associated entourage of entertainers, was not complete until the middle of the nineteenth century.[7]

36 A Renaissance stage design (after Peruzzi);
37 The banqueting house of Henry VIII at Calais, France, 1520. Drawing by James Fitzgibbon

There are two basic forms of large circus tent: the framed structure and the tension structure. The first consists of a structurally independent timber or metal frame, on to which a tent is spread purely as a weatherproof skin. One example is the Cirque Palisse which lasted for more than 30 years from 1911. The 3,200 seat building had a 36 metre diameter timber frame which was covered with canvas. It took a foreman and four workers between two and six days to erect, and two days to dismantle.[8] The architectural form was typical of this type of building: a circular vault (which forms the perimeter of the circus ring on plan) upon which a continuous apse (which encloses the audience space) is supported. Metal frame buildings are built in the same form but are more robust (as the material is more suitable to erection and dismantling procedures, particularly at the joints), and less bulky to transport. The principles are, however, similar, as are the advantages: the building is structurally independent and relatively lightweight, requiring no foundations and minimal tethering against wind uplift; the building structure is contained within its own plan; no external guys or supports are required. This makes this form of tent particularly suitable to city sites with hard-paved areas which cannot accept fixtures, are limited in space, and have the necessity for a secure perimeter which can be attained by fixing solid panels to the outside of the frame at ground level. The Napoleon Rancy Circus, first built in 1955, is typical of this sort of building. Tubular steel frames enable the entire building to be erected in four days. It is 41 metres diameter and 15.6 metres high and can seat 3,000 people. The building weighs 120 tons and the entire circus is transported in 18 medium-sized vehicles.[9]

38

39

The tension-structured tent is a much lighter solution to the same problem; however, it is restricted in siting as it must be located on a relatively flat field and security must be achieved in a different manner. This form does have the potential to produce large dramatic structures with the minimum of materials. The simplest type is the 'umbrella', a single central pole from which a conical tent is suspended.[10] However, the most complex and largest circuses also use this form. The Barnum and Bailey Greatest Show on Earth was a mammoth attraction at the turn of the century which toured Europe several times in the late nineteenth and early twentieth centuries. The 1897–1902 circus utilised fourteen tents on sites that had to be a minimum of 200 by 300 metres. The largest tent was 130 by 54 metres and could seat 10,000 people. This building had three rings and two stages, and the entire outfit required 70 wagons towed by four trains for transportation. This spectacle set a precedent that others such as Buffalo Bill's Wild West Show and the Circus Sarrasani tried to emulate. Europe's major cities became halting points in a giant caravanserai of entertainment shows, each bringing its own tented cities together with wild and exotic inhabitants.

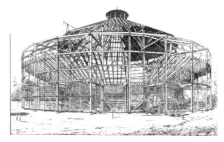

40

To erect a tension structure tent, the main mast or masts are fixed at the base and hoisted to a vertical position with a winch or manpower. They are then guyed to the ground so that they are stable. Next, the tent is laid out on the ground around the mast and its seams tied so it makes a continuous piece. After securing with ropes at its perimeter, the centre of the tent is hauled to the top of the main poles. Internal and perimeter poles are now slotted into their places in the tent to give it its final form and help stiffen and brace it with ropes and guys. It is essential that the entire skin is as tight as possible and that there are no loose areas of canvas that can flap and act as a sail to weaken the rest of the structure. There are many different tent patterns to fit any type of entertainment situation, and development continues with new lighter and stronger materials. Canvas is now replaced with stiffer, more weatherproof and longer lasting synthetic materials, and masts are now aluminium framed structures braced by cables and able to accommodate lighting and other services.[11]

Colonial and Emigrant Buildings

There are many early examples of buildings which were pre-manufactured then transported to site for assembly, for reasons of convenience or necessity, situations which could be described effectively as: 'the classic situation of prefabrication, a sudden unpremeditated demand, and negligible local resources with which to meet it'.[12] Mediaeval frame buildings often utilised timber components shaped at the location where the trees were felled then transported to site to save in the

38 Nineteenth century circus with an umbrella tent at Villié-Morgan, France; **39** Tubular steel circus structure, the Napoleon Rancy Circus in Grenoble, 1955; **40** Demountable wooden circus structure from *La Construction Moderne*, February, 1893

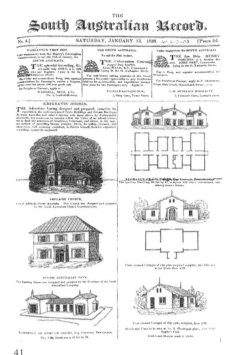

41

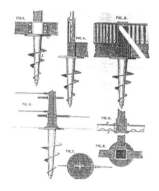

42

effort of transportation of wood which would not be used in the construction. In the eighteenth century, at the beginnings of British colonialism, there were many examples of specific buildings being made at home and shipped abroad for erection in far countries. In 1787, Samuel Wyatt built 12 movable hospitals which could be dismantled and re-erected inside an hour without the use of tools.[13] Buildings like this were essentially unique responses to specific situations and, though interesting in terms of their logistical approach to the problem, cannot be recognised as developed componentised systems. For this, repetitive elements that utilise interchangeability and dimensional coordination are significant characteristics.

The first manufacturer to address the more general issue of the mass-market demountable building was John Manning, a London carpenter and builder who in 1830 conceived the 'Manning Portable Colonial Cottage'. This structure was designed to utilise a small volume for effective use of shipping space, to be easy to erect, and, as repetitive parts were of the same dimension, modular. Manning stated that: 'as none of the pieces are heavier than a man or a boy could easily carry for several miles, it might be taken even to a distance, without the aid of any beast of burden'.[14] The practical benefits of such a building were manifest. A contemporary commentator, John Barton Hall, was farsighted enough to have transported one of Manning's products to the settlement at Holdfast Bay, South Australia in 1837, and he observed:

If you were to see the miserable shifts our good friends and neighbours are put to, you would think us well off; we are almost the only people in the colony who possess wooden houses, all the others living in rush-huts and tents. The other day, in a gale of wind, we saw some people running after their house that had blown away; let no one come to a new colony without one of H Manning's nice portable wooden houses.[15]

Manning advertised in the journals and newspapers of the new found colonies worldwide with illustrations of the completed buildings that enabled his customers to order their prefabricated home by post, complete with all the components necessary for its erection. Manning's innovative and successful methods were soon imitated by others, most notably Peter Thompson, who not only manufactured dwellings but churches, banks and other buildings. The advantages of prefabrication were also used in the home market and Thompson built a prefabricated, temporary church in Kentish Town, London in 1844.[16] The Manning cottage can be seen as the beginning of the prefabrication industry which produced products that utilised standardised interchangeable components and dimensional coordination to form easily erected flexible structures.

The prefabricated building industry began in North America in much the same way. Buildings were at first shipped from Britain, but the country's vast source of readily available timber, the independence that resulted from the American Revolution and the vast distances still to be covered from the Eastern seaboard meant that local products became far more important. The first major market for the prefabricated house was the California Gold Rush of 1849 which resulted in the creation of instant boom towns for the exploitation of the mines and the miners. From the 1860s the settlement of the prairies in the vast midwest states, where timber for building was scarce, led to the importation of building materials and the need for prefabricated products. The creation of the 'Chicago method' or 'balloon frame' construction process helped establish timber framed buildings as the cheapest and fastest mode of fabricating shelter. This process was so called because the house could be erected so fast that it appeared to be inflated like a balloon. It utilised factory-made nails to join corners, instead of the more laborious mortise and tenon. With the establishment of the railroad network, transportation became much more efficient and Sears, Roebuck and Company introduced a system of purchase and supply using a mail-order catalogue. Because of the convenience of the system and the reliability and quality of its products, Sears established a strong market that provided the settlers with most of their requirements by mail order including, from 1895, the mail-order home. Sears manufactured many of their own products in factories built close to reserves of labour and materials, and they set about producing buildings in exactly the same manner with a series of factories devoted to various aspects of the building process: timber

41 Front page of the *South Australian Record*, 13 January, 1838. Advertisement for prefabricated emigrants' buildings by Peter Thompson of London; **42** The Calvert and Light Portable Building System of 1860 from the *Mechanics' Magazine*, September, 1860

machining, nail-making and plumbing components. The houses Sears sold varied greatly in style and size, meaning that almost any budget could be accommodated. The product was guaranteed (Sears called them 'honor-built homes') and in many cases included the comparative luxuries of indoor bathrooms and fitted kitchens. A house kit contained approximately 30,000 components, all transported by rail. Though a typical house could be fitted into two box cars it was common to stagger shipments to arrive on site when required and when the budget allowed. Sears also made farm buildings, outhouses, garages and during the First World War shipped hospital buildings to the Red Cross. Between 1908 and 1940 more than 100,000 families bought homes by mail from Sears, selected from over 450 designs. Many more, based on a similar system of manufacture and marketing, were acquired from Sears' competitors, The Hodgson Company, Alladin Homes and Montgomery Ward. Many thousands of these homes still exist in cities and towns across North America.[17] Once erected they were not intended to be mobile. However, the construction of these buildings is so strong and flexible that it is quite feasible to raise the complete structure intact from its site and move it elsewhere if desired. There are many specialist house moving companies that exist for just this purpose and it is even possible to purchase a second-hand house from a sales yard and relocate it to your own site.

The Industrial Revolution

The single great technical innovation to take place in building before the twentieth century was the invention of cast and wrought iron. This made the concept of substantial lightweight buildings possible. Banister Fletcher identified these developments:

> far-reaching innovations in building were often related to progress in general technology, eg, in metallurgy, and some were of great architectural importance … one was the development of structural iron, dramatically illustrated by the construction of the Iron Bridge.[18]

The bridge, which crosses the River Severn at Coalbrookdale in Shropshire, was built in 1779 by Abraham Darby III (1750–91), who was an iron-founder and therefore implicitly understood the capabilities of the new material. The structure is made solely of cast iron, all prefabricated, and assembled on site with component fixings such as nuts and bolts. Colin Davies describes the Iron Bridge as: 'the favourite candidate for the title "first High Tech structure".'[19]

In 1807, the Coalbrookdale Company shipped 50.8 metric tons of components to Jamaica to build an iron bridge. It was another iron bridge building company, the Horseley Iron Works of Tipton, Staffordshire, that built the first iron boat for the Oxford canal which was transported in component form to the Surrey Canal docks in London in 1821. Many more boats were built in component form, transported abroad in a dismantled state and assembled for use at their destination, or even, when occasion demanded, assembled to cross water, disassembled to be carried across land, then, reassembled at the final destination.[20] These examples provided the model for the use of this material in building construction. The casting technique meant that the requirements of prefabrication, the ability to make dimensionally coordinated repetitive parts, was readily achieved. Cast iron began to be used extensively in the construction of buildings though, at first, only in those of a thoroughly practical nature which served the new industries of the Industrial Revolution. It was used for the multistorey buildings (often up to eight or nine floors) of the mill industry, chosen for its lightness, relatively small footprint on plan, and fire resistance. At first it was only rarely that the capabilities of the material for componentised construction in building were realised fully. One of these early examples was a modest building, first erected as a prefabricated toll house on the West Bromwich–Birmingham Railway in 1830. It was later dismantled and re-erected as a lock-keeper's cottage at Tipton Green, Staffordshire where it remained until being demolished in 1926. This humble building has been described as: 'not simply the first prefabricated metal house in the history of the world, but the prototype for generations of cladding systems'.[21] The building consisted of a series of flanged full-height wall panels bolted together. A system similar to this was used extensively for the first commercially available demountable componentised buildings. These cast-iron and galvanised sheet buildings

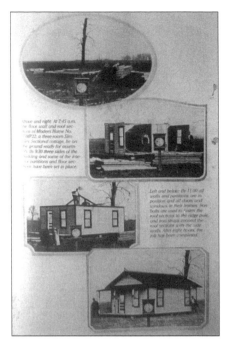

43

43 The Sears Simplex Portable Cottage assembled in just over two hours, from the Sears mail order catalogue of 1919

44

45

44 Prefabricated lighthouse by Alexander Gordon, erected in Cottam and Hallen's yard in London, 1844, before dismantling and shipping to Bermuda for erection on Gibbs Hill. From the *Illustrated London News*, 31 August 1844;
45 The Great Conservatory at Chatsworth, Derbyshire, Joseph Paxton, 1837–40. From the *Illustrated London News*, 31 August 1844

were created for export to the colonies. From a catalogue you could buy houses, barns, sheds, even a church building. Buildings were shipped all over the world, and some were employed for unlikely local uses – one was used for a temporary ballroom at Queen Victoria's house at Balmoral in Scotland, though like many successful 'temporary' buildings it has remained in use and still stands there today.

A dramatic early example of the use of cast iron was the 40 metre high lighthouse built by Alexander Gordon for Gibbs Hill, Bermuda in 1844. The manufacturers, Cottam and Hallen, fully erected the structure in their central London yard prior to shipping, a dramatic and unmistakable example of the portable capabilities of the new systems now being devised. The practicality of metal buildings was soon understood by both manufacturers and users and a whole range of demountable buildings was designed both as commercially available products and as solutions to specific problems. Dwellings, churches, army barracks, shops, hotels, theatres, custom houses, banks, hospitals and even palaces were built. In the 1850s, a complete gas works was built in Buenos Aires constructed entirely from components shipped from Britain.[22]

Cast iron excelled in its lightweight provision of structure. A purpose for this arose in the Victorian fascination with the collection of exotic plants from the British Empire. The first glass-houses were made of timber framing, but the potential of cast iron with its repetitive componentised construction methods was soon realised. One of the first glass-houses was built by a gardener, JC Loudon, at Bretton Hall, Yorkshire in 1827. This building had a dome spanning 30 metres, and depended on the interaction of metal and glass for its rigidity, one of the first to do so. In 1831, Loudon proposed a 60 metre diameter conservatory for the Birmingham Horticultural Society.[23]

The first of the greenhouse structures to draw significant public attention was Sir Joseph Paxton's (1801–65) Great Conservatory at Chatsworth, Derbyshire. Built between 1836 and 1840, it was 84 metres long and 20 metres wide. Queen Victoria visited it on 1 December 1842 and in her journal referred to it as: 'the most stupendous and extraordinary creation imaginable', and Paxton: 'quite a genius'.[24]

The most beautiful of these great nineteenth-century conservatories may be that by the Dublin iron-founder Richard Turner and architect Decimus Burton (1800-81) for the Palm House at Kew Gardens, London. Built between 1845 and 1847, the building has a smooth machine-like surface and featured dramatic innovations in its construction such as thermic welding and post-tensioning.[25] These buildings are lightweight in nature, prefabricated and componentised in construction but are essentially intended to be permanent. However, the capabilities of their system as a medium for the construction of temporary buildings were soon to be explored in the most profound way possible.

Nineteenth Century Exhibition Buildings

In the early nineteenth century France had a tradition of holding regular exhibitions displaying national industries at regular intervals (the first was in 1798). In Great Britain the only exhibitions had been held by the Society of Arts: manufacturers' shows in 1847, 1848 and 1849. Prince Albert, who was the president of the Society, was approached by civil servant Henry Cole with the idea of holding a much larger exhibition. The idea grew into a proposal for a great international exhibition and a building committee was established in 1850 which included CR Cockerell the architect, and the engineer IK Brunel. A competition was held and 245 entries were received. The first prize was awarded to two designs, one by Richard Turner who had been involved with the Kew Palm House, and the other by Hector Horeau, a French designer who had submitted the same design for the Paris Exhibition in 1849. Both designs were constructed from cast iron and glass but contemporary illustrations of Turner's design show a truly lightweight solution with delicate structural supports and a skin that takes on the form of a continuous, bubble-like section.[26] However, neither winner was commissioned. The Building Committee decided to present its own design described by Pevsner as: 'a mongrel affair of a long, aisled nave with *Rundbogen* everywhere'.[27]

When Paxton saw the official design he was unimpressed and made enquiries to see if his ideas might be considered. On 11 June 1850 he made his first sketch, on the 20th he took his ideas to London, and on the 24th presented them to Prince Albert. On the 15th July they were accepted by the Building Committee and on the 30th contractors started earth-moving on the site. The building, 563 metres long by 124 metres wide and 33 metres to the top of the transept, was complete by January 1851. Pawley calls this building: 'an epic of prefabrication, standardisation, precision and construction management unprecedented in its time and hardly matched since … a display of technological mastery'.[28] Banister Fletcher describes it as: 'an astonishing achievement … excellent for its specialised purpose, and a forerunner of twentieth-century concepts'.[29]

The Crystal Palace was built in just six months. A complete revolution in building methods had to be introduced in order to achieve this remarkable objective. The building was designed on a 7 metre module and incorporated 3,300 iron columns, 2,150 iron girders, 372 roof beams, 38.6 kilometres of gutter, 402 kilometres of sash bar, and 293,635 glass panels. The roof was glazed by operators working from specially designed trolleys that ran in the grooves of the glazing bars like railway lines.

At the 1851 Great Exhibition, the exhibition building itself became the prime attraction. With the Queen's patronage, the building received tremendous popular acclaim, visited by over 6,000,000 people. The building was not innovative in the field of large spans, iron construction, or the use of glass (though it utilised all these to dramatic effect) but in the unprecedented use of a 48 component system in building manufacture and site assembly which allowed its rapid construction, remote from its manufacture, and the subsequent dismantling for reassembly on another site. Every item of the building's construction was meticulously planned for reuse in the new structure; even the temporary timber fencing was reused as floorboards inside.

The building was dismantled in 1852 and reerected in a slightly altered and improved form on its new site in Sydenham, London, as a permanent exhibition hall.[30] But even without this reerection and continued existence as a physical example, the building had a profound effect on the creation of subsequent exhibition structures, the first of which was the Bogardus project for the 'Crystal Palace of New York' in 1853. This building involved a 91 metre high tower at its centre with a tension roof supported by iron chains. Many more great exhibition projects followed the spirit of the 1851 exhibition, increasing in size year after year until by 1889 the Paris Exhibition spread over 21 hectares – more than twice the area of the one in Britain in 1851. At this exhibition, two structures were most impressive: the Eiffel Tower (designed by Gustave Eiffel), at a height of 300 metres, the highest structure in the world at that time, and the Galerie des Machines (by Dutert and Contamin), at 420 metres long and 111 metres wide – the largest span to have been achieved to that date.

The feature of the Crystal Palace which makes it unique to this day is that it is still the largest building to have been designed to be specifically demountable, and to have proved its practicality unequivocally. It is the 'world's greatest prefabricated building',[31] still, after nearly 150 years, when fantastic innovations in virtually all other fields of science and design have taken place. It is a great precedent for designers of today who wish to design lightweight, movable building systems, but it emphasises the inadequacy of our own era in that nothing better has been produced since the nineteenth century, that 'epoch of bewildering innovation'.[32]

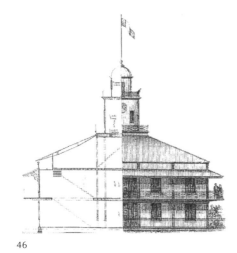

46

47

48

46 Prefabricated Iron Customs House for Payta, Peru,1854, made by Edward Bellhouse and Company of the Eagle Foundry, Manchester, England. From the *Civil Engineer* and *Architects' Journal*, 1854; **47** Design for the 1851 Exhibition building, London, by Richard Turner, 1850; **48** Joseph Paxton, The Crystal Palace, 1850–51

CHAPTER IV
TWENTIETH CENTURY INNOVATORS

... if we observe the historians' convention of running the nineteenth century from the defeat of Napoleon in 1815 to the outbreak of the Great War in 1914, then virtually every significant element of modern life, from antisepsis to railways, from electricity to turbines, the aeroplane, the motor car, the radio, the telephone and even the fax machine and the computer, were properly speaking nineteenth-century inventions. With the exception of electronics, our own century has made only developmental contribution; and our process of development has slowed to a crawl.[1]

This statement by Martin Pawley made in 1991 can be seen as a cynical summation of technical progress in the twentieth century. Perhaps it is even surprising for those of us so used to the constant effect of new technology in our everyday lives. The general impression is that today the pace of advancement is faster than it has ever been. Yet upon examination, the point Pawley makes is true, and in architectural terms it is particularly true. This is so even if the one exemption, electronics, develops as predicted and, through the creation and growth of computer technology, makes half the other things on the list redundant! The Modern Movement is that architectural epoch which has most strongly influenced building in the twentieth century and although the designers of that movement strongly professed support for technological advance, Reyner Banham could confidently criticise them in 1960 as having 'produced a Machine-Age architecture only in the sense that its monuments were built in a Machine Age'.[2]

What Pawley is advocating and what Banham sees lacking in Modernist architects' work is a truly inventive approach to architectural design which challenges and meets building design problems in the same way that the best engineers and applied scientists do in their respective fields. This ambition has been recognised and even professed during the twentieth century. One influential example was Sant'Elia, who stated in his 'Futurist manifesto' catalogue for the Città Nuova exhibition:

> We no longer believe in the monumental, the heavy and static, and have enriched our sensibilities with a taste for lightness, transience and practicality … We must invent and rebuild *ex novo* our modern city like an immense and tumultuous shipyard, active, mobile, and everywhere dynamic, and the modern building like a giant machine.[3]

Designers in the twentieth century have certainly embraced the *image* of the machine but regarding its purpose and intent there still appears, at least in some cases, confusion.

In his statement, Pawley dismisses the contribution of those who make only developmental contributions in the advancement of technology. This is misguided. The recognition of the potential in an idea, invention or discovery, often takes quite different skills from those of the inventor. As a nation, Great Britain has been strongly criticised for letting great inventions slip away to be developed elsewhere; the electronic computer is probably the most recent and most important example. The application of technology in a meaningful and beneficial way is surely the most important part in its development, for after all, what good is knowledge without a use?

In the twentieth century, there have been some creative personalities in the architectural field who have produced new and innovative ideas, particularly directed at the development of lightweight building systems. These designers have not been 'obliged to invent movements to advance careers'.[4] Though they come from diverse backgrounds and their contributions have been in different forms, all have possessed a common approach in that they have attempted to look on their architecture as work without precedent – not without inspiration,

49 Buckminster Fuller, US Marine Dome, 1954 – a seminal image that commumicated the qualities of the geodesic dome: lightness with strength

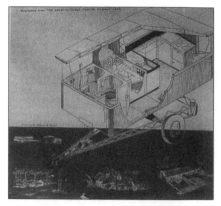

50

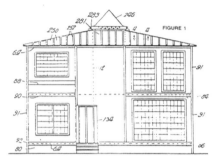

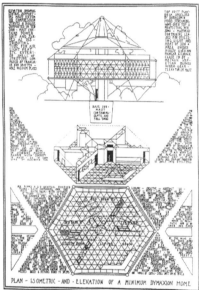

51

50 Buckminster Fuller, the Mechanical Wing servicing trailer, from the *Architectural Record*, 1940; **51** Above: Buckminster Fuller, April 1928 design for the Dymaxion House; Below: May 1929 design for the Dymaxion House

or without external influence – but as a completely contemporary solution appropriate to a problem.[5]

WR Lethaby, an architect of the nineteenth century, described accurately and concisely the approach that a designer must take if he is to draw from technological advance those features which are going to be of value in his work, and in the long run to society: 'The method of design to a modern mind can only be understood in the scientific, or engineer's sense, as a definite analysis of possibilities – not as a vague poetic dealing with poetic matters'.[6]

Buckminster Fuller

In 1928, when Buckminster Fuller offered the patent rights of the 4D prefabricated house (an air-deliverable dwelling built using industrial manufacturing techniques) to the American Institute of Architects in order to further development of affordable, high-quality housing, they refused with a rebuff that not only conveyed their disapproval of his ideas, but also showed their disregard for his abilities to take part in what they regarded as an architect's privilege to design houses.[7] In fact, for most of his life Fuller was regarded as an outsider by the architectural profession – an eccentric inventor and purveyor of unrealistic products. It is only in the latter half of the twentieth century that his work has come to be understood, appreciated and recognised as an important forecast of the application of new principles in architectural design.

His [Fuller's] comprehensive and knowledgeable use of materials and technology borrowed from other industries ... his insistence on a global view of building performance ... and his refusal to have anything to do with the conventions of traditional, academic architecture – these have all been built solidly into the ideological structure of High Tech [architecture].[8]

Fuller's career encompasses a bewildering array of ideas and projects yet his work can be divided quite simply into two main concerns: the desire to introduce new methods of producing affordable housing, and the relevance of weight as a design component in building. He quotes his early upbringing in Penobscot Bay, Maine, USA, as an influence on his work, particularly his association with the 'deft tension techniques as spontaneous as those of spiders', found in the boat building and fishing work of the community.[9] From 1917 to 1919 he served in the US Navy which was then undergoing a technical revolution with the introduction of radio aids and the aeroplane, and this, coupled with his involvement for five years with the Stockade building system, inspired his concern for the possibilities of technological transfers into the building industry.[10]

Fuller saw the building industry as an outdated wasteful series of unrelated processes that produced expensive products in an inefficient manner. At this time, his personal experiences led him to understand the tremendous burden that poor housing brought to those who could afford no better.[11] His first active attempt to address housing as a design issue was with the Dymaxion House project, which he patented in 1928. Fuller did not invent the Dymaxion name which was in fact a public relations exercise devised by the Marshall Fields store in Chicago (made up of dynamic/maximum/ions: Dymaxion) and only applied to the design in 1929. Fuller's first drawings of the concept are crude and show his lack of formal training in the design field. But the revised, and widely published image of the 1929 version shows a futuristic and compelling vision of 'future' living, especially once it had been transformed into a shiny metallic model for the exhibition. Fuller described the house (and the other permutations of Dymaxion design)[12] as: 'air-deliverable, mass-producable, world-around, new human life protecting and nurturing scientific dwelling service industry as means of transferring high scientific capability from a weaponry to livingry focus'.[13] He told the organisers of the 1933 World's Fair that to build a prototype Dymaxion House would cost $100 million, based on a figure of $45 million that had been required to develop Henry Ford's Model A automobile, but that once in production each house would only cost $1,500. The average cost of a new house in the USA was then $8,000.

The Dymaxion House never went beyond a design idea, yet its publicity brought Fuller into the public eye and led to invitations to contribute to more 'futuristic' projects. In 1940, for a special issue of *Architectural Forum* entitled 'The Design

Decade', Fuller designed the 'Mechanical Wing'. This was a capsule containing a fully fitted kitchen, bathroom and generator that could be towed behind a car and plugged into a remote tent or cabin. Throughout the great farming lands of the mid-west of the USA, grain was stored in Butler Bins: 5.5 metre diameter, circular steel containers. Fuller realised that this structure, coupled with a 'Mechanical Wing', could make a simple mass-produced dwelling, which he named the DDU, the Dymaxion Deployment Unit. The unit included a redesigned segmental top surface to allow extra headroom, windows and a convection ventilation system. It was delivered in fully furnished, but demounted, form and erected on a removable steel mast. The interior was lined up to roof height and divided by canvas curtains. Originally, the DDU was marketed in Europe as military housing, but once the USA entered the war it was acquired in thousands to be used by the US military and for domestic purposes, such as factory worker housing.

52

The DDU was the undoubted prototype for Fuller's most influential contribution to housing development, the Wichita House, though only two of these buildings were actually manufactured, compared to the thousands of DDUs which saw service all over the world. The Wichita House was made by the Beechcraft aircraft factory which was seeking diversification ideas for production once the war was over. The building was to be made on a production line and of Duralumin, the lightweight alloy from which aircraft were manufactured. It was to be air-transportable in a single Douglas DC4 (the standard transportation aircraft of the period) and to be capable of easy and speedy assembly. The house would contain a higher specification of conveniences than were then common in dwellings and was intended to be substantially cheaper than the price of a one-off new house.

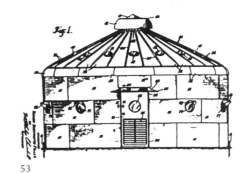

53

Fuller developed a series of performance criteria that went back to first principles, deciding that he could 'make "house" do much more than a house ever did before ... the house is to be conceived of scientifically as man's initial advantage relative to forces of the environment'.[14] The 'house' could be considered:

> the first line of defence against the large category of elements ... such as fire, earthquake, tornado, flood, pestilence, politics, selfishness ... bacteria, accident, laziness and habits ... and the routine inevitable functions of man as a process, that is eating, sleeping, being clean, refusing, etc., ... Technology can help him to gain great advantage over the routine necessities.[15]

Fuller was adamant that 'new postulates stem from observation which reveals the inadequacies of our previous concepts'.[16]

The Wichita House was a remarkable re-invention of the dwelling. In its standard form it incorporated automatic natural ventilation, air-filtering, electrically operated roller cupboards, movable partitions, plumbed-in vacuum cleaning, fully fitted kitchen and two Dymaxion bathrooms. It fitted into a reusable stainless steel tube that could be carried on a single truck, and no single component weighed more than 5 kilograms. It took six men one day to assemble, or one man six days. The components cost $1,800. Retail cost, on site and assembled, was $6,500 compared to $12,000 for a conventional new house. The first prototype was assembled two months after the Hiroshima bomb was detonated – the Second World War was at an end, and timing for the introduction of the new design could not have been better. Initial publicity led to unsolicited orders being placed with the Beechcraft Company for 37,000 houses, with a predicted production target by the factory of 6,000 units per year.

Why, therefore, were only two prototypes made? The cause for this can be attributed solely to Fuller. The man who had created the concept and realised the potential of the transportable factory-made dwelling could not let the idea move from under his own direct control. In his contract with Beechcraft he had stipulated that nothing could be decided without his approval and he refused to meet the market demands while they were there. He insisted on continued development of the house before manufacture began, valuable time was lost and money spent went unrecouped. Eventually his partners lost patience and interest and the project died.[17] At only 3,500 kilograms, the Wichita House was a prime example of Fuller's concern for the weight of buildings. He believed that weight was a crucial factor in architectural design and argued that the architect was unaware of the weight of the object he designed, unlike engineers who designed aircraft, ships and cars:

52 The Wichita House, 1946, made by the Beechcraft Company in Wichita. One of the two prototype buildings was erected permanently in Wichita, Kansas but was relocated in 1992 to the Henry Ford Museum in Dearborn, Michigan; **53** Buckminster Fuller, Dymaxion Deployment Unit (DDU), 1942. Fuller's conversion of the propriety grain storage bin made by the Butler Manufacturing Co

54

55

56

the fact that weight considerations are not primary in buildings tells us how far building is from the industrial equation. No one should think that because we build big buildings and use some industrial materials, industry has therefore embraced the building arts.[18]

At a talk to the Women's University Club in New York in 1930 he compared the weight of the transatlantic ocean liner, the *Mauretania*, with the Hotel Belmont, a building of similar function and capacity, in New York city. Despite being self-sufficient in food and power for 30 days, the liner was one fifteenth the weight of the hotel.

Fuller's interest in weight led him to recognise the potential of the geodesic structure in relationship to its behaviour in the form of a dome. Fuller is often mistakenly credited with the invention of the geodesic dome as he did manage to patent the device in the USA in 1954; however, the principle and practice have several earlier precedents. The great circle principle upon which geodesic dome design is based was known in antiquity.[19] The first industrial example of the application of the geodesic principle to building dome design was at Jena in Germany in 1922. There, Dr Walter Bauersfeld of the Carl Zeiss works designed an optical device designed to show the movement of the stars and planets – the first planetarium projector. A hemispherical surface was required, onto which the image could be projected. On the roof of the Zeiss building, Bauersfeld created a light iron rod framework with iron connectors, precision-built in the factory below. The construction had bolted fixings in the form of a highly subdivided icosahedron with great circle arcs, and was composed of 3,480 struts accurate in length to 0.05 millimetres and spanned 40 metres. The framework was covered with a new advanced sprayed concrete layer of only 3.8 centimetres, its thickness determined by the ratio of an eggshell's thickness to its diameter.[20]

Fuller was therefore not the creator of the geodesic dome; however, his name is synonymous with its form and he was responsible for its acceptance as a valuable and practical building system. Fuller produced a multitude of dome designs constructed in new and diverse materials – from early hand-built examples constructed while working with students at Washington University, St Louis and at Black Mountain College, he developed the dome into an accepted symbol of technological ingenuity. Between 1954 and the early 1960s Fuller devised a whole range of lightweight and portable building types based on the dome principle. The magnesium-framed, Dacron-clad, air-transportable helicopter hangars he devised for the US Marine Corps in 1954 were the first of many projects he would undertake for the US government. He also produced 16.5 metre span polyester/fibreglass Raydomes to protect radar installations, and a demountable 30 metre (later 60 metre) dome for the US Information Service. Peter Cook, writing in 1970, stated that: 'The vision of the helicopter with the dome dangling beneath still summarises the whole point of minimal effort for maximum effect.'[21]

The US Information Service domes could be transported in a single aircraft and erected in 48 hours by local labour. In June 1956, a Trade Fair Pavilion of aluminium tubing and stretched nylon-neoprene skin was shipped to Kabul in Afghanistan, then on to New Delhi, Burma, Bangkok, Tokyo, Osaka, Manila, then back across the Atlantic to South America. Fuller claimed that because the local people had erected the buildings themselves they associated their construction with a product of their own society and that this made the buildings an unexpected 'prime local friends-winning factor'.[22] The culmination of Fuller's built domes was the American pavilion at Expo '67 in Montreal – a three-quarter sphere of 76 metres span which the editors of the *Architectural Review* thought one of the best two pavilions.[23] The building was composed of structural steel components covered with hexagonal acrylic 'lenses' with filters that opened and closed with the path of the sun to provide shade.

Between 1954, the date of Fuller's patent, and 1984 more than 300,000 geodesic domes were built.[24] Some of these structures were very large, for example the 135 metre span enclosure for the flying boat *Spruce Goose* at Long Beach by Temcor, a company of which Fuller was a director; however, nothing surpasses the unbuilt (but fully proven by calculations) project for a 3.2 kilometre wide dome over Manhattan Island which he proposed in 1960. The dome, which

54 The *Queen Mary* in Trafalgar Square, London, from the *Modern Boy's Annual*, 1937. A dramatic illustration of the engineering achievement of ocean liner construction in comparison to buildings; **55** The geodesic dome structure created by Dr Walter Bauersfeld on the roof of the Carl Zeiss works at Jena, Germany, 1922; **56** Buckminster Fuller and Shoji Sadao, US Pavilion at Expo '67, Montreal

would be 1.6 kilometres high, could be put into place by 16 Sikorsky helicopters and would take three months to erect.

In his later years Fuller toured the world tirelessly lecturing on his favourite subjects which by then had homogenised into a whole world approach to design issues summed up in the concept of 'synergy' – a system of cumulative technical advantage. He believed that 'all the deficiencies of human society and all the dangers it feared, could be overcome, resolved and miniaturised into a vast and seamless man-made service technology'.[25]

> Technology represents philosophy resolved to the most cogent argument. If man did this, such would result. In technology man is empowered to explore and develop his own 'if' without reference to the limiting response of other preoccupied egos. Through technology alone the creative individual can of free will arrange for the continuing preservation of mankind despite individual man's self frustrating propensities.[26]

Though Fuller was eventually reconciled with the architectural profession he still suffered from a lack of acceptance as a major architectural influence. He is well known, primarily through the development of the geodesic dome but also because of the potency of the Wichita House as an image, but his writing is difficult to follow and his personal drawings fail to convey confidence in the man as a designer. Where Fuller was unique was in his approach to the issue of building design as a reborn problem, new today for today's conditions. He understood the efficiency of industrial production and saw in that the solution to the physical problems of the provision of fully integrated building systems. Many of his logistical assertions cannot be faulted, and his principles of prefabrication and transportation of demountable buildings have provided excellent examples for contemporary designers approaching the same issues.

Where Fuller's work was deficient, and why he proved generally unacceptable to the majority of designers, was in his lack of awareness of the subjective aesthetic and symbolic factors in his designs. Factory-made products can be made beautiful, appropriate and desirable, as has been proven over and over again, but Fuller's designs, primarily for houses, did not meet these criteria except by chance.

Charles and Ray Eames

Unlike Fuller, American designers Charles and Ray Eames undoubtedly gained the respect of their architectural contemporaries around the world and, with the aid of considerably less built architecture and a fraction of the published material, had a profound international effect on the development of constructional techniques in architecture.[27] Known primarily for the house they designed for themselves in Los Angeles and the extensive range of modern furniture for Herman Miller, they also took part in a wide range of related creative fields as 'architects, inventors, designers, craftsmen, scientists, filmmakers, educators'.[28] Derek Walker, writing for *Architectural Design* in 1981, stated: 'Although their work in architecture has been minimal, their influence on architects has been extraordinary'.[29]

One reason for the general acceptance of their work is that, though it is diverse, it stems directly from an architectural aesthetic. Charles Eames was an architect who struggled with the Beaux Arts system at Washington University in St Louis where he was educated, preferring the theories of organic architecture expressed by Frank Lloyd Wright. Much of the Eames' time was spent in architectural education as teachers exploring new methods of communicating learning processes, and they were therefore strong advocates of 'the belief that a wide-ranging architectural training can be an unrivalled background for success in allied arts and techniques'.[30]

While teaching at Cranbrook Academy of Arts, near Detroit in 1945, the Eames', in collaboration with Eero Saarinen, started to investigate the possibilities of technology transfer from industry (primarily the motor industry) into furniture design. This led to the projects for the Case Study Houses sponsored by *Arts and Architecture* magazine. Preliminary designs were first published in 1948 and the construction was followed in subsequent issues during 1949, until being published when complete in December 1949.[31] Eames worked with Eero Saarinen on the design for these two houses (one was built close by at Pacific Palisades

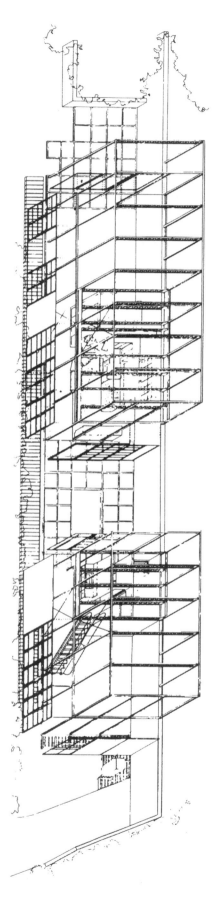

for the editor of *Art and Architecture*, John Entenza) as an experiment to explore the potential of building with completely prefabricated commercially available products. The structure involved an asymmetrical prefabricated steel frame on a prepared concrete base and retaining wall which held back part of the sloping site. Proprietary steel decking was used for the roof, and the walls were in-filled with a variety of steel, glass, plywood, asbestos and plastic panels. Michael Brawne commented in 1966:

> It also posed again all the problems we had hesitantly but still persistently been asking; in particular, whether a system of factory-made parts could be devised in which the components were small and variable enough to make them equally useful and valid for all the buildings within the village, town, city; and then at what point, if any, some new order was necessary among this deliberate diversity within unity. Was, in other words, the unique delight of the Eames house on its California hillside extendible into a whole urban area?[32]

This was obviously a factor which interested many architects who saw in the beautiful and harmonious interiors, and subtle, almost Japanese sensitivity with which the house was fitted into the landscape, a model for the development of industrial building techniques and the application of them wholesale to buildings of any purpose in any situation. What many other architects subsequently missed in their personal exploration of industrial building techniques is the Eames' search for what Brawne calls an: 'attitude more appropriate to the present high level of technology' and Fuller would call 'synergy'.[33]

The Case Study Houses were not the only such buildings erected during this period. The Herman Miller showroom in Los Angeles opened in September 1949, just before the house was completed. The showroom used the same principles of construction and was built for just over half what it would have cost to build a similar building by conventional methods. It presents the image, even today, of a thoroughly sophisticated commercial building, a type which has been copied the world over. The Eames' interest in technology transfer continued in their immensely influential furniture designs, introducing innovative patterns in new materials like moulded plywood, bent steel, and plastic. The moulded plastic chair which Charles and Ray Eames designed has been duplicated universally to become an archetypal twentieth century design icon. Their use of industrial techniques and materials in beautiful and seductive forms had a profound influence on designers:

> What Eames has shown is that it is possible to exploit the highest available levels of industrial production to whatever ends are considered correct within a given design context; that, in other words, the machine can be controlled, and that, through its use, a designed world can be created in which choice, the delight of visual wit and a high appropriateness between form and use are all possible.[34]

Charles and Ray Eames had the aesthetic sensitivity which Fuller lacked but like him they believed: 'design ... starts from a performance specification'.[35] What Fuller had, which the Eames' perhaps did not, was a crusading belief in the ideas he professed – that they could help mankind and alleviate suffering, that the use of appropriate technology could 'prevent much of the present inroads of physical and mental and moral diseases into good health and well-being and general happiness'.[36]

The Eames' value to designers of lightweight and demountable buildings is in two areas. First in the clear use of differing and alternative technologies to solve architectural problems – the use of all industries as a palette for the sensitive designer. Second, and less easy to grasp, that the additive method of assembling components into a unified whole so that all the parts act in concert to produce a harmonious and practical composition. Eames was described as the man who realised the twentieth century 'wish for universality [which Fuller expressed] by the fact of versatility and resourcefulness'.[37]

Frei Otto

The work of Frei Otto is evidence of a career in architectural design which displays an unusually consistent nature, for all that he has been responsible for – whether built project, theoretical, or research work – has been founded on the principles of efficiency in form, lightweight in nature, flexible in purpose. His ideas are unique in the twentieth century in that they demonstrate a profound insight into the functional opportunities shown in the form of the tent. The recognisable and transferable properties of this traditional mobile dwelling outlined by Faegre: 'the very qualities that are the essence of the tent – portability, lightness, and flexibility – are qualities that can be useful to a variety of design problems'[38] have also been recognised by Otto.

Otto is best known for the dramatic cable-net structures that he devised for the German Pavilion at Montreal Expo '67 and the Munich Olympic Games in 1972; however, his work also extends to fabric tent systems, pneumatic structures and lattice domes. Architectural observers of Otto's work might come to the conclusion that it is merely the provision of engineering solutions for problems of enclosure; however, his design attitude is shaped by a belief that lightweight building systems form a definitive design route for all building types set in the particular circumstances of the twentieth century. Before any of his major projects had come to fruition, he stated in 1961:

> We need buildings which fulfil their task today and will do so tomorrow, which, in other words, do not age in adhering to their forms and this becomes a drag upon the economy as well as the visual environment. But in order to build adaptably we must try to build as lightly, as movably, as possible and with the greatest perfection technically available.[39]

Otto was born in Siegmar, Saxony, Germany in 1925, the son of a sculptor. He initially began to train as a sculptor, but as Fascist Germany rearmed he became a glider pilot (between the wars Germany built the most advanced designs of these lightweight flying machines) and later, a fighter pilot in the Luftwaffe. After the Second World War he was interned in France and filled the post of architect to the prison camp where he lived, responsible for the erection of structures with the minimum of resources common to the post-war rebuilding period. From 1948, he studied architecture in Berlin with brief periods in the USA, and although he began in practice in 1952 he set the pattern for his working life, in both his method and theme, by continuing research into tent forms for which he received his doctorate in 1954.[40]

The early work by Otto was based purely on the precedent of the tent and sail maker and his early designs show this influence even though the resulting structures reveal a sophistication that clearly sets them apart from traditional forms. They are delicate, freely suspended forms that seem to touch the earth gently and reluctantly, held aloft by the thinnest of compression members and tension cables. As the ambition for more complex forms developed in both the designer and his clients, Otto began to develop research techniques that would enable the design of more complex buildings to be completed in the studio with the necessary assurance of success on site.

The first larger structures were designed in 1956–57 for the 1957 Federal Garden Exhibition in Cologne where Otto prepared designs for a number of structures including the entrance arch and the exhibition hall, and the Berlin Interbau where he built the Interbau Café and the roof of the 'City of Tomorrow' exhibition hall. Due to the mathematical difficulty and spatial complexity of these structural forms the design process was based on developing a series of study models, devised to test all the performance characteristics of the proposal. This was not unlike the system used by Antoni Gaudi in creating the unique organic structures for projects such as the chapel at Colony Guell and the Cathedral of Sagrada Familia in Barcelona.

Otto tested forms by the use of soap bubble models which provided a naturally resolved physical model of the shape generated by tension structures stretched between specific defined points. In the design for the entrance arch at Cologne, the first permanent model was made of fabric which was followed by a 1:50 replica set on a precision ground marble slab. This model was made incorporating 1 mm steel wire which could be loaded in different ways and then measured using special small calibrated steel springs. Photographs were made of the model under stress, aiding in the analysis of deflection in various circumstances. The final model resulted from these tests, and took the form of a 1:25 solid quadrant of the roof structure, from which patterns for the skin material could be made. This

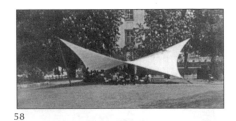

58

59

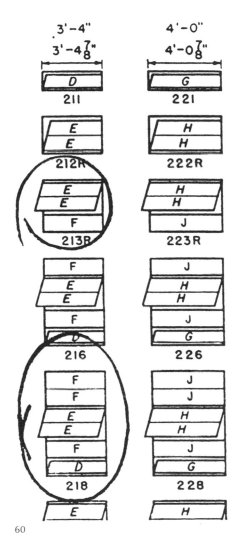

60

57 Charles and Ray Eames, the Eames House, Santa Monica, 1949. Drawing by Charles Lee from *Architectural Design*, 1981; 58 Frei Otto, Bandstand at Kassel, Germany, 1955; 59 Frei Otto, German Garden Exhibition Pavilion, Cologne, 1957; 60 Contemporary manufacturer's catalogue identifying industrial components used in the construction of the Eames House

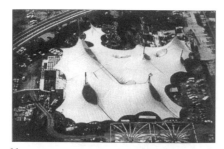

61

method of design undoubtedly led to developments in the form of the buildings. As they were revised, models took on unexpected shapes that suggested alternative design routes when alternative proposals were required.

The first truly international project of Otto's career was the German Pavilion at Expo' 67 in Montreal, Canada. The design process developed for the early tent structures was seminal in the generation of this building's organic, free-shape form. Philip Drew comments on the design of this building: 'The design evolution [of the Montreal Pavilion] was a trial-and-error process of developing a form that defined architectural spaces and corresponded as closely as possible to a minimal surface.'[41] The theme of Expo '67 was 'Terre des Hommes', the relationship of Man with the Earth, which inspired the Otto team to create a series of related, overlapping landscapes, sheltered beneath an organic floating form. The shape was wholly determined by model iterations, seven complete models made, and dozens of part studies. Otto's design team made scaled down measurements of all loadings with calibrated springs, explored deformations with double exposure photographs, and built solid models for wind loading tests. These tests led to the crucial decision to make the structure into a cable-net system instead of a fabric membrane system. This latter system could accommodate the loading associated with fair weather but the fear of high snow loading in Montreal resulted in higher performance criteria.

The Montreal building was the culmination of more than ten years' research and development into lightweight structures and all the main advantages of working with lightweight, prefabricated, demountable structures were taken full advantage of. The date of announcement of the competition winner to completion on site before the onset of the Canadian winter in October 1966 was fourteen months. In this time the building was designed, prefabricated, shipped and erected. The building took Otto's team 20,000 hours to design, but it took just three and a half weeks to erect.

The building was received enthusiastically by both the architectural and the lay press. JM Richards wrote in the *Architectural Review* that the German Pavilion was 'the work of architecture at Expo that is likely to be longest remembered. Looks as temporary as it is and exploits the opportunity an exhibition offers of taking experiments a stage further in practice.'[42]

Life magazine thought it: 'a major architectural innovation ... a lasting influence on the planning of stadiums and exhibition halls of the future'.[43] This statement was unusually prophetic in that Otto went on to design the huge enclosures for the stadia at the Olympic Games in Munich in 1972. Robin Boyd also remarked at the time: 'There is just a suggestion that they are demonstrating a principle which is really more applicable to much bigger problems.'[44] He also recognised the big problem with cable-net structures, that of cladding. In this case it consisted of a polyester fabric membrane that was hung below the steel mesh:

> the fit is not always Savile Row, and the miles of seams ... are vulnerable at every stitchhole ... and they bear no apparent relationship to the equally strong overlaid patterns formed by the hundreds of points where hangars from the steel mesh penetrate and support the membrane.[45]

The Munich stadium suffered from this problem to an even greater degree. Whereas the Montreal Pavilion was definitively temporary, this was not a requirement of the German Olympic Stadium.[46] The non-uniformity of the stress nets and their nodes and geometry meant that uniform cladding systems could not be made to fit easily. Under consideration at Munich were such diverse systems as polyester fabric on a timber frame, bituminous layers with metal foil finish on mineral wool panels, liquid plastic sprayed on lightweight (but not in comparison to its supporting structure) concrete, and a separate structure to support acrylic glass domes. Eventually, the final solution was tinted acrylic glass set in wide flexible joints – a crude system which has resulted in cracked, difficult to replace panels. Boyd's preference was for the tent structures of Interbau more than ten years earlier: 'the purity of form revealed by the surface of the white canvas membranes' led him to surmise that for large structures 'the new tensile epoch is not quite here yet. It is still waiting for the chemists'.[47]

Recent history has shown this statement to be a valid one. Development of tent structures has taken place in line with the new synthetic-based fabrics that can be

61 Frei Otto and Rolf Gutbrod, the Federal Republic of Germany Pavilion at Expo '67, Montreal, Canada

relied upon for continuity and uniformity of strength, and the computer design techniques that reduce the 20,000 man hours that Otto's design team spent on the Montreal Pavilion to a reasonable and economic limit. The latest version of Trevira High Tenacity, the fabric manufactured by the German company Hoechst, has a specific strength higher than steel: each one-metre wide strip can support 15 tonnes. Computer programs not only produce spatial designs and calculate all loads, including snow and storm loads, but also determine the dimensions of the textile segments with great accuracy. The latest systems send instructions direct to cutting machines that automatically create accurate membrane patterns (for examples of contemporary tensile membrane architecture see Chapters VII and XI).

As well as tension structures, Frei Otto and the Institute for Lightweight Structures which he founded at the University of Stuttgart, Germany, have been involved in the development of other associated innovative structural forms, notably pneumatics and lattice frames. Lattice structures, as explored by Otto, are square, mesh frames, deformed to form a dome surface, and are a stiffened version of an inverted tension net. They are of interest in that the simple square plan form types bear a remarkable resemblance to the Tuareg mat tents (see Chapter I). At Expo '67, two lattice structures of up to 20 metre span were incorporated as auditoria. These were based on information found by measuring 1-20 inverted chain net models. The domes were made from Canadian hemlock pine strips laid out at right angles on a 50 centimetre grid and connected at the nodes by a single nut, bolt and washer. This meant the unerected structure could be folded like a concertina into a much smaller space for transportation.

Once erected it was restrained by a ring beam around the perimeter. This structural system is reminiscent of that used in the construction of the walls of the traditional demountable dwelling the yurt – (see Chapter I).

The demountability aspect of Otto's work at Montreal and elsewhere[48] shows an involvement with the requirements of lightweight structures that stems not from an exploration of form as an architectural aesthetic but as a result of the physical factors affecting general construction in the twentieth century.[49] The Montreal structure was designed to be demounted, transported and reerected elsewhere in the original or modified form:

> It could be re-employed as a museum cover, as industrial premises, or as a roof above a recreation centre with swimming pool. The individual sections of the net could be rearranged and part surfaces provided with retractable skins.[50]

The pavilion showed a reduced cost in materials and manufacture, transportation and erection in return for a greater investment in design time and innovation. Unlike the great majority of buildings at Expo '67, the life of the German pavilion had the potential to begin anew when theirs was complete. Robin Boyd commented:

> When this pavilion has done its Expo job it can be dismantled, rolled up, and returned to Germany. There is something disturbing – actually aesthetically disturbing – about some other pavilions done in massive brick and concrete for only six months' life. Almost before their mortar had set, three months before they were seen by the public, tenders were being called for their demolition.[51]

Today, in a world more aware of the ecological effects of our manufacturing decisions this strategy of reuse has even more significance.

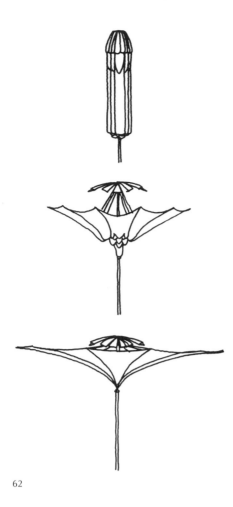

62

62 Electrically operated automatic umbrella roof, 16 m diameter and 9.5 m high, for the Federal Garden Exhibition, Cologne, Germany, 1971 (after Glaeser)

CHAPTER V
MILITARY ENGINEERING

Up until the 1850s it was colonisation, mainly of Australia and South Africa, that provided the main foreign use of British demountable buildings. However, by the time of the Crimean War in 1854, British industry had developed 'a significant technical competence and production capability for the manufacture of prefabricated buildings from modest wooden or corrugated iron huts to the most elaborate iron villas, churches, and commercial buildings'.[1] This capability was now used to support the war effort. In mid-November 1854, 14,000 prefabricated huts were ordered to house British forces. By Christmas, the first batch had arrived and by February all were in place. The famous designers of the day became involved in the war effort – Paxton raised an army of 1,000 construction workers, from the team who had assembled the Crystal Palace, and created various types of portable buildings including a special tent which utilised the flue of a central stove to act as its main support. At Renkioi, in the Dardanelles, Isambard Kingdom Brunel built a hospital for the wounded, the design of which was based upon remarkably astute principles that still make sense today:

First – That they [the buildings] should be capable of adapting themselves to any plot of ground that might be selected, whatever its form, level or inclination, within reasonable limits.

Secondly – That each set of buildings should be capable of being easily extended, from one holding 500 patients, to one for 1,000 or 1,500 or whatever might be the limit which sanitary or other conditions might prescribe.

Thirdly – That they should be very portable, and of the cheapest construction.[2]

These principles might be paraphrased as: adaptive to site conditions, flexible in layout and form, easy to transport and deploy, and economical to manufacture. The provision of these buildings, which though not particularly innovative construction, shows that the values of prefabrication and portability were firmly recognised by those in authority and were utilised in a situation that received maximum publicity.

The use of prefabricated buildings to such a large extent in the Crimea is an example of the principle that technological innovation and invention receives a dramatic boost in wartime situations. Keith Mallory and Arvid Ottar in their book *Architecture of Aggression* draw attention to this:

In civil construction, there always has been this gap created by the system between designer, manufacturer, researcher and client. There has been little

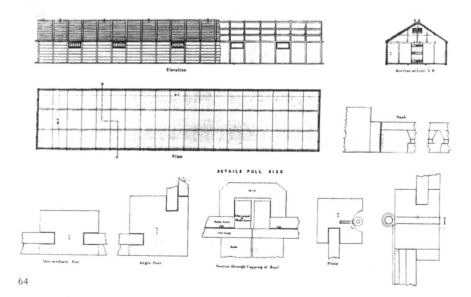

63 Erection process of a typical mobile timber hut of the First World War, in this case, the Weblee Portable Hut of 1918; **64** A British design for a demountable wooden hut, 1855

64

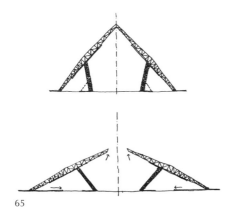

65

66

65 An 82-metre span demountable Zeppelin shed. Assembled on the ground, a winch is used to draw together the base of each wall member until they meet at the ridge; **66** USAAF Second World War transportable aircraft hangar made by the Butler Manufacturing Co

attempt at market research in the building industry, nor is the social environment of peacetime conducive to innovation. Military construction and war, conversely, provide excellent conditions for innovation. Boundaries between research, design, use and manufacture are broken down. The matter of speed and urgency provides an excellent climate for innovation and more important – its implementation.[3]

During both the First and Second World Wars technological innovation became the key to success on the battleground, where battles were increasingly won by machines rather than manpower. However, innovation does not just take place in weaponry but in many other aspects of support and supply, some of which have subsequently found applications in related civilian industries.

Aviation Buildings

The relationship between the development of innovative architectural concepts and the technological developments required to create light and strong structures for use in aviation has already been noted (see Chapter II). However, the buildings associated with the protection of aircraft also deserve mention as the mobility of these structures often possessed great strategic advantages.

Zeppelins were used for military purposes during the First World War. These huge aircraft were structural feats in themselves, although their fragility meant that they could not be left exposed to extreme weather conditions. In addition, their manoeuvrability was strongly dependent on the direction of the wind and moving such an aircraft in and out of a static hangar could only be accomplished with a favourable head wind. It is for this reason that experiments were made to create moving buildings that could shift position to allow access for the aircraft at any time. Some sheds were built that could float on water which, although effective, restricted their location significantly. A more practical idea was a rotating shed that was constructed on wheels, but the huge cost and lengthy construction period meant that this solution also had limited potential. As Zeppelin design improved dramatically during the war years, more than double the rate it would have done during peacetime,[4] smaller and more manoeuvrable aircraft were developed. For strategic reasons, it therefore became more important to move the entire shed to a new location.[5] This led to the development of the demountable airship shed. The sheds near Namur navy base were constructed from relatively lightweight lattice beams that were erected by drawing the outside ends together with a winch at ground level to elevate the central ends to form a ridge. The whole structure could therefore be assembled from ground level even though its height was more than 40 metres. Though only a few of these sheds were made, the principle they used for erecting large structures quickly, without recourse to extensive associated works, has been used repeatedly to the present day.

By 1917, the airship had been abandoned due to the increased effectiveness of heavier-than-air machines; nevertheless, for the aeroplane squadrons, mobility in the field was valued even more highly. The famous travelling circus of Baron von Richthofen received its name because all personnel, spares, offices and workshops travelled by train from sector to sector behind the lines. The hangar design they used consisted of a three-pin arch with a canvas skin. The building was assembled on the ground, then raised into position by drawing the two bottom ends together. These ends were tied together with a rope that spanned the width of the hangar at ground level.

The success of the mobile air bases in the First World War, which allowed the German forces to maintain air superiority despite being outnumbered by the Allies three to one, undoubtedly led to the development of mobile hangars in the Second World War.[6] Both the German and Allied mobile hangars were remarkably similar in principle to the earlier designs, though far greater in scale. Named after its designer, the German Hünnebeck hangar was clad in corrugated sheets but still utilised a lightweight steel lattice truss that was drawn together at the bottom ends to raise the centre. The American Air Force mobile hangar was built by the Butler Manufacturing Company which had also collaborated with Buckminster Fuller to produce emergency housing (see Chapter IV). It was described in *Engineering News Record* in 1944 as:

a lightweight steel, demountable hangar claimed to possess the mobility of a circus tent ... using [a] three hinged, steel arch truss of 130 feet [39.6 metres] span tied at the base as the principal framing ... a cleverly designed hinge bolt reducing erection time to a minimum.[7]

Since the Second World War relatively little research has been carried out in this area that has resulted in fully developed innovative buildings. The development in aviation technology has meant that the greater range and flexibility of the aircraft itself can be used to replace the movement of bases. The use of aircraft carriers, the increased efficiency of in-flight fuelling and the extension of aircraft range has meant that very few locations are too remote for the aircraft to reach.[8] Helicopters are one of the few military aircraft types that still require mobile maintenance facilities. In this area development has concentrated on the provision of light-weight, air-supported structures for ease of erection and transportation, though the actual development work has been carried out by industrial contractors rather than the military.[9]

Floating Structures

The value of large floating structures was perceived by the designers of the Zeppelin sheds and this method of making normally static construction projects movable has been used in other military arenas. The traditional fort is a substantial building built at a crucial military location for protection of established territory. In the Second World War the necessity for increased coastal defence at a location further towards the source of the threat led to the development of 'Sea Forts'. These structures were designed to be half-way between a building and a vessel, a pre-manufactured structure that could be fully constructed and then deployed at its permanent site complete with provisions and garrison. Sir Winston Churchill first made the suggestion in 1917, but the real impetus did not appear until the Second World War when the threat to the ports required extra defences at the Thames and Mersey estuaries.[10] Two types were manufactured: the Naval fort and the Army fort. The Naval fort consisted of two hollow concrete towers constructed on a concrete caisson which supported a steel superstructure containing guns and radar equipment, while the 'crew' lived in the towers, which were mostly below the water line. The Army fort also had a concrete base, though because of the shifting sands in Liverpool Bay where it was to be deployed, these were designed on different principles that enabled them to become buried and therefore remain in a static position.[11] Four precast concrete legs supported a steel box-like superstructure that contained all the accommodation and defence equipment. The Army fort was arranged in a group of seven separate structures linked by light-

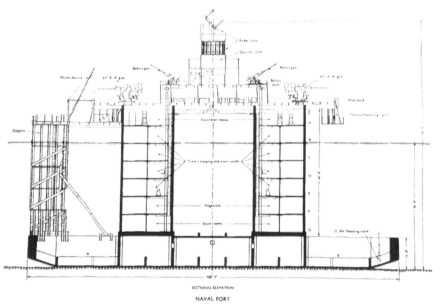

SECTIONAL ELEVATION

NAVAL FORT

67

67 The Naval sea fort, cross-section. The two hollow towers and the caisson were made of reinforced concrete; the superstructure, steel

68

69

weight walkways. Each fort structure had a different defence purpose: guns, searchlights, or command post, and because of their design, a superior standard of living accommodation that could take advantage of natural light and ventilation. The buildings that still remain in situ to this day maintain an intense charismatic imagery. This is particularly so for the Army fort which, because of the techniques used in its construction, appears to be an assembled object. It therefore exhibits connections with technology as well as a gathering together of communities with a separate yet linked purpose. This structure also possesses an easily understood formal arrangement with anthropomorphic qualities – an obviously habitable structure supported on legs that somehow appear as though they might begin to carry it away! To the fertile imagination, it therefore appears to preview a profoundly different way of making architecture.[12]

By 1943, although the initial purpose of the Army forts had now passed in terms of protecting an island under siege, the logistical success of their remote prefabrication, assembly and deployment was still a valuable lesson for those planning the D-Day operations. If a successful follow-up campaign was to be carried out after a bridgehead had been established, port facilities would be required. The Germans, realising this fact, had placed their most significant defences surrounding the French Channel ports. Again, Churchill's earlier ideas in 1917 were an inspiration in the strategy to pre-manufacture an entire harbour in Britain which could then be deployed on site within days of the invasion operation. Two harbours were to be built, code named Mulberry A and B, each with a handling capacity of 12,000 tons of stores and 2,500 vehicles per day.[13] The harbours not only had to be deployed extremely quickly; they also had to protect the moored ships from enemy fire, extreme weather and breakwaters, and accommodate tides of more than 7 metres. The solution was a system of components, each intended to carry out a specific purpose – breakwater, harbour pier, gun platform and bridge, all primarily constructed of reinforced concrete. The project's portability requirement was mainly because of its remote deployment; however, such portability had other advantages. It meant that construction could be spread between a number of contractors, which was essential if the work was to be completed in time, yet also in secrecy. The main harbour 'Phoenix' units alone required the labour of 15,000 workers and 630,000 tons of concrete, a substantial commitment of personnel and materials in war-time Britain.

The harbours began to be deployed just a day after the D-Day landings and initial installation went just as planned. However, on 18 June 1944, 12 days after D-Day, the largest storm seen in the English Channel in 40 years nearly wrecked

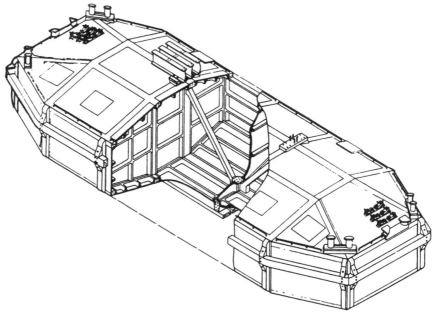

68 Deployment of the Naval fort in 1942. The fort was towed to site, then valves were opened in compartments in the caisson to enable the structure to settle gently on the estuary bed; **69** Army fort under construction in Liverpool, 1942. The structure was assembled from precast concrete bases and legs. The superstructure was made of steel; **70** Floating, concrete Beetle Bridge pontoon

70

the entire project, destroying many of the components which were in transit and some of those which had already been placed in situ. By grouping the components of the two main harbours, a single harbour was constructed which, along with the beaching of coasters at low tide, served its purpose until the coastal ports could be captured.

Military Bridging

The Mulberry harbour project also led to the creation of the largest mobile bridge ever built: the 'Whale', a 1.5 km long pontoon bridge consisting of 80 floating concrete pontoons called 'Beetles', interconnected by steel structures with telescopic legs stabilised on the sea bed. As the bridge was required to resist the movement of the sea, every sixth span had telescopic connections to allow flexibility of movement. The whole structure was prefabricated and deployed in sections and could take the heaviest tanks of the period.

71

Once inland, the problems of bridging are not dissipated. The permanent routes afforded by roads and railways, whilst invaluable in peace time, are useless to the military in times of war because they form easily identifiable targets. Military mobility is thus dependent on being able to cross barriers and impediments in the terrain, notably canals, rivers and chasms. Military engineers have therefore developed a range of portable and demountable bridges capable of being deployed at very short notice. Development has been rapid since the end of the Second World War, when a whole night could be given over to the construction of a bridge; now the same task should be undertaken in less than an hour and be capable of supporting heavier vehicles.[14]

72

One type of portable structure that is capable of coping with this task is the track-vehicle mounted scissors bridge, which is self-propelled to its site and provides an instant span of up to 20 metres. An additional requirement for bridges of this type is the ability to be deployed surreptitiously. For this reason, though air-transportable structures are available, they possess severe disadvantages if required to be installed in action.

A larger span can be achieved with the medium girder bridge, which arrives fully assembled and is launched via a roller beam and a launching nose that carries the weight of the bridge on the opposite bank until it is fully supported. These bridges normally span 30 metres but this distance can be extended using demountable link reinforcement or a transportable floating pier.

The third type of transportable bridge is the type that makes contact with the surface of the river or chasm which it is spanning. Wet support bridges make use of transportable pontoons but have the disadvantage of being relatively easy to

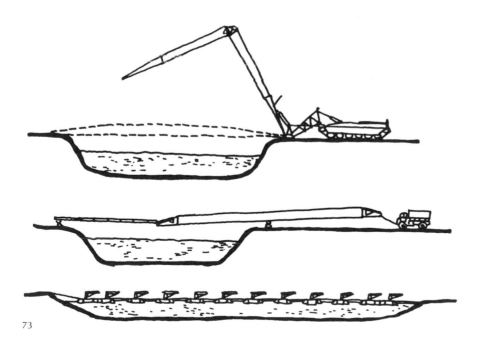
73

71 Red Sands Army Fort showing the arrangement of separate structures into a community with connecting bridges; 72 Prefabricated Floating Pontoon Bridge used after the D-Day landings; 73 Mobile military bridging a) track-vehicle mounted scissors bridge b) medium girder bridge c) wet support bridge using floating pontoons

damage. Difficulties are also encountered in launching and coping with bank conditions, although in theory there is no limit to the distance they can span. The quickest deployment of these bridges is by the use of pontoons, which automatically unfold on contact with the water. A 100 metre span can be crossed in less than 30 minutes in this way.

The latest bridge design to come into use with NATO forces is the General Support Bridge, which can be deployed in less than 20 minutes for a span of up to 50 metres. The bridge can support a 105 ton wheeled load and deployment can take place with all personnel staying within armoured enclosure.[15]

In all these bridging structures the factors that have driven the design have been speed of erection coupled with rugged reliability. What is surprising is the considerable level of portability achievable in what most would consider a permanent design issue. In addition, many of the solutions, whilst referring to a specific problem, utilise standard military equipment such as vehicles, engines, winches, which have been redefined to fit a new role. All bridges are categorised into a set of standards common throughout all NATO forces and are designed to fit specific roles within their classification so that any vehicle approaching from any country will be able to determine if it can cope with the load.[16]

Shelter Buildings

Although these feats of engineering can be seen as dramatic examples of the capabilities of portable structures, it is in a less dramatic sphere of construction that military building can be seen to have had most influence on general demountable building construction. The provision of shelter is a universal requirement for all types of people that has many practical similarities, though psychological and social factors may differ dramatically.[17] Nineteenth century portable shelter provision greatly improved the lot of the soldier both in terms of living conditions in the field and also in the provision of suitable medical facilities. In twentieth-century conflicts, the dramatic increase in the numbers involved in military operations, the lack of availability of conventional materials for logistical reasons, and the impact of technology on the approach to warfare instigated new techniques in the provision of portable shelter. The functional requirements for economic, quickly deployable, easily transportable, effective solutions remained the same.

In the early days of the First World War many soldiers were still accommodated in tents behind the lines, although plans were under way for the provision of portable hutting for winter accommodation almost immediately after war was declared. At first, numerous types of portable buildings were used. Most, like the Aylwin and Armstrong, were timber structures: 'heavy and awkward to construct and transport'.[18] The Liddell Portable Hut was designed by Major Guy Liddell of the Royal Engineers and though it was based on similar principles to the earlier designs, it did give greater consideration to the transportation factor, using hinged panels which enabled the building to be taken down and reerected more quickly. These early buildings were, however, overshadowed by the implementation of the Nissen Bow Hut, designed by an officer of the Canadian Engineers,

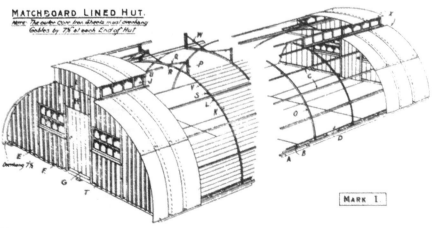

74 The Nissen Portable Bow Hut, 1917. Elevation and section of the typical accommodation hut

74

64

Captain PN Nissen, and 'a triumph of minimum material for maximum enclosed volume'.[19] In 1917, Filson Young, a war correspondent, wrote:

> At about the same time as the tanks made their memorable debut on the battle field, another creature, almost equally primeval of aspect, began to appear in the conquered areas. No one ever saw it on the roads; it just appeared. Overnight you would see a blank space of ground, in the morning it would be occupied by an immense creature of the tortoise species, settled down solidly and permanently on the earth, and emitting green smoke from a right angled stem at one end … in a week or two you would find a valley covered with them … The name of this creature is the Nissen Hut.[20]

The building was manufactured from a small number of components, a semicircular roof, a floor, and two ends – one with a door and two windows. The roof, and internal lining on later models, was made from three interchangeable pieces of corrugated iron, while the floor was of interchangeable wooden panels resting on longitudinal sleepers. Heating was by a Canadian type drum stove. The whole building, which measured 8.2 metres by 4.9 metres, could be erected in four hours by four men using a single spanner. It could be carried on a single army lorry and could comfortably sleep 24 men or double that in extreme circumstances. Variations were devised, such as the Nissen Hospital Hut (which was also used for dining and recreation), basically the same design, although made larger by the inclusion of a continuous ventilator/roof-light down the centre. By 1917, at least 20,000 huts were in use, providing accommodation for more than 500,000 soldiers. The Nissen Hut can be seen as 'one of the forbearers of prefabrication and mass-production of buildings'.[21] The structure utilised simple components that were not only easy to assemble but also easy to manufacture. The interchangeability of parts and the dimensional coordination made for an efficient erection process and reliable deployment in the field.

At the outset of the Second World War, steel was in great demand for the production of machines, weapons and munitions with the result that the search for new shelter systems using available materials began. As Britain settled into the defence of its island territory, it became clear that portability could be a crucial factor in the application of limited resources in construction requirements. Buildings manufactured from prefabricated components could provide the most efficient method of providing shelter using available materials, and to avoid the components becoming redundant at a later date, thought was given to relocating and reusing them as replacements for at least part of the building stock lost during hostilities. A contemporary journal commented: 'Cost; speed of erection; economy of scarce materials – these are primary factors which must be considered in designing war-time buildings. Added to this, there are considerations of use for after the war for peace-time buildings'.[22]

Pre-manufactured panel systems used mainly concrete but also asbestos and composite materials like 'Lignocrete', a mixture of cement and chemically treated sawdust. These buildings were not easy to transport because of the lack of suitable lightweight tension materials. Even the Tarran system hut, which was supposed to be 30 per cent lighter than a comparable building made from prefabricated timber construction, required five lorries to transport it to its site. Nevertheless, so effective were these buildings in solving a shelter problem that they had a profound effect on the way in which post-war governments dealt with the housing problem by the introduction of industrialised building methods (see Chapter VI).

By 1943, thoughts had once again turned to more transportable designs as preparations for the invasion of Europe began. At this time the US forces brought their own portable buildings to Britain, made from home-grown timber which was available in North America in vast quantities. At the peak of preparations for the D-Day invasions, 3,500,000 men were stationed in the South of England. As steel became available, the Nissen Hut proved itself once again, and was used in preference to contemporary designs, in its original form and in developments such as the 'Iris' and 'Romney' huts.

Post Second World War developments in shelter requirements for the armed forces have been spearheaded by manufacturers responding to requirements established by the procurement sections of various military units. This has led to a diverse range of products, some using new materials and technology,

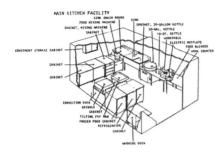

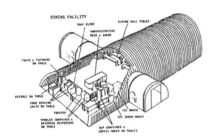

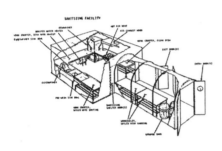

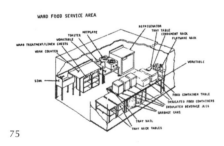

75

although usually within a familiar logistical framework. An extensive US Army research report carried out in 1968 commented that:

> Not much advancement has been noted in the prefabricated building technology used by the military since World War II. Procurement and installation of conventional types of buildings field assembled from prefabricated parts have now become a tradition. Inertia has become well established ... Even where special military criteria have been set up, these have often been bypassed in order to obtain quick delivery of manufacturer's standard stock items.[23]

One successful design has been a combination of portable and demountable units to form a deployable combat support hospital, MUST (Medical Unit, Self-contained, Transportable). A MUST hospital consists of an inflatable dual wall Dacron enclosure, 6.1 metres by 15.2 metres, that is packed in containers ready for shipment by air. The structure becomes rigid at 1.5 pounds per square inch and can withstand an 129 kilometre-per-hour wind load. It comes complete with other rigid expandable enclosures made of aluminium-faced, paper honeycomb sandwich panels, including equipment and an operating room. MUST hospitals have been used in many conflict arenas around the world from Vietnam to the Gulf War and have undoubtedly saved many lives due to their speed of deployment and ability to be used close to the scene of operations.

Military engineering forms a large part of the world's technological development. Spin-offs regularly make a profound impact in many areas of civilian life and industry. Radar, created for the defence of Britain during the Second World War, is now the basis for the successful flow of air and maritime traffic throughout the world. The most successful airliner of today, the Boeing 747 is a direct development of the military bomber, the B-52.

The development of prefabrication techniques, particularly those associated with concrete buildings, made a dramatic impact on the civil construction scene in the post Second World War rebuilding period; indeed, Churchill recognised the adoption of these techniques as 'military evolution'.[24] Buckminster Fuller also recognised the relationship between technological advancement and military development and recommended a shift from 'a weaponry to livingry focus' and expressed frustration at the way the world received its 'technical advantage gains only as a second-hand event'.[25]

The most significant feature of technological development during war-time is that it shows that the speed of advancement is increased when, due to an emergency, innovative solutions to problems are taken seriously, their development given priority, and their implementation is seen as the natural end result of this process. Conservative design development may be perceived as a safer economic option but innovation results in a greater design advantage, although there are higher risks that a percentage of the ideas will not be applicable. In war-time, many apparently exciting ideas do not work; however, because so many new ideas are constantly being tried out, the overall result is a net gain in technological development.

In many situations, industry and governments take advantage of war-time technological developments for subsequent peace-time opportunities. If the opportunities of technological development are so clear, why does the human race have to wait for conflict to create the circumstances for its genesis?

75 MUST mobile food service system. The main dining area is a pneumatic shelter; the remainder of the accommodation is housed in demountable and portable units. The entire facility is transported complete with all appliances;
76 MUST portable hospital by the Garrat Corporation, USA. Interior of the pneumatic hospital ward

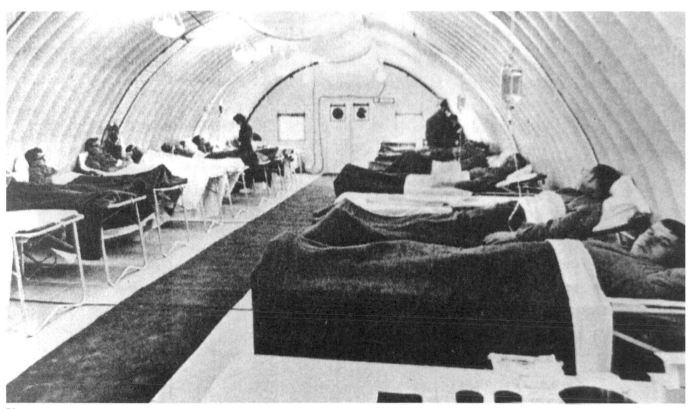

76

CHAPTER VI
THE CONSTRUCTION INDUSTRIES

The practice of utilising prefabricated components in the building industry is inextricably linked with the design of portable and demountable buildings. Innovative and diverse examples of prefabricated demountable buildings in history have been examined in earlier chapters. However, an exploration of the development of the philosophy of prefabrication in contemporary building practice reveals opportunities that may be shared with the manufacture and implementation of portable architecture. The contemporary basis for the use of prefabrication systems in construction is greater economy, speed of erection, a higher-quality product due to factory manufacture and a reduction in skilled labour at the site. Though the simplest form of prefabrication can be the use of standard, commercially available components in the construction of a traditionally made building, the term is more commonly associated with the mass production of large parts of the building envelope. In order to be worthwhile it therefore requires a high degree of continuity, repetitive use of individual components, assemblies and, ultimately, building forms.

The genesis of prefabricated construction for buildings began in two distinct areas. First, the need to produce an effective demountable building type for use in distant locations where there were few resources for a local solution. These buildings were a response to a logistical requirement of the building's function rather than to an economic or manufacturing problem, and their development led to the instigation of repetitive components and dimensional coordination. Second, the desire to develop the potential inherent in the application of a new building material: cast iron. This made the development of mass production possible, as once the component design was complete and the manufacturing process established, repetitive production was no longer the task of a skilled craftsman producing one-off (though identical) components, but an automated machine based process. This was the beginning of the end of human error as a factor in reducing tolerances in the manufacture of the building component. With a few important exceptions, the development of prefabrication techniques has, for economic and social reasons primarily followed the demands of building for permanent solutions. However, it is important to examine these examples if the full potential for portable architecture is to be understood.

Building Prefabrication

Industrial production in the nineteenth century proved its value in the construction of large impressive structures such as the Crystal Palace and in the more domestic scale buildings that were required for the effective management of an empire (see Chapter III). The idea of the effective management of machine production as an aid to human existence in terms of the dwelling began to attract the interest of designers in the early twentieth century. Le Corbusier was involved with the automobile and aeroplane company Voisin in the design of factory-built houses. In L'Esprit Nouveau he stated that it was 'impossible to wait on the slow collaborations of the successive efforts of excavation, mason, carpenter, joiner, tiler, plumber ... houses must go up all of a piece, made by machine tools in a factory, assembled as Ford assembles cars, on moving conveyor belts'.[1] In 1919 he stated: 'Industry on the grand scale must occupy itself with building and establish the elements of the house on a mass-production basis'.[2]

Jean Prouvé was an early collaborator with Le Corbusier who later established a reputation as an industrial designer who profoundly influenced the way in which metals and glass could be used in building, particularly in the development of the curtain wall. After the Second World War Prouvé's factory at Nancy began to manufacture prefabricated metal dwellings for those made homeless by war damage. Prouvé built many other prototypes for portable dwellings, his most

77 Tower crane on a difficult site, New York City, USA

78

significant the Maison Tropicale, a flat-packed, air-transported steel house for the tropics that made use of passive cooling techniques.

Like Prouvré, Walter Gropius believed that more, better and cheaper houses could be built by utilising industrialised processes. He was involved with Konrad Wachsmann in an effort to manufacture a prefabricated panelled house by the General Panel Corporation of California in the 1940s.[3] This project, like Fuller's Wichita House (see Chapter IV), was an attempt to utilise the latest technological manufacturing capability during the Second World War to fill the dramatic need for new housing. Although North America had not suffered the damage to housing stock that Europe had, very little investment had been made in this area during the five years of hostilities. The most successful ventures, however, proved to be those products that were direct developments of proven designs developed during the war years. An important American example is the mobile home, which because of its impact is studied in detail later. Another was the Nissen Hut, the house version of which was mass-produced by the Great Lakes Steel Corporation for home use and export.

After the Second World War, the most significant attempt to introduce mass-production manufacturing techniques originally developed for the production of machines to the building industry in the USA, was by Carl Strandlund in the development of the Lustron House. This was a completely prefabricated factory-made dwelling built almost exclusively from vitreous enamelled steel panels.[4] The design of the building was conventional apart from its construction method and the high standard of fitting-out, which included domestic appliances and complete environmental services. Influence in the government resulted in substantial loans, nearly $40 million, to establish a company based in a wartime Curtis-Wright aircraft factory. The objective was to build and sell the house like a car, using franchised employees based around the US who would then act as a specialist sales force, taking orders and advising clients, and as erectors, receiving the house package and assembling it on prepared foundations. The entire house arrived on a single truck, the components arranged in sequence for off-loading related to the order of assembly. There were over 3,000 components, many specially developed and produced for the house, although ultimately this was one of the factors that led to its downfall as the building was more complex to make and erect than had been originally anticipated. Only 26 houses could be made each day during peak production whereas the prediction had been a hundred. It took 350 hours to assemble, considerably less time than a conventional house, but considerably more than the 150 hours originally specified. The specialist parts mass-produced in the factory could also find no market elsewhere to ease the payback on the vast tooling costs. Lustron promised 17,000 houses by January 1949 – by 1950, when the company collapsed, only 2,500 had been built. Carl Koch, a gifted architect experienced in manufacturing technology, was brought in and made proposals that could have solved Lustron's design and

78 The factory-manufactured metal Lustron House, 1949; 79 The Acorn House designed by Carl Koch, Huson Jack and John Callender in 1945. Designed for transportation by truck as a narrow unit with folding panels that formed living spaces. Despite its ingenuity, the building was never manufactured in bulk

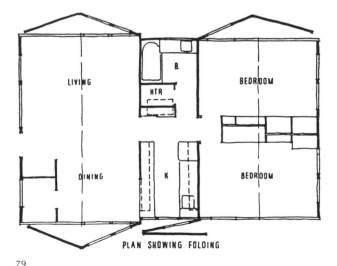
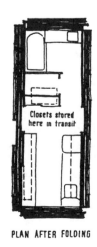

PLAN SHOWING FOLDING

PLAN AFTER FOLDING

79

production problems.[5] These resulted in a more attractive building that took greater structural advantage of the materials used, was made from just 37 factory assembled components and used substantially less material. However, it was too late for the company, which ceased production in the spring of 1950.[6]

In Britain, the housing shortage was just as serious and the government also turned to industrial methods. However, in this case it was to methods which had already proven so effective in solving the problem of housing troops in preparation for the D-Day landings.[7] In the period from VE day to January 1948, 156,677 temporary houses made by 11 different manufacturers costing more than £200 million were made and deployed. The AIROH (Aircraft Industry Research Organisation) house was the most interesting of these in that it used all the production line assembly techniques of the aircraft in whose factories it was made.[8] It was constructed of riveted aluminium sheet sections, and was delivered to site in volumetric units which were assembled and fixed together in the same way that wings had been joined to the fuselage. The four sections were off-loaded by crane at the site and installed complete with wiring, fitted kitchens and bathrooms. One unit was completed every 12 minutes of the working day. The houses were very popular with their tenants, many of whom enjoyed for the first time indoor fitted plumbing, refrigeration, and the convenience of a detached house set in its own garden. These buildings were intended to be temporary solutions to a specific problem; however, because the quality was high and the design was well tuned to its function, they became permanent, many remaining in use until the 1980s.[9]

This was not the case for all developments in prefabricated building constructional applications. Precast concrete was promoted extensively as a cheap and efficient building method, but as can be seen with hindsight, in many cases there was insufficient investigation into the new forms of architecture this could lead to, and in particular, the effect that repetitive and anonymous building patterns would have on the dwelling and the way people respond to it. The individual factory houses that were set out in conventional communal patterns enabled people to relate to their individual homes. Often they were set into small cleared bomb sites within existing communities of older housing stock. The widespread creation of new housing areas without reference to communal patterns left people alienated and isolated. What had been seen as a liberating new building method actually produced an alien architectural environment that instead of being flexible and user-friendly was resistant to change and hostile in its response to community and individual.

Systems Building

Despite the very real problems of the large precast concrete housing estates, the concept of a flexible approach to industrialised building design has, however, shown its value and continues to the present. The use of industrialised components as a palette from which the sensitive designer can compose an appropriate and efficient building was most effectively first seen in the Case Study houses by Charles and Ray Eames (see Chapter IV). The systems approach to building took this idea a stage further with the introduction of a range of components designed to fit together. A Cornell research project in 1968 expressed the dissatisfaction that was already being felt with the lack of flexibility of the undedicated prefabrication system: 'A systems approach defines and relates all elements which must function together to achieve desired goals ... Existing industrial building techniques are sometimes called systems but are far from being comprehensive environmental systems. They are at best partial systems and should be seen as distinct from total systems'.[10]

A serious attempt to take advantage of the benefits of systems building was undertaken in the UK by the consortium of Local Authorities Special Programme (CLASP) first set up in 1957 by a group of county and city councils primarily to build schools. Based on the experience of Hertfordshire County Architect, Donald Gibson, this system aimed to provide the mechanism for making buildings that could respond to site and brief and yet retain the benefits of mass-produced components assembled without skilled trades personnel. Though there were many undoubted successful aspects to the CLASP programme, unfortunately, the systems approach also has the effect of multiplying problems. For example,

80

81

80 ARCON housing site at Great Yarmouth, England; **81** AIROH housing production in the Bristol Airplane Co factory. Weston-super-Mare, England,1946

71

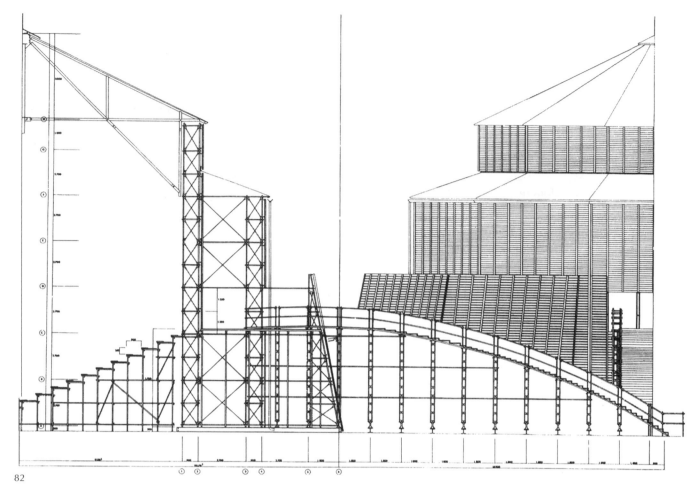

82

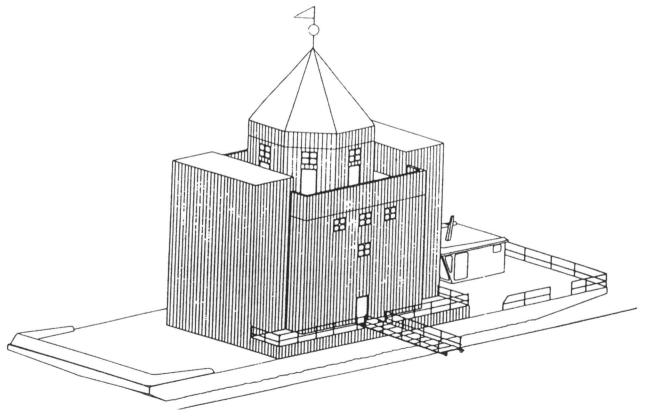

83

when a design failure occurs it may be repeated many times, causing catastrophic failure. The cost benefit of being able to use unskilled installation teams can result in on-site constructional problems because operatives do not understand the basis of their tasks and therefore are not able to recognise errors in construction.

Where industrial building techniques have been a success is in the assembly of high quality components in patterns created by knowledgeable designers. Site work is carried out using specialist contractors who are familiar with their products. Though many of these buildings have been essentially permanent buildings (the relevance of being able to change a component either for functional reasons or for maintenance has been an important factor), some systems buildings have been specifically created to take advantage of assembly techniques for disassembly. Michael Hopkins' own house in Hampstead, London follows the principle of the Eames house as an aesthetically and functionally controlled assembly utilising a diverse set of components from various manufacturers. Cedric Price's Inter Action Centre in Kentish Town, London, uses the steel frame as a loose-fit structure which can be changed to respond to the requirements of the people who use the building. Skin, services and plug-in elements can be moved if desired to alter the operation and appearance of the building (see Chapter IX).

Architects have predominantly been in the vanguard in exploiting the systems approach in building, although there are now many companies that operate a ready-made 'design and build' service for clients. These buildings use restricted components and skilled operators who can assemble products with which they are completely familiar. The benefits they offer to their clients are speed and economy. Design is restricted within strict parameters and is now often done within a simple computer program. These non-dedicated designs, though slicker in appearance and without the manifest constructional problems of the earlier systems, do not generally take advantage of the opportunities that systems building can offer in terms of dedication to a specific purpose, environment and site and flexibility of operation. Far from reducing the importance of the designer and his personal response to a client's requirements, all the evidence points to the fact that the designer is even more important in a construction industry scenario that is complicated by a seemingly endless choice of components. If an appropriate solution is to be found to a specific problem it needs a direct and personal response rather than selection from a loose-fit range of ready-made products. Martin Pawley, in his search to describe the way architects might respond to the challenge of new technology, quotes Edgar Kaufmann Jr:

> Within the great impersonality of the world of mass-production and new disposability there becomes clear for the first time the possibility of an intense personalism as a proper balance and as a proper enrichment of life. The future of design lies in situation design and not in product design; products merely implement the situations.[11]

Temporary Works

Temporary works are an important yet surprisingly little regarded part of the construction process and have a 'critical effect on the speed, safety and quality as well as the profitability of a project'.[12] All construction projects, without exception, have some form of temporary works associated with their completion, and in some cases the necessary investment in design, effort, and cost will exceed that for the permanent structure that remains. *In situ* concrete bridge structures in particular require a large investment in temporary works, up to 60 per cent of the total cost.[13]

The most obvious form of temporary works that relates to this study is the portable office set-up which enables the work to be supervised on site. In many cases this extends to on-site workshops for the creation and preparation of components and materials associated with completion of the project. In remote sites this may also include accommodation for the site team. These facilities are usually provided by readily available pre-manufactured units. There are, however, other forms of temporary works that have much greater ambition in terms of portable structures.

Scaffolding is the most common form of temporary works used in the construction industry, yet the basis of this modular system which is often designed and

84

82 Tadao Ando, Karaza Theatre, part section and part elevation showing scaffolding construction; **83** Aldo Rossi, Teatro del Monde, Venice, Italy, 1979; **84** Tadao Ando, Karaza Theatre, erected at Sendai in Miyagi Prefecture, Japan in June 1987 and Taito Ward, Tokyo in August 1988

85

erected by specialists in large contracts has great potential. Complex scaffolding structures can be erected to great heights, though the cost of doing so can be prohibitive, so alternative forms of construction utilising the permanent structure to support the remaining construction procedures have been devised. Scaffolding is therefore used most often for safety and protection reasons, protecting the workers from the danger of falling, and surrounding property and people from construction dirt, noise and danger. The potential of scaffolding's simple assembly procedure has been recognised by the Japanese architect Tadao Ando, who created the Karaza Theatre, built in 15 days in 1987 using readily available local scaffolding, clad with timber. The building is designed to be portable but not in the conventional sense as only a few special components are actually moved from site to site, the vast majority of the structure being made by locally sourced standard components and: 'If the drawings and a set of instructions are sent ahead by FAX, construction will be possible anywhere'.[14]

86

The Karaza Theatre is, however, not without precedent. Perhaps one of the best-known portable buildings ever made is the Teatro del Monde made for the Venice Biennale in Italy in 1979, designed by Aldo Rossi. Based on sixteenth century floating pavilions (see Chapter III), the 250 seat theatre was built from steel scaffolding using a steel barge as a floating foundation. It was 17 metres high and 9.5 metres square and clad in timber boarding to present a clearly monolithic architectural presence with no reference to its kinetic nature. For this reason it appeared to melt into the city as it approached the land's edge. Indeed, Rossi's drawn proposals for the building, which show it situated amidst an urban setting of towers, bridges and substantial buildings, emphasise that his ambition was to alter the landscape of the city with a temporary impostor. After the Biennale, the theatre embarked on a maritime tour of other coastal towns and cities that were once part of the Venetian State.

Plant associated temporary works are those that utilise special large scale tools that must be able to be deployed to different sites. Tower cranes are impressive structural objects that are readily movable not only from site to site but within sites too. Some cranes are built on temporary tracks that enable them to move within the site perimeter. Tower cranes designed for high-rise construction are required to climb through the structure as it is completed and therefore incorporate a self-lifting system that lifts them from floor to floor as the building progresses. The most versatile tower cranes are those that are built on a mobile caterpillar track platform and are based on a rotary tower. This crane has minimal erection and deployment costs, is self-powered and self-transported from site to site. Other mobile plant facilities include site batching plants, hoists and lifts. A complete portable factory for manufacturing concrete has been made for oil jacket construction in the North Sea.

The method of transporting a prefabricated product to its place of erection can also be described as a form of temporary works. One remarkable example is the Flotation Collar built by Highland Fabricators Ltd for transportation of oil rigs to the Forties oil field in the North Sea. This giant movable steel object is 200 metres long by 75 metres wide. The rigs are fixed to the collar and towed to site. Compartments in the collar are then filled with sea water and the whole assembly tilts into a vertical position, the rig being ejected into the water by explosive bolts at the critical moment. The collar is then towed back to the manufacturing plant for construction and transportation of its next load.

The scale and importance of temporary works in conventional construction projects is manifest, and when construction is carried out in extreme climates this importance is magnified. Contractors who build in countries with long winter seasons such as Alaska in North America have had to devise temporary enclosures that enable the process to continue when external temperatures are continually 20 degrees below freezing at night and never rise above freezing in the day. One solution has been to manufacture air-supported structures that enclose the entire building site in an artificial environment unimpeded by structural supports. The system uses a translucent vinyl-coated polyester weave fabric which lasts for 15 to 20 years. The structures are laid out at the site and anchored to the ground at the perimeter by earth augers before being inflated with warm air to eight pounds per square inch. Air-locks permit the entry of any size vehi-

85 Aldo Rossi, Teatro del Monde, Venice, Italy, 1979; **86** A modular portable building on site adjacent to the Lincoln Memorial, Washington DC

87

88

cle. The structures have to be maintained to ensure good service, which includes manual sweeping of snow to prevent snow-loading problems. If internal air quality becomes a problem the space can be vented at the top with the use of extra fans to reinstitute pressure before deflation occurs. The size of the area covered is infinite if it is covered in sections. One project in North New York State, USA in 1987 covered 22,000 square metres of site area and extended to a height of 25 metres.[15]

Manufactured Portable Buildings

In the developed world, commercially manufactured portable buildings are used in many diverse locations for a range of widely differing purposes. The most significant of these, particularly in North America, is the mobile home, which because of the unique factors involved with its design and implementation, and the significant and continuing impact it has on the nature of new dwelling provision, is discussed in detail later in this chapter. Portable, relocatable and demountable buildings are used in nearly all areas of life and work. In health care, portable buildings are used for wards, operating theatres, locally based health centres, mobile screening and medical check-up facilities, and blood donor stations. In education they are used for classrooms, sports facilities, nursery units, specialised adult training programmes and mobile libraries. Industry makes use of portable buildings as field stations for natural resource exploitation, secure storage of tools and materials and personnel facilities for engineering and building projects. Commercial portable buildings have a particularly wide range of uses, portable sanitary facilities, catering, banking, display and exhibition, offices and many more. Government operations include police control centres, electoral stations and even prison facilities.[16] Though the military have played an important part in the development of the genre of portable architecture and continue to do so to a certain degree, they are also significant users of standard manufactured products.

There are a great many different methods used in the industry to solve the basic problem of enclosure with portability; however, these can be divided into five basic strategies: module, flat-pack, tensile, pneumatic, systems. Most companies depend on a single strategy though a few combine more than one into the manufacture of a single product or make separate products based on different systems. Buildings that involve similar strategies may use quite different materials in their construction. These materials, however, are invariably used in similar ways: in compression, tension or as a skin.

Modules are enclosed building units which are delivered to site in a largely complete state and are the type of portable building most familiar in the manufactured building market. Portakabin has become the market leader of this type of building, so much so that like Hoover, the company name has become synonymous with the product and is used for all buildings of this type, whether manufactured by that company or not. They can basically be divided into two types: fully complete independent units and volumetric units. Both types are delivered to site whole, usually on a truck that has its own lifting crane to deploy the unit, but they can also be delivered by helicopter to locations remote from a road. This independent building unit is then ready for use, though it may be connected to services if these are required. Some units are delivered empty to accept the user's own furniture and fittings, but many come complete with lighting, heating, telephone connections, hot and cold water and sanitary fittings, movable internal partitions and loose furniture.

Volumetric units are used when the requirement is for an overall space that is larger than that which can be transported by road. These units are of the same size as the independent unit but with one or two side walls missing so that similar units can be abutted to form a larger space. Large volume buildings, though limited in height and span, can therefore be made. They are fitted together on site by specialists and are usable almost instantly. Timber and steel are the most common materials used in the construction of module units, though some now use a composite skin panel of metal and plastic based insulation. All steel units are used where security is a particular requirement and many smaller kiosk type units are made of GRP or vacuum formed plastic.

87 A series of volumetric units assembled to form a temporary two-storey structure on a building site in Dresden, Germany; **88** Flat-pack prefabricated building by National Partitions and Interiors Inc of Florida, USA

Once erected, many flat-pack units appear very similar to modules; however, they are delivered to site in a collapsed form, which means that their size when transported is much smaller. This can have distinct advantages if delivery distances are great and efficient use of volume, for instance in a cargo aircraft, is necessary. Another advantage of the flat-pack strategy is that it can be used in limited access situations where size, weight or volume is restricted. Flat-pack units can use two strategies for erection. The easiest to erect, though more complex to manufacture, is the pre-joined hinged strategy in which most of the components are arranged in simple surfaces such as walls, floor and roof, which, when opened in a predetermined manner, fold into place and, after simple fixing, form a rigid volume. In large units this process can be carried out with the aid of a crane or in smaller systems by hand. Additional internal and external panels may then be added to the basic structure depending on its purpose. The other strategy is to deliver the unit as a kit. This can be a relatively simple solution with the walls, floor, and roof being identifiable complete elements that are assembled in a clear hierarchical process. A more complex kit system has separate parts for structure and skin and even for components like doors, windows, services, etc. Flat-pack units can be assembled by skilled operatives or by local labour following a set of instructions. This can be seen as a clear advantage to the user, who may have labour and transportation available or may be able to provide them at a reduced cost. Construction materials are generally similar to those used for the module type of building though the quality, efficiency and deployment of the system depend far more on the design of its assembly procedures.[17]

89

Module and flat-pack portable buildings are the most common form of manufactured portable buildings in use, although they are not suited to the many instances where more flexible spaces are required. The traditional solution for these problems has been the marquee, generally a rigid frame that supports a thin skin membrane. Many manufacturers still produce and market these simple tensile buildings; however, here the tensile strategy is used to describe all taut membrane structures (excluding pneumatic) including those commonly identified as tents. All of these products consist of two basic elements: a stiff compressive frame, strut or series of struts, generally steel or aluminium, and a stretched tension skin. Traditional skin materials are canvas and more recently, PVC coated polyester. However, this is one of the few areas where technological developments have significantly influenced manufactured portable building design and higher performance specifications now utilise PTFE (polytetrafluoroethylene) coated glass fibre skins. This, despite its translucency and lightness, is a permanent building material because the Teflon is a non-deteriorating plastic and the glass fibre (which is the load carrying element) has the characteristics of glass and is therefore comparatively stiff. The quality of the building is directly related to the quality of the skin material used, poorer quality skins being used for loose-fit situations in terms of function and constructional strategy. Higher loadings from larger spans and live loads like wind and snow require taut, minimal movement, and skins which are finely tuned to their support structures. These buildings can take many forms and the larger and more complex products take advantage of computer aided design programs to develop cutting patterns for the manufacturer. Standard marquee functions generally employ the lower-quality products where simplicity of erection and dismantling are the main criteria.[18] The most impressive tensile structures have been developed in liaison with designers, and specialist manufacturers providing an expert service in the solution of specific problems. This part of the industry is without doubt the one most open to new ideas from clients, designers and related industries. Manufacturers involved in the field make specific reference to the beautiful organic shapes made possible by their high-technology materials and sophisticated computer generated design methods. Visualisations of completed forms are available at the design stage for subjective assessment prior to production. The nature of the manufacturing process means that the skins for special designs can be made alongside standard products.[19]

Pneumatic structures also achieve their stability from a skin under tension, however, in their case the tension is provided by air pressure. Pneumatic structures have the advantage of being capable of large spans and speedy erection

89 Framed, tension skin structure by Cannobio, Milan, Italy

90

without specialist equipment. There are two basic strategies: the support of an entire skin by a difference in pressure from outside to inside, or by the use of relatively high pressure structural sections that take the place of compression members. The quality of the product is based on the quality of the skin material used (generally an impervious PVC or PTFE coated polyester), the nature of the tie-down system for the building, and the reliability and efficiency of the inflation device. These buildings can be very easy and light to transport and simple to deploy; however, problems are associated with making the building resistant to wind load (which can lead to catastrophic destruction) and accidental deflation in the event of puncture or air-input failure.[20] They also require a constant reliable power supply, though this can be associated with heating and cooling requirements. Pneumatic structures have the capability to cover large areas more cheaply than any other system and because up until recently it was not generally possible for them to be made without competent engineering advice, there have been relatively few failures. However, it is now becoming possible to buy impervious material direct from the manufacturer, to assemble or buy-in inflation devices, and make and install a structure without expert advice or quality control. Consequently, calls are now being made to regulate this type of building.

Demountable systems buildings are generally derived from permanent building construction techniques and can take many diverse forms. Demountable buildings of this type use familiar, bolt-together components in order to produce a building that can also be disassembled for relocation. The implementation of these systems is usually the result of a manufacturer already producing components for one market and seeking new markets for the same tooling. All the products use steel or aluminium based structural systems in coordination with a range of cladding materials such as glass, PVCs, plastic, metal, timber. These buildings can take many forms and quality may vary widely between system and function. The nature of their portability is, however, generally compromised by the lack of dedication to this purpose, and deployment costs are a major part of the total building budget. Hybrid solutions are possible utilising a systems approach that incorporates several techniques to provide more finely tuned solutions.[21]

A large number of manufacturers exist to cater to the portable building market more than a hundred separate dedicated companies exist for the sole purpose of building and selling portable and demountable buildings in the UK alone. These companies are, however, very different in the way they approach the operation of manufacturing and marketing their product. Some products are aimed at a reasonably defined sector of the market, and may be further restricted by the method of manufacture. For example, vacuum formed plastic mouldings are particularly suited to small-scale portable toilets and shelters, whereas a lightweight geodesic-based structural system is more suited to large open spans. All, however, have to conform to construction standards set at local, national, or international level, though in some cases these may be less stringent than for permanent buildings. In the UK, buildings do not have to conform to the Building Regulations unless they remain in the same position for more than 28 days. Some manufacturers have been able to obtain type approval for their products, which makes it no longer necessary to apply for separate Building Regulation approval for each site. Portable buildings also have to comply with relevant Codes of Practice dealing with items such as fire and wind loading. British Standard 5750 contains specifications concerning design, development, production, installation and servicing to ensure specific standards of quality which manufacturers find useful in marketing their products. Other British Standards refer specifically to particular products and materials.[22] Agreement Certificates indicate that a product has been independently assessed and found acceptable for fitness of purpose.[23] Companies wishing to export their product are put to considerable expense in complying with foreign regulations, although efforts are being made to establish European product standards which will lead to greater opportunity for transfer of products between countries.

Some companies have developed their market in a particular way for historic reasons. Timber hutting is the traditional form of builders' on-site enclosure. These have largely been replaced by the vehicle-delivered secure enclosure that

90 Pneumatic sports hall by Cannobio, Milan, Italy

provides on-site accommodation that is vandal and thief resistant and available for instant use. Companies which formerly made steel shipping containers have diversified into high-security site storage enclosures and from there into site personnel enclosures. In most cases it appears that products have developed in an undetermined manner, based on accidents in the company's trading or manufacturing history, or in response to the identification of a similar adjacent market.[24] There are few instances where a mass-produced product has been designed to fulfil a specific identified purpose. Even when manufacturers have a dedicated design team involved in the manufacturing process, design changes are generally made in response to external factors, for example the need to make economies in production or comply with new regulations. Except in specific cases, there appears to be little regular interaction between the manufacturers and the users of the product.[25] Users typically explore the market availability and select the product they deduce is closest to meeting their needs; there is little or no impartial informed advice available on the possible options that may be available. In a similar manner, there is little or no feedback on the operational qualities of the product. It would appear that most manufacturers assume that if a product continues to be in demand it is meeting a given market and is therefore successful, although in fact it may be because it is the best available but not the best possible. Except in the case of tensile and pneumatic structures there is very little dedicated research and development in the industry and there are very few instances where the opportunities of technology transfer have been exploited. In an industry where lightness and fast response mean everything, the implementation of new materials, manufacturing techniques, and systems of erection or operation could lead to dramatic advances in the nature of the product.

The military, one of the few users that consistently make specific demands on the industry to produce new more effective developments, still generally resort to the use of standard products due to an apparent lack of response to their demands and the need for expediency (see Chapter V). For these reasons, an industry which is dealing with solutions to dynamic and kinetic situations is in general responding with new products which are modifications of old and existing lines rather than real examples of innovation. A classic example of the failure of the industry to respond to the opportunities raised by the nature of its product is the case of the recent British Antarctic Survey installation at Halley Base. This project has all the conditions to which a portable building solution should be able to respond effectively – remote manufacture, difficulty of transportation and erection, minimal planning controls. However, the £9.4 million station cost £4.2 million more than was estimated and ran two years late because of lack of understanding and communication between the Germany-based contractor Christiani and Nielson, which carried out the design, and the British-based subsidiary of the same name which procured the components and supervised construction.[26]

Manufactured building in Japan has responded more effectively to the opportunities of new technology. Driven by the lack of skilled site labour, the rapid turnover in the housing market, and the restrictive nature of sites, specialist companies have developed new techniques of making buildings based on extensive research and development work. The Sekisui company operates by taking orders direct from clients who can virtually design their own layouts by using a sophisticated computer program that not only provides plans, but costing and finance packages, and will even transmit the order direct to the factory. The company uses both flat-packs and modules assembled on a 400 metre long assembly line. A house is built from about 12 modules and about 300 are made each day. At the end of each day all the units are transported to their site for erection. Using this system Sekisui, which is about the same size company as Laing, produces 60,000 houses compared to the British company which builds about 4,500.[27]

The Mobile Home

The American mobile home is the most successful example of a factory-built building to be found in the world. Out of the 1.1 million new homes sold in 2000, 250,000 were 'mobile' homes and more than 9 million have been sold since 1977. The building type provides 25 per cent of all dwellings in North America – homes for 12,500,000 people – and is by far the largest section of

91

affordable housing. In the past, this building type has not generally been accepted as 'real' housing, and until relatively recently suffered from prejudice from the design profession, local and central government and the lay person. However, it has now been recognised as a realistic option within the housing market, one that is recognised generally on a vernacular level, i.e. by those who build and use the building.

> The mobile home may well be the single most significant and unique housing innovation in twentieth-century America. No other innovation addressing the spectrum of housing activity – from construction, tenure, and community structure to design – has been more widely adopted nor, simultaneously, more broadly vilified. The mobile home is the dream of the factory-built house come true, yet few advocates of that dream are proud to acknowledge its manifestation in the present form.[28]

The mobile home is a factory-built building ranging in size from 2.5 metres by 10 metres to 7.5 metres by 25 metres. On average, it takes 100 man hours and a single working day to build a single mobile home unit. It is generally transported to its site on its own chassis and wheels, though some of the larger units, called 'double-wides' are transported in sections and assembled by specialists. Nearly half of all homes are placed in mobile home parks of which there are 24,000 in the USA. The average size of each is 150 to 175 spaces, though there are many with only a few units and some with many, many more.[29] The industry now prefers the term Manufactured Housing, which is in fact a more accurate description as 97 per cent of new buildings will actually only be transported once, usually within 480 kilometres and, though the potential for removal will always exist, will remain permanently sited for the remainder of their life. This change of name also corresponds to a change in appearance, from the obviously transportable 'trailer' (which would be recognised in Britain as a large caravan) to a finished product which now possesses a more building-like image, with pitched roofs and square house-like windows. However, there has been little change to the basic construction; the lightweight timber superstructure is still made on a chassis which simplifies the towing procedure, usually on a permanently fixed set of wheels.

The historic precedent for the American mobile home is the Conestoga Wagon which was mass-produced for freighting goods to the frontier in nineteenth century America.[30] Converted by their owners to provide mobile dwellings, sometimes called Prairie Schooners, they became both a practical necessity and a moving symbol of home. This quintessential moving house is redolent of the national characteristics of determination and courage that led to this great exodus and retains a potent imagery used with respect but casual familiarity throughout the US Midwest.[31]

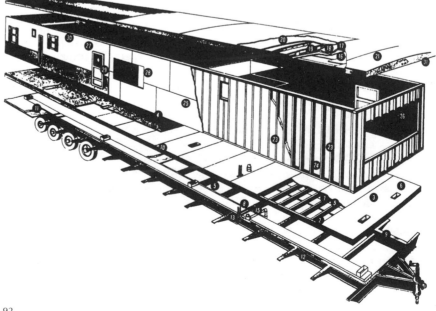

91 The Conestoga Wagon, perhaps the single most significant artifact used in the settlement of the North American West; **92** Lancer Home single-wide mobile home by Lanchart Industries, USA

92

In the 1920s, the advent of the readily available motor car led to a new type of traveller: one who did so for pleasure. These Tin-Can Tourists (named after their principal food) initially used simple tents and the inside of their vehicles for shelter, but soon individuals began to build towed enclosures at home. Many variations of these trailers were made, with a great variety in form and level of sophistication and comfort. The popularity of auto-camping was such that wealthy people (even the President) were involved and they were able to commission specially built units to make their travel more comfortable, the *Aerocar* of 1919 by the aeroplane manufacturer, Glenn Curtis, being an early significant example. Part of the pleasure of touring was to meet up with like-minded people and one natural topic of conversation was the design of trailers. Inevitably, cross-fertilisation occurred between different travel trailer builders and the best ideas became incorporated into their designs. The first volume producer of a travel trailer was Arthur Sherman, a chemist who had built a trailer for his own use on family trips. He saw the potential and went into business in 1936 manufacturing and marketing his design, called the Covered Wagon in homage to its nineteenth century counterpart. A ready market made this commercial trailer a success and other manufacturers soon became established, for example the Auto-Kamp Trailer Company whose brochure for its 1923 line promised the motorist would be able to 'take even the longest of tours with independence and comfort. It is a completely equipped home, affording absolute protection from the elements'.[32]

93

94

The internal arrangements of the various designs of travel trailers were largely similar, greatly influenced by the Pullman car developed by George Pullman in 1856 – a railroad carriage that contained furniture that was demountable and convertible to berths for overnight rest. There were also connotations with yachts; for instance the term galley was used for the kitchen. The exteriors could, however, be quite different though all made distinct associations with readily understood imagery, generally the romance of the Gypsy Caravan, denoting freedom from responsibility, and the technological advancement of the motor car or aeroplane, while also expressing the excitement of the future. The Airstream Company, perhaps the most famous trailer company, was founded in 1935 by Wally Byam. A contemporary description of this sleek, shining representative of the future notes: 'the front was rounded to present an easy edge into the air, vertically and horizontally. The tail was tapered off to eliminate suction in the rear, it was streamlined underneath as well as on top ... and planned to give an extremely low centre of gravity'.[33] The Airstream is still seen today as a timeless

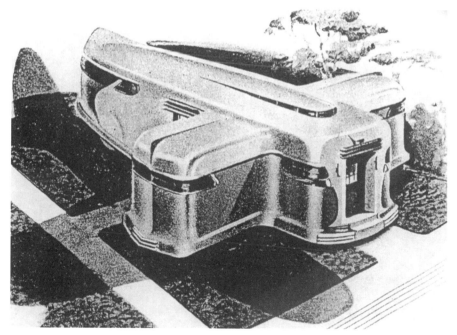

95

93 The Aerocar Land Yacht, designed and made by Glenn Curtis, aviation pioneer and aeroplane builder, 1928; **94** A contemporary Airstream Trailer; **95** A prediction of post Second World War mobile home design from a Palace Corporation advertisement

second floor plan

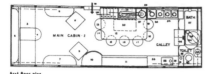

first floor plan

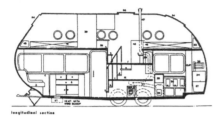

longitudinal section

transverse section

96

example of appropriate design coupled with potent imagery, and is seen as an iconic landmark by design historians.[34] A more ambitious trailer (though probably considerably more difficult to tow) was the 'Mobile House' by Corwin Wilson, a 1936 design published in *Architectural Record*. This double-storey trailer incorporated all the conveniences of a home, including bath, dressing room, fitted kitchen and four beds.[35]

Until the Great Depression of the 1930s there was relatively little use of the travel trailer for year-round occupation. However, as the population began to shift in larger numbers in search of employment the problems of affordable, available accommodation became acute and the travel trailer became a necessity rather than a luxury. At this time new manufactured trailers were still far too expensive for most people to buy, particularly if unemployed, so home-built trailers or truck conversions were still common. However, the industry had been able to show that it could produce a workable and desirable product which became a ready solution to the critical housing problems that arose when the United States joined the Allies in the Second World War. The establishment of large war supplies plants required large shifts in the population to provide labour. The work-starved population were willing to make these changes but resources and labour could not be spared for constructing conventional housing. The Government turned to the trailer industry. During the war years over 200,000 trailers were manufactured, more than 60 per cent for placement in defence production areas. For example, the bomber factory established in Ypsilanti, Michigan in 1941 required 42,000 workers, who naturally brought their families. More than half of these made their homes in an instant city of trailers. After the war, the value of the trailer as an affordable, quickly available housing unit had been established. The US government located 722 trailers in Portland, Oregon after a disastrous flood in 1948 and over 1,000 units in response to a similar disaster in Kansas in 1951.[36] Large construction projects also used trailers to house their workers and families. The Atomic Energy Commission project at Savannah River in 1954 required 45,000 workers. Four thousand rental trailers were provided by the employer but over 5,500 private ones were also used.[37]

Virtually all trailers until this time had been seen as a primarily mobile form of housing, but it was now clear that they could also provide continuous homes for a large sector of the population who either preferred to buy a ready-made house, required one quickly, or could not afford the more expensive conventional building process. The industry responded to these requirements and the size of the units began to grow from the minimum space required for towing the vehicle behind a normal car to a factory delivered unit of much larger dimension fitted out inter-

96 'The Mobile House' by Corwin Wilson from the *Architectural Record*, 1936; **97** Owner modifications to a mobile home, Arizona; an early stage, with a simple protective roof and porch canopy

97

nally with all the facilities of a normal house. There were, however, problems with the acceptance of the mobile home as a legitimate form of housing. Although wide sections of the population are represented in mobile home occupants, there was much prejudice shown by potential neighbours living in conventional housing. Local zoning laws were introduced to prevent mobile homes being sited on normal house plots in residential areas and to relegate them to marginal locations on the outside of town. Differences in building codes also caused problems in terms of the acceptability of the units as habitable structures. In many ways, mobile homes were treated as vehicles, which led to problems with the financing of their purchase and insurance and in some cases they were subject to both property and vehicle tax. Transportation of the units was also limited by laws governing the width of units allowed on the highway, exacerbated by the introduction in 1955 of the 'ten-wide', a ten foot (3 metre) wide trailer, which allowed much greater freedom to the interior layout but also led to battles with individual States to allow their transportation on the road.

It was only in the 1970s that these problems began to be overcome. Legislation was introduced in all States to establish codes of quality in building that brought consistency to the construction and safety aspects of the homes. Public support for the industry by the President and the Department of Housing and Urban Development led to the gradual disintegration of unfair zoning and tax conditions. Mobile homes are now generally accepted as a realistic affordable housing option.

Throughout its history, the mobile home has been developed not through the expertise of professional designers but through the pragmatic and aspirational desires of its owners and users. The early examples were created by amateur designers building in accordance with what their first-hand experience told them was required. The manufacturing industry, right to the present day, is still governed by this idea that the success or failure of its products is governed by the purchasers' requirements. Although many suggested plans and layouts are given to the prospective purchaser, there is a great deal of freedom in terms of customisation of their own unit. Buying from new, colour schemes, internal layout, appliances and furnishings can be selected. The nature of its manufacture, without expensive specialist tooling, enables these changes to be made. It is a relatively low technology process that allows change within specific standardised limits, to individual units or to whole ranges, without dramatic implications in terms of cost or time.

Once the home is purchased, the owner can then state how the unit is to be placed on the site and of course what site it is placed on: in a mobile home park, a private site or close to a relative's home. They are then free to create their own landscaping details and also to build additions and make alterations. The afford-

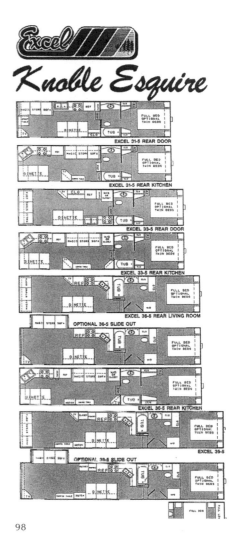

98

99

98 Interior options for Excel recreational vehicles manufactured by Peterson Industries Inc, Kansas, USA; **99** Owner modifications to a mobile home, Arizona. A late stage with roof, stone fireplace, concrete chimney stack and mature landscaping

ability of the mobile home makes it less precious in the eyes of the owner; it is theirs to customise in the same way they might alter their car. Like the car, it can also be seen as a ready-made consumer durable, compact and efficient, a space for everything yet economical, and complete with internal fittings and furnishings. Alison and Peter Smithson described these attributes effectively:

> Against the standard solution to the permanent dwelling, the caravan is neat, like a big piece of equipment, has a space for everything like a well run office, has miniature appliances in scale with the spaces like a toy home, is as comfortable as this year's space heated car. And like the car, the caravan represents a new freedom. It has become a sort of symbol as well as a sign of 'population in flux'. It has something of the cheerful, safe transient feeling one gets driving along in a car.[38]

Its relative cheapness also means there may be more money available for alterations and because it is a homogeneous building type, they may be more necessary in order to respond to a particular climate. Virtually all mobile homes that have been occupied for even a short length of time have had significant changes made to their external appearance: the disguise of the wheels and chassis, landscaping for access and establishment of personal space, step entry usually with a porch, shed addition for storage. Other more substantial alterations are the addition of extra living space, canopies for a carport and above the home for protection from sun, rain and snow. In many cases the mobile home can be seen as the 'seed' of the house from which a gradual construction project can establish a much larger self-built dwelling. The mobile home is expedient in that it is instant and affordable, but it is also flexible in that it can be fully appropriated by the owner for the expression of his own understanding of home. It has no official cultural place in society's understanding of the built environment and is therefore a simple usable product. It does, however, still have connections with the flexibility and mobility of the frontier which is inherent in many aspects of North American culture, of being able to make your own changes to your physical circumstances when necessary – a primary characteristic of vernacular design. The mobile home can therefore be seen as an innovative yet evolved form of technology – a building type that uses production techniques developed in other industries to provide a solution in housing, yet because it has been developed from pragmatic models developed by the end-users themselves and has remained close to their requirements, it has also retained relevance and popularity. Observers seem unanimous that the mobile home industry is succeeding where conventional methods of providing affordable housing are not:

> The mobile home industry is the most efficient building industry in the world. The industry has achieved what the rest of the building industry has not because of its continuing readjustment and reorganisation. The message for the rest of the housing industry is that the mobile model must be emulated to obtain effective results.[39]

(Arthur D Bernhardt, 1980)

100 Mobile home design for National Homes by the Frank Lloyd Wright Foundation, 1970

100

An innovation's ultimate contribution is not simply that it meets some need more effectively, but that it alters a socially constructed sense of reality and broadens it to accept new forms of action and thought as an innovation, the mobile home's contribution in reshaping the American understanding of housing is unfinished.[40]
(Allan D Wallis, 1991)

Architects' observations on the buildings produced by the industry are that they are badly designed: 'Theirs is a conservative industry that competes fiercely on the basis of how long they take and how much they charge to deliver their product. The quality of design is not a major issue'.[41] Though there has been interaction between architects and the mobile home industry in the past (notably by the Frank Lloyd Wright Foundation and Paul Rudolph),[42] these have not had lasting impact. Until recently, the opportunities that might arise from the involvement of professional designers who understand the positive qualities of mobile home/manufactured housing products had not been tested. However, in 1991, the US journal *Progressive Architecture* sponsored an initiative to explore the possibilities for increased quality in the affordable housing market. Their objective was to build a family home for $65,000. They turned to industrialised housing as it is this sector of the construction industry that has the major share of this market but also because it still possesses clear development possibilities:

> The potential is perhaps obvious. Because it is built in a factory, industrialised housing is often more comfortable and precise, less wasteful and costly, and more rapidly installed and secured than most site-built work. And the modules, typically no more than 14 feet [4.3 metres] wide and 11 feet [3.4 metres] high (to allow for highway shipment), lend themselves to placement on narrow urban infill lots, which most large cities have in abundance.[43]

Abacus Architects of Boston won the competition to produce a design utilising the industry's techniques; however, only one manufacturer could be found to build the house within the budget: Stratton Homes of Knox, Pennsylvania. The house was designed as a piece of product design, working in detail with the manufacturer. The product needed to be flexible as, if put into production, it would have to meet different building codes dependent on its deployment location. It was built on an assembly line in two modules – a typical double wide strategy; however, because the architects wanted the building to be compatible with compact sites and to fit easily into existing communities in terms of pattern and building form, the modules were positioned one above the other. The lower module is built on a chassis and the upper features on a collapsible roof which lies flat when being transported, then is unfolded on site to form a conventional pitched roof. Because the building was a prototype, there were hitches on the production line as the architects became accustomed to the manufacturing habits of the industry. However, production line work began on 23 March 1992, the building was delivered to site on 14 April 1992 and both modules were set in position in a single day. The house was finished by the end of the month, five and a half weeks after starting down the line. The design process took three and a half months, which has resulted in a proven product ready for delivery from the manufacturer at relatively short notice.

The house plan is conventional, and obviously builds on traditional North American family home types, particularly the 'shot-gun' house.[44] However, this conventionality also meets the aims of the designers for contextuality.

The logistical decisions made regarding its construction are where the differences lie – differences that enable the placing of a well-designed product within the grasp of the mass-market. One of mass production's marketing tools is making high quality products available to many because quantity of numbers means economy in production. The *Progressive Architecture* affordable house is a realistic proposal to use this tool for the benefit of the housing industry.

In the UK prefabricated housings consists primarily of high-quality, expensive kits imported from Germany and Scandinavia (though the development as web-based construction packages is beginning to introduce the possibility of flexible user-involved designs; see Chapter XI). However, modular construction using pre-assembled room-sized components has begun to be used for hotels, student

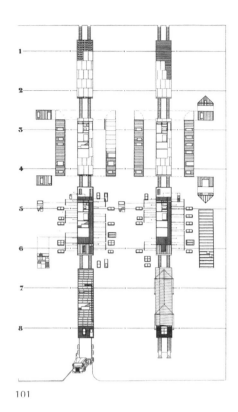

101

101 The *Progressive Architecture* house designed by Abacus Architects, Boston USA, 1992; exploded axonometric showing factory construction sequence

102

102a

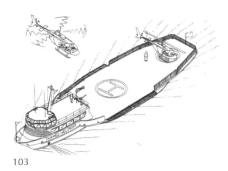

103

accommodation, and even prisons. Perhaps the most interesting recent project has been the Peabody Trust's Murray Grove Housing, London, designed by Cartwright Pickard Architects. The designers collaborated with a subsidiary of Portakabin UK to build a prototype housing system utilising prefabricated modules for each flat, stair towers, and lifts.

Engineering

Portability has often been a key factor in engineering projects. It may be a strategy to enable the assembly of a structure which is ultimately to be located at a permanent site, or as a by-product of the necessity to make a structure economical and flexible in manufacture and use. Engineers have created dynamic examples of lightweight structures for economical or logistical reasons. The suspension bridge is an example of these strategies, producing exciting examples of lightweight structures that other designers have used as a source in the creation of lightweight architecture.

The first suspension bridges originated in East Asia, resulting from the necessity to span large voids between the mountain passes. These bridges were manufactured of plaited strips made from bamboo and other natural fibres by the local inhabitants and spanned up to 240 metres.

The metal suspension bridge originated in China. The Kuanhsien Bridge over the Min River was built in 1177 and consisted of eight spans of up to 70 metres, totalling 320 metres in all, and using iron chains for suspension. This feat was not matched in the West until 1809 with the construction of the suspension bridge over the Merrimack River in Massachusetts, USA. By 1889, the suspension bridge was made to span 486 metres with John A Roebling's design for the Brooklyn Bridge, New York. By 1940 when the San Francisco Golden Gate Bridge was built, the span had increased to 1,280 metres. The dramatic imagery of these great structures is based on the same structural principles of the lightweight tension bridges in East Asia, yet the potent message they convey is also associated with the power of modern technology. In turn, these tension cable structures influenced the tension cable-net structures developed by Frei Otto in the 1950s.

The ability of water to support large structures has been exploited throughout history. On Lake Dal in Kashmir, rich fields that float on the water, supporting market gardens and shelters for their farmers, have been in existence for many generations. A contemporary version of this principle has been proposed by the French architect Francis Soler for a series of floating gardens 3,200 metres long on the San Francisco waterfront. Soler's ambitious plan includes pedestrian promenades and vehicle routes.[45] The necessity for transporting large engineering structures from their place of manufacture to their place of installation has led to the

102 Aquapolis floating pavilion, Okinawa, Japan, 1975; designed by Kituake Architects and built by Mitsubishi Heavy Industries Ltd; **102a** Polyconfidence Floating Hotel, designed and built by Mitsui Engineering and Shipbuilding Company in 1987. This mobile hotel is based in the North Sea to rest oil rig workers; **103** First City Air mobile heliport designed to operate on the River Thames by naval architect and marine engineer, Bill Williamson, 1993; **104** The Progressive Architecture house in Cleveland, completed prototype built by Stratton Homes of Knox, Pennsylvania

104

development of remarkable towing techniques that have enabled virtually any object to be moved via the sea. Barges, flotation collars, and special heavy-lift vessels transport objects far larger than buildings at an economical cost. The proposed First City Air Heliport in London, designed by naval architect and marine engineer Bill Williamson, will cruise the River Thames enabling helicopters to land and depart from a series of locations. This strategy provides a facility which is not acceptable on land due to safety and noise pollution problems, and allows passengers the flexibility of several departure points as they will be ferried from the shore to the movable facility.[46] However, this project appears conservative in comparison with the installation of the 70 megawatt hydroelectric power plant at Portsmouth, Ohio, USA. This 6,500 ton structure was built by the French firm Alsthom Atlantique and transported across the Atlantic Ocean on a heavy-lift vessel. At New Orleans it was then off-loaded and floated up the Mississippi and Ohio rivers nearly 2,575 kilometres before being nudged into place on prepared foundations at the site. The only significant problem with the project was local opposition to the power lines that transferred the electricity to the city grid.[47]

The exploitation of oil resources from off-shore oil fields has resulted in dramatic engineering developments in the creation of stable platforms at sea. These structures must be movable because they are completely prefabricated before deployment on site and also because they can subsequently be moved to a separate field or brought back into port for refurbishment. The engineering capability developed in this area has started to transfer to associated fields of development where land is not available for construction, or it is logistically desirable that the development is located out at sea. It is the Japanese engineering companies that have proven that this technology can be transferred successfully. In 1975, a prototype marine city titled Aquapolis was constructed as a government pavilion at the Okinawa International Ocean Exposition. The structure was supported on 16 columns that rested on four semi-submersed buoyant foundations which could be raised or lowered by pumping water in and out. The structure was moored by a series of long chains that spread out in four directions, and it could be moved horizontally to weather storms by lengthening or shortening the chains. Services were all contained within a closed system, which meant there was no chance of pollution.

A major cost of North Sea oil exploitation has been for relief of personnel who experience extremely severe conditions during their shifts on the rigs. Greater savings could be made if a rest station were provided close to the rigs' location. This has resulted in the creation of *Polycastle* and *Polyconfidence*, which are portable sea-based hotels specially designed to withstand extreme weather conditions. *Polycastle* was commissioned in 1982 and is a 600-bed hotel with eight recreation rooms, a 190-seat cinema, a gym and a sauna. The building is supported on columns that are based on fully submersed floating buoyant foundations. *Polyconfidence* (commissioned in 1987) is built in the same manner but has space for 800 residents and an advanced set of submerged thrusters that counteract pitching in rough weather and can also be used to move the position of the platform.[48]

The North Sea hotels are undoubtedly hybrid structures, part building/part oil platform, but more recent projects have begun to take on the characteristics of genuine 'floating' architecture. The Barrier Reef Floating Hotel opened for business in March 1988 as the first permanent facility situated adjacent to Australia's Great Barrier Reef. The building was built in Singapore and was taken to site by the heavy-lift carrier, *Mighty Servant 2*. This vessel was submerged, the hotel floated into place above its lifting platform and then refloated to transport its burden to the mooring site. The 200-room hotel has a main substructure built in the form of a steel barge. Two floors are contained within the barge and a further five above contain lobby, restaurant, kitchens, shops, disco, bars. Public spaces within the hotel are large and open plan but the *en suite* bedrooms are made from cellular prefabricated modules slotted into place in the superstructure. All services are operated on a closed system, sewage and waste is compacted and incinerated, then treated water is removed to open sea and released, an essential operation as the building was moored in an extremely sensitive conservation area. The buil-

105

106

105 The Barrier Reef Hotel built by Consafe Engineering, Sweden. Originally located over the Great Barrier Reef, Australia, the hotel is now moored in the harbour of Ho Chi Minh City, Vietnam; **106** Floating Island theatre and aquarium, Hiroshima, 1989. Designed by Crayon Associates and Eiichi Yanagita of the Tsuneishi Shipbuilding Co Ltd and constructed by Tsuneishi Shipbuilding Co Ltd

ding's strength was proven shortly after it was established on site as it was subject to a typhoon immediately and another six months later.[49]

The novelty factor of such buildings initially meant that the quality of their aesthetic design was not important; the fact that they existed at all was sufficient to ensure their success. However, the quality of planning and appearance has now begun to be more important and specialist designers are becoming involved in their construction. The Floating Island project is in the Japanese inland sea adjacent to Honshu. The building, completed in 1989, consists primarily of a theatre, a gallery and an aquarium and is situated away from the shore so that its structure will act as protection for a marina. The engineering element is a large floating platform, of 130 metres by 40 metres, which has been used as a base to support a dramatic superstructure consisting of a rotunda, walkways and 30 large vertical steel columns. The image of this building is far from a simply engineered solution but appears to emphasise conventional land-built forms despite the obvious fact that it floats. Unlike the earlier, obviously engineered solutions like Aquapolis, the fact that this is a floating structure is not seen by the developers as sufficient to ensure its success. It is required to have its own distinct image, in the same way that any new leisure building would.[50]

One of the most remarkable examples of lateral design thinking ever to have been constructed is the part vessel/part operations platform/part living space/part laboratory created by Frederick Fisher and a group of fellow scientists to make precise measurements on the ocean using sound waves. They required a platform far more stable than anything so far created and reasonable mobility that would allow the structure to change location without excessive trouble. The result was *Flip*, a 108.2 metre long craft which could cruise to station in the horizontal mode and, when it reached station, take on water in tanks and flip to a vertical mode with 91.4 metres of draft. This draft affords remarkable stability, the structure then being able to withstand 24 metre waves with little disturbance. The laboratories and living quarters on board must be able to accommodate a shift in orientation of 90 degrees. The first model of *Flip* was made from a baseball bat, which it resembles quite closely. It has been very successful as an operating platform but less so in terms of living and working, these considerations being worked out on an ad hoc basis. Proposals are now established to build *Flip II*: 128 metres in length, able to withstand 30 metre waves, and with the added feature of deployable submersibles from the bottom of its 103.6 metre draft.[51]

The sea is a vast arena of possibilities for architectural design. Large structures have utilised the sea for centuries, but this has been a medium for transport, the prime purpose being to get from one land-based place to another. Ocean liners were required to compete with each other in the opulence of their comforts and interior compartments, but this was only while the passage time remained significant.[52] Today, there are new reasons for building large portable structures not associated with a transient purpose. The portable maritime structure has become a destination and, therefore, clearly the architect's province. The value of engineering structures to designers attempting to create this new genre of portable buildings is that they show quite simply that it can, and in some cases, has already been done. In many cases these solutions are inventive, even audacious in their approach to creating a practical, economic and successful solution. They use as their precedent experience drawn from engineering traditions in naval architecture, structures and materials technology. In many cases, the solutions are hybrids of several technologies, working together to form a composite working prototype.

It is not just the ingenuity which is impressive; it is also the scale of operations. To move a 6,500 ton object over many thousands of kilometres takes planning but is easily achievable. The approach of the engineers is 'if it needs to be done, it can be done'. Designers are beginning to be involved in these projects for their skills as space planners and interior designers, although it has generally been other disciplines that have established the logistical approach and the form of the structure. If architects recognise the capabilities of these structures they might be able to offer them to clients as appropriate solutions. The flexibility of buildings that require no other site than the sea can result in long-term ecological benefits, and in a growing number of cases, make short-term economic sense.

In 1965, Buckminster Fuller put forward ideas for ocean cities, of which Tetrahedronal City was a project for a 3.2 kilometre wide floating city in San Francisco Bay. This earthquake proof building had 20,000 apartments gathered in the walls of a giant tetrahedron. In 1968, The US Department of Housing and Urban Development financed a detailed study for Triton City, a series of neighbourhood-sized floating communities for between 3,500 and 6,500 persons. It was Fuller's intention that these structures should be produced at shipyards, and floated to their eventual location.[53] In his book, *The Man-Made Future*, CH Waddington predicts that ocean cities are a probable urban development in the future.

Cities on the sea surface, extending down a few hundred feet, may develop in the first place from the existing small drilling platforms used for mining oil (and probably later other products). In shallow seas the town structure would extend right down to the sea bed, although its upper part would be at and above the sea surface … In the last two or three centuries, several coastal cities have been built to serve as nodes of sea transportation, located at previously unused areas of the shore line – Singapore, Hong Kong, Aden and Bombay. These cities were conjured up out of mud flats and waste along the sea's edge … If we needed any further communication nodes, we could now construct them as floating islands in the middle of the deep ocean.[54]

107

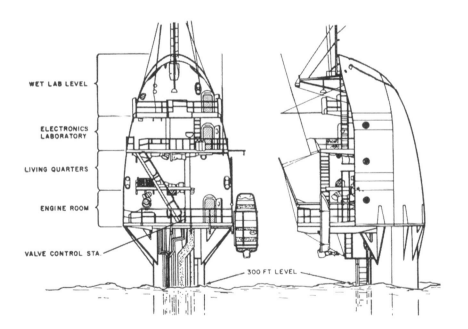

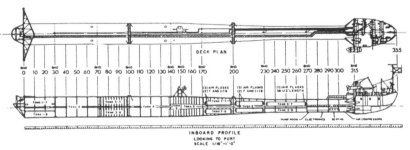

108

107, 108 *Flip*, a vessel that in the vertical position has a large draft which gives it remarkable stability at sea. *Flip* was designed by the Marine Physical Laboratory of the Scripps Institute of Oceanography, built by the Gunderson Brothers Engineering Company, Portland, Oregon, USA. The vessel was first deployed at sea in 1962

CHAPTER VII
CONTEMPORARY DESIGN

Most architectural work consists of a response to a specific commission or brief. This has proved restrictive on the development of portable architecture as many briefs are initially prepared by the client, and fail to take account of the possibilities offered by this genre of design. In spite of this, architects and designers do seem to have an interest in this type of building; indeed, those who are involved in experimental work see the process of producing such lightweight, functionally unique products a useful exercise in the development of new and valuable expertise. The work of designers who challenge the perceived limits of their profession is bound to be of interest and it is significant that the work of architects who have created innovative ideas for portable architecture are innovative in other areas too. It would appear that these designers are striving to break boundaries in all their work, and technology transfer and innovation are seen as logical approaches in design – an attempt to make the most of current capabilities in industry and manufacture with a strategy that has the possibility of creating a truly contemporary image. Expressing a radical, yet logical summation of the technologists' approach to design, Richard Rogers has stated that: 'a more innovative solution would carry less risk than a mundane one because to innovate one must start from basic principles with nothing taken for granted'.[1] The influence of such work can far exceed its importance in terms of scale, cost and function. Innovative work finds a ready publicist in the design press; therefore relatively small budget work can have a dramatic influence on architects who are actively working on live projects on a daily basis, even though these effects may take some time to filter down to a more conservative client body.

Though the work of architects is important in this area it must be stated that they are frequently, if not always, most successful when in collaboration with other disciplines. Innovative engineers such as Peter Rice, Tony Hunt and Atelier One have been intimately involved with projects that break new ground, and often utilise their experience with one designer to great effect when working with another.[2] Another source of important collaboration is the expert adviser, in the form of the specialist contractor, whether in glass, steel, aluminium, timber, or plastics. Materials technology and the applied use of new techniques form a complex resource for today's designers, and the relationship of the expert in these fields to the contemporary architect is comparable to that of the master craftsman in the past. In fact, the emergence of new routes in architectural design should be seen as an evolved *technologically based craft*, which, based on the engineering traditions, has led to some of the greatest man-made artifacts, rather than a new unproven strategy.

The architect's house has long been understood as a vehicle for experimentation by its designer. It is a universally understood design problem and innovation, in its execution, is therefore perceived more clearly by observers. The subject of the dwelling, which of course is affected dramatically in relation to culture and society, is also perceived by designers as an unending and intriguing problem. Buckminster Fuller's search for an economical demountable housing solution achieved through mass production and industrialisation is just one example of the many precedents in this area (see Chapter IV).[3] In the late twentieth century some architects have taken their search for applied, transferable, technological systems into other industries, with the direct purpose of building truly contemporary houses. This has become more than just a search for techniques of production that may be appropriated, but also for the value inherent in the products themselves. This work, though initially intended to develop new ideas for permanent buildings, has in some cases led the designers to question the efficiency of permanency in the provision of the contemporary dwelling.

Richard Horden's innovative yacht house projects incorporate the products and assembly techniques of the lightweight technology developed for the manufacture

109 UNESCO Urban Reconstruction Laboratory, Otranto, Italy, 1979

of yachts. John Winter cites Horden's influences as hang gliders, Tensegrity sculptures by the artist Kenneth Snelson and, especially, his own Tornado catamaran sailing yacht which can be assembled and dismantled in one hour: 'Small boats … are highly stressed, lightweight, corrosion-free and colourful: why do we bother with rusting steel and damp bricks when the materials of the boat-builder perform so much better?'[4] Horden has used yacht components made by Proctor Masts which have been designed to accommodate the requirements of a kinetic object powered by dynamic forces. The first house, built in Woodgreen, New Forest in 1984 from an assemblage of recognisable yacht components, resulted in a transferred, yet fresh image. In their normal situation these components are required to be regularly assembled, disassembled and reassembled depending on the direction and state of the wind and the yacht. Used for a new purpose, they lend the building a sense of lightness and dynamism, proof that 'a true architecture of technology transfer need be neither impoverished nor primitive'.[5]

The building is assembled as a series of simple and separate sequences. After the foundations are made the masts and spars are erected into an independent framework into which prefabricated roof and wall panels are fixed. Horden has used 'the elements of yacht technology to produce an interchangeable arrangement of parts which can be easily assembled with unskilled labour – "like a windsurfing kit for the building industry".'[6] Horden, in collaboration with students and staff of the Technical University of Munich, has experimented with truly portable buildings, demountability and mobility becoming an intrinsic part of their purpose. The air-lifted ski-haus utilises similar components to the yacht houses but takes advantage of their lightness and dry assembly techniques in a more significant manner. The building can be dismantled for conventional transportation but is deployed by helicopter to its site on the mountain where it can be tethered in less than an hour. The total structure weighs 300 kilograms and is electrically heated by solar rechargeable ni-cad batteries.[7]

The main influence of Horden's work has, however, been in the development of a new market for these lightweight, finely crafted, industrial components in the wider area of architectural design. Many more architects have recognised the potential of these components and the manufacturers themselves have begun to apply their marketing to the building industry and tune their product design to this area.

Dutch architects Benthem and Crouwel have approached the problem of building temporary and portable building in a different way, selecting components

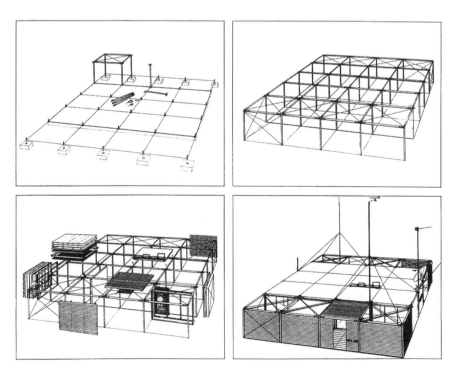

110 Assembly sequence of the yacht house, Poole, Dorset, designed by Richard Horden

110

92

already available and developed for the building industry specifically for their demountable capabilities. Their first project which explored these issues was also a house, built at Altmere in 1984. The building was created as a competition entry in which the prize was the free use of the site for a five year period. It is a composition of commercially available components which have been assembled in a way that allows the building to be moved and relocated at a later date. The single storey building is lightweight in construction but also in appearance. It is primarily a glass box tied down via a space frame supporting structure to four concrete pads. To the rear is an opaque metal-panelled area that conceals the services, while the glass walls are structural and support the roof. Glass is also used as a structural material in their sculpture pavilion built at Sonsbeek, Arnhem in the Netherlands in 1986. This building was built in response to the theme of the 1986 exhibition, 'The Skin', and presents an almost ephemeral image that appears and disappears through the refraction and reflection of light and the building's surroundings on its edges and surfaces. Appropriately, the impression is that this building is more of a sculptural object than a piece of 'architecture'. Though it is made of glass, traditionally perceived as a fragile material, it is an assembled structure, all connections made with steel bolts, with only the glass sealed with silicon joints.[8]

The functional diversity of architecture has resulted in some commissions which have enabled the architects to respond with buildings that have portability as a main part of their concept. Often, when small temporary buildings are required, clients turn naturally to readily available products which can be rented or purchased. However, in a few cases, particularly when the use is to be prestigious or image is an important criterion, architects have been asked to prepare individual designs. A recent example is the Buckingham Palace visitors' pavilion by Michael Hopkins, a portable structure which, though it does not exhibit innovative imagery, manages to convey the quality of craftsmanship and continuity suitable for its site without resorting to pastiche or imitations of permanency. The building is redolent with references to transportable objects, a tented roof braced by spars, exposed repetitive timber structural ribs, a simple horizontal box-like form – each refers to sails, a hull, and a caravan respectively: 'A structure of poise and charm, it holds its own beside its grandiose neighbour and acts as a nicely understated advertisement for British craftsmanship at its best'.[9]

The work of Renzo Piano is characterised by a similar direct response to the circumstances surrounding each individual design problem. The result is a body of work that does not exhibit an obvious house style but a series of solutions that are responses to individual conditions. However, the work of the Piano Building Workshop based in Genoa, Italy and that of the Piano Atelier based in Paris also show a more developed understanding of the making of buildings, indicating that lessons learned from previous projects influence subsequent designs. Renzo Piano states: 'In my way of working, I never start a project merely on the basis of just a philosophy. Right from the first moment I think about materials, modes, tekné, about which process to adopt and the right materials for it'.[10] Piano's designs usually utilise dry assembly techniques as a method of construction, perhaps most famously shown in his work with Richard Rogers for the Pompidou Centre in Paris. This technique is, however, also manifest in his most humble work. The attention to detail that is a characteristic of this work enables the smallest problem to be approached with the same level of intensity as the largest issues. In 1979, the Workshop was commissioned to prepare a strategy for the urban reconstruction of Italy's historic town centres. Its proposal for the communications aspect of the project was to build up a relationship with the local inhabitants in order to establish relevant issues and convey information on restoration techniques utilising new technology which the residents could carry out themselves in their own homes. The designers created what they called a 'mobile laboratory' to act as a convening point for residents and designers. First erected at Otranto, South Italy, in 1979, the laboratory's ephemeral, dynamic, 'open-ended' image was used to break down barriers between client and advisor. The aim was to provide a responsive venue for a series of important discussions, but it also provided a valuable asset by showing the inhabitants that the team they were to work with had no pre-set ideas about the conventional developer/architect

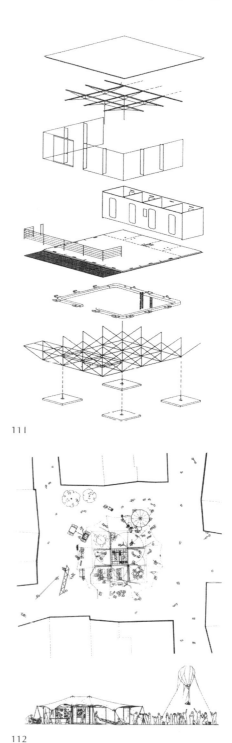

111

112

111 House built at Altmere, the Netherlands by Benthem and Crouwel Architekten, 1984;
112 Urban Reconstruction Laboratory for Otranto, Italy, 1979. Renzo Piano Building Workshop; engineer, Peter Rice

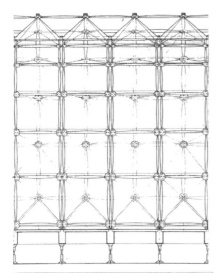

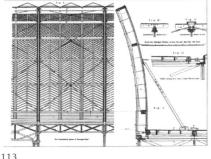

113

relationship (the developer in this case being the government) and favoured an end-user/architect relationship.[11]

In 1982, the architects responded to another portable building problem for a very different client with a completely alternative solution. IBM, the international computer company, required a mobile pavilion that could provide a focus for its technologically advanced products over a four year period at a wide range of venues across Europe. For such a client with such a purpose, the response was unexpected in that it was not overtly technical. The building was a formally simple crystalline tube assembled from commercially available, and relatively familiar, pyramidical polycarbonate roof lights. This component was assembled in an unconventional repetitive manner as a continuous skin system, supported by a structural system using a beech ply and aluminium frame. The floor system utilised a deep lightweight metal frame that allowed space for most of the services and a firmly braced platform for the supporting telescopic legs, which accommodated variations in the supporting surface. The temporary nature of the building enabled it to be deployed in dramatic and usually unavailable sites, close to significant European landmarks such as the Eiffel Tower. The building therefore took advantage of a unique feature of portable architecture, the ability to utilise an easily recognised 'address'. Such a temporary venue enables the visitor to know where the building is, even if it is only there for a short length of time, while also providing valuable publicity interest for the client.[12]

A more recent building to benefit from this advantage is the Cardiff Bay Visitors' Centre, the result of a competition won by Alsop, Lyall and Störmer. The design strategy for this building, initially intended as a temporary structure but since relocated to another site due to its popularity, took advantage of the opportunities afforded by the use of a portable building rather than a permanent one. In form it is a simple extruded tube that has been raised above ground level by a continuous triangulated steel support. This enables the building to be cantilevered over the water at the edge of the dock wall as a dramatic termination related to the subject of its exhibition. The structure of the building itself is a series of steel ribs, prefabricated and then assembled on site and clad with a layer of insulation bonded to plywood. A PVC coated polyester membrane then forms the weatherproofing. The smooth, simple shape forms an unusual and charismatic image that helped entice 28,000 visitors to the Centre in its first three months of operation.

Like Piano's IBM pavilion, the Cardiff Bay Visitors' Centre is a temporary structure (though it is still in use more than five years after it was first opened) that has not only been permitted to be deployed on sensitive sites, but also possesses an image and appearance that do not conform to local planning restrictions. Buildings of this type, if they are made with the same care and attention as permanent

113 Above: IBM travelling pavilion elevation by Renzo Piano Building Workshop, architect Shunji Ishida; Below: Crystal Palace barrel vault sectional elevation. Both the appearance of these two structures and the approach to utilisation of repetitive elements are similar; **114** IBM travelling pavilion in Milan; **115** IBM travelling pavilion in Paris, taking advantage of a unique landmark for its temporary 'address'

114

115

ones, can therefore become an infiltrator for innovative forms of architecture. This also affects the architect's approach to the design in that he is designing for a new set of criteria, in which concern about long-term litigation may not be as important: 'as so often with temporary buildings, the architect, freed from the strait-jacket of at least ten years' liability, has allowed himself to be more innovative than he might otherwise have dared'.[13] Actual built examples of contemporary innovative architecture situated in important or historic settings could provide a focus for the debate about the necessity of conforming to homogenised local building patterns. The attractive alternative is to approach each building as a unique solution to a unique problem while still adhering to the principle of rational and sensitive diversity.

Commerce and industry, in the search for more efficient methods of working, can be effective users of portable architecture. Nicholas Grimshaw and Partners, who have been one of the leaders in the introduction of innovative architectural construction techniques, have utilised demountable assembly methods in their building solutions. Kenneth Powell states that Grimshaw is 'a radical exponent of the engineering tradition in architecture that, in Britain, has a noble ancestry extending back to Brunel, Paxton, and the great industrial architects of the nineteenth century.'[14] Grimshaw believes an architect's office should be 'a cross between a workshop, a studio, an office and a manufacturing plant', and one small project which the office realised together as an example of this philosophy was the design and assembly of a staircase made primarily from components found in the building, yacht, and oil industries.[15] The Herman Miller factory, built at Bath in 1976, utilised a dry fixed panel and structure system that enabled the skin of the building to be altered easily. The IGUS factory, designed for a German industrialist who required a totally flexible manufacturing plant, further develops this principle in terms of its structure and skin. However, it also includes a series of completely portable two storey office pods that can be relocated within the factory building, allowing changes in production line operations to take place without hindrance. The initial strategy was to make the pods demountable so that they could be relocated over a holiday period; however, the later phase buildings will:

> rest on air cushions, so the pods may be moved over a weekend. The pods' splayed feet spread their load, which avoids the need for local foundations. Each pod has its own services box, which can be plugged into the building's overall system through flexible ducts … Inside the basic structure there is virtually nothing that cannot be moved or altered.[16]

Exhibition architecture is one area in which the combination of functional imper-

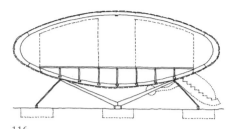
116

117

117a

116 Alsop, Lyall and Störmer, Cardiff Bay Visitors' Centre, cross-section; **117** Nicholas Grimshaw and Partners' IGUS headquarters and factory, Cologne, 1992. The office (left) can be dismantled and moved in two weeks. Later variations may include air-supported pods that can be moved in a weekend; **117a** Nicholas Grimshaw and Partners' Herman Miller factory, Bath, 1976. The practice also completed a distribution centre for the same client based on similar principles in Chippenham in 1982

118

manence and a requirement for a building that shows a clearly contemporary identity has been repeatedly demonstrated.[17] These buildings are especially significant in their influence on mainstream architecture in that they form a venue which often attracts extensive attention from architects, building professionals and the general public.[18] Buildings erected for celebration or exhibition may be a focus for cultural and social celebration and therefore take on a significance that is more profound than for a simple functional solution. One recent example is the portable pavilion designed by Mario Botta for the Swiss centennial celebrations in 1991. This building takes the form of a crown supporting 26 poles representing the 26 existing cantons of Switzerland, which in turn is supported by 13 hinged trussed beams that signify the 13 original cantons that formed the country. The structure seats 1,450 people and covers 1,500 square metres. The crown is assembled at ground level, connected to the truss ends and then raised into the air by three hydraulic rams. The other ends of the trusses are fixed to precast foundation blocks and remain in the same position as the trusses fold out into their erect position. By using this ingenious system, a building able to contain large numbers of people can be made of relatively compact, transportable components. The building is clad in a PVC polyester fabric and is heated by self-contained mobile units.[19]

The Swiss people have their roots in several different geographic backgrounds and they also use different languages. The diverse nature of this society means that the image of the building had to be one that was not only acceptable to all but also spoke of a common identity. Botta described the design as 'a physical sign for collective values'.[20] The temporary nature of this building has supported this aim in its design – as it is to be relocated in each region it is not necessary to respond to one particular location's environmental and physical parameters in a site-specific way. In this case, the ideal solution was to respond equally to each of the communities the building sought to link and promote. Though the building is not site-specific in nature, it is located on a specific site within each community, is adopted by the community for the duration of its stay and should thus stay in their memory forever. A successful building of this type should therefore possess a desirable commonality and be acceptable to all its users, yet also retain a specific identity for its visitors unique to any given location. Luca Gazzaniga comments in *Domus*: 'A tent always is a tent, and its *raison d'être* lies in having to stand on sites that always differ, creating new equilibriums and interpretations each time; "Born to last a moment", it is perceived as a happening, then it lives on in one's memory'.[21] The shared, yet specific experience of the portable building means that it has the potential to become an expression of cultural and communal unity where a permanent building in just one location would fail. It also has the potential to defuse the conflict between central and regional demands which is a

118 Mario Botta, Swiss seventh centennial pavilion in Bellinzona's mediaeval castle, 1991; **119** Renzo Piano Building Workshop, temporary auditorium within the 1595 Renaissance church of San Lorenzo, Venice

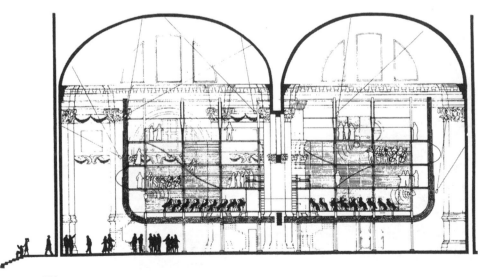

119

common problem in all forms of organisation, whether political, social or commercial.[22]

Buildings for performance provide another area where portable structures have proven their value (in this architectural genre there is an impressive history of circus and theatre structures that are the predecessors of those used in the present day. See Chapter III). In 1984, Renzo Piano created a temporary auditorium in Venice for the interior of the Renaissance church of San Lorenzo, built in 1595 by Simone Sorella. This structure was to accommodate audience, orchestra and singers for a special choral work by the composer Luigi Nono. In the piece, the performers wandered around a three-dimensional framework that surrounded the audience so the location and volume of the individual sounds that made up the complete composition were constantly changing. Piano designed a robust structure of laminated timber ribs that are reminiscent of a ship's structure. The perimeter metal framework is light in contrast to the ribs and contrasts in the same way a ship's rigging does with its masts and spars. The whole assembly was pre-manufactured and 'rigged' within the church space. This temporary addition to a respected historic architectural masterpiece expresses contemporary ideas about what architecture has become in the intervening four hundred years yet also relates to technology and craftsmanship that would have been very familiar to sixteenth century Venetians.[23]

Another portable musical pavilion that has a very different image is the Carlos Moseley Music Pavilion devised for the New York Philharmonic and the Metropolitan Opera to stage outdoor shows at different New York parks during the summer. As the shows could be at different venues on subsequent evenings, the building needed to be erected in under six hours and taken down in even less. The building, designed by FTL Happold Design and Engineering Studio, is transported on seven articulated trucks, five of which actually become part of the structure. The stage, which consists of a series of hinged and folded panels, is deployed automatically with hydraulic pistons and supported by truck trailer beds. The canopy structure consists of three trusses, two of which unfold automatically and connect at low level with the third. This is then unfolded and in the process all three trusses are raised to form a tripod with the peak more than 20 metres in the air. The fabric membrane is also attached at low level and is hoisted into position and stressed so that it will not flap. Although the audience is not contained within the structure, the aim was to achieve concert hall acoustics with a set of 24 battery powered, state-of-the-art, electronic acoustic systems that are dispersed amongst the audience. Project architect Nicholas Goldsmith comments:

> Our design approach to this project was to let the engineering of the mechanism dictate the forms and geometry of the structure. We consciously tried not to create arbitrary architectural compositions, letting the steelwork express its essential character. The fabric membrane, too, took its shape from the reflective acoustic requirements and the need to provide rain cover for the stage. The architectural poetry was in the proportions and the relations of these elements to each other. The design became a mixture of architecture, industrial design, and engineering ... This project put us on the edge of our profession by raising the question: When is a structure a machine and when is it a building?[24]

Intentional or not, the pavilion certainly possesses the excitement of a transitory performance, not only in its fully erected state, but as a performance in itself with mysterious hydraulically operated structures speedily and efficiently erecting large impressive structures. In this way it attracts attention to the more conventional performance which it supports. In its first year the pavilion was host to 30 performances. It is stored each winter and is expected to be deployed until at least 2005. As a result, it is a transient yet familiar sight in the city's parks.[25]

There is one design practice that, since 1977, has produced regular, huge transportable structures with budgets of up to $10 million for live audiences of 250,000 people. Mark Fisher is an architect whose design work is primarily concerned with the impressive stage sets that are used for contemporary rock music concerts. These performances, which must be the ultimate present day versions of the traditional circus, often include a wide range of visual, aural and live effects that must be coordinated into a stage area to make sense to huge

120

120 The Carlos Moseley Music Pavilion, a mobile auditorium for the New York Philharmonic and Metropolitan Opera, 1991, designed by FTL Happold

121

audiences often viewing from great distances.[26] The set Fisher devised (with engineer Jonnathan Park) for the Pink Floyd concert *The Wall*, in Berlin's Potsdamer Platz in 1990, utilised a wall 80 metres long by 35 metres high which was destroyed each night as a symbolic act. Large cranes were used to manipulate huge inflated figures at either side and above the stage. The U2 *Zoo TV* tour travelled throughout Europe and North America with a giant set that manipulated Trabant cars attached to the end of hydraulic cranes. The backdrop to the stage contained huge projection screens that were used to reinforce the message in the band's music, but were also reminiscent of billboards on large semi-completed (or semi-destroyed) buildings. Each night of the tour this structure was recreated, along with its complex servicing arrangements.

U2's 1997 tour *Popmart* demanded an even more spectacular design from Fisher. The set image appropriated consumer imagery such as a single 'golden arch', a billboard, and a giant lemon complete with cocktail stick. As before, every element was componentised for assembly and disassembly, the most ambitious task being the huge 50 by 16 metre 'billboard'; actually a ground breaking Light Emitting Diode (LED) powered video screen which alone cost more than $6 million.

The design for these structures was a complex affair, involving up to a hundred consultants with diverse areas of expertise, and clients who sought to emphasise the message of their music and to create a spectacle for the audience. This form of portable architecture must be the most visible ever created, with shows regularly having a single night attendance of 70,000 people, and on many occasions being televised nationally and internationally.[27] Although the spectacle cannot be doubted, can these ephemeral stages be treated as valid forms of architecture? They primarily consist of standardised components, some used in the building industry, some specifically prepared for the music business. Yet each show must convey a very different image if the specific identity of the band is to be retained. In many cases the appearance of the stage is developed with the use of sets and lighting, which makes the design closer to theatrical work than architectural, although this too can undoubtedly influence architecture (see Chapter IV). However, as in the Pink Floyd and U2 examples given here, some designs use the actual physical elements themselves in the creation of the image and this is no different from the way in which architecture is understood – by its tectonic qualities.

The examples described here show that architects do exhibit interest and expertise in the creation of portable architecture. However, it would appear that there are only a few acknowledged experts in this area producing a string of related and

121 Stage design for Pink Floyd's 'Division Bell' World Tour by Mark Fisher; **122** Stage design by Mark Fisher and Jonathan Park for the outside broadcast unit for rock group U2's international tour, *Zoo TV*

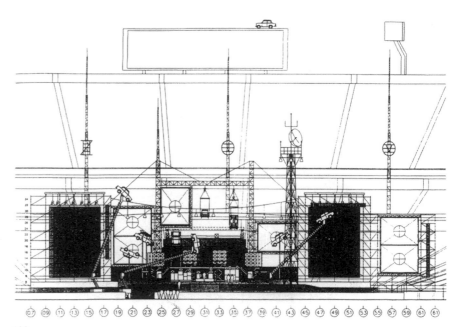

122

influential built projects. This is probably because the built solutions, as opposed to experimental work are, in general, individual responses to an individual problem (experimental work is examined in Chapter IX, and the relevance of the most recently realised portable architectural projects to new economic and social trends is explored in Chapter XI). In cases where portable buildings are required repeatedly in similar situations, specialist manufacturers fulfil the market's perceived requirements. For the same reason that innovative portable architecture has been allowed to be deployed with limited aesthetic control, manufacturers are allowed to deploy buildings of poor appearance. Design quality, which is unconnected to operational requirements and is determined by building regulations, codes of practice and international and British standards, is not understood as a central issue in the creation of these products. In the conventional client/architect relationship, it is generally the architect who has recognised the potential of portability as a factor in the design process and that with innovative and sensitive design, it can be used to create an appropriate solution. However, it must also be understood that for the few good quality portable building solutions described here, there are countless more that have been tackled using either a commercially manufactured, loose-fit solution, or even worse, by the creation of a temporary building using conventional construction. Such a solution is destroyed when its function is no longer required in that particular location – an unacceptable waste of resources.

The positive aspects of the specifically designed, innovative portable building therefore include a wide range of architectural issues: constructional, economic, legislative, social, aesthetic, and cultural. One of the most significant quantifiable benefits, and one which seems in some way to encompass all the rest, is the ability of such a building to appear instantly in an important and familiar setting to make visitors re-evaluate their relationship with the environment in a way that favours contemporary architecture. On describing the impression of Botta's Swiss Confederation Pavilion at its first site within the walls of the mediaeval castle at Bellinzona, Switzerland, Luca Gazzaniga fluently describes the inspiration that can occur in the bringing together of the temporary and the permanent, modern and antique, kinetic and static:

> Perhaps here, more than anywhere else, this design flourishes on the conspicuous tension created between the new and the ancient ... Dynamism opposes static qualities, artificial materials oppose natural ones, skyward lofting opposes ground hugging, geometric form opposes the organic one, frailness opposes solidity, cool colours oppose warm ones (especially at night), and the ephemeral opposes the eternal.[28]

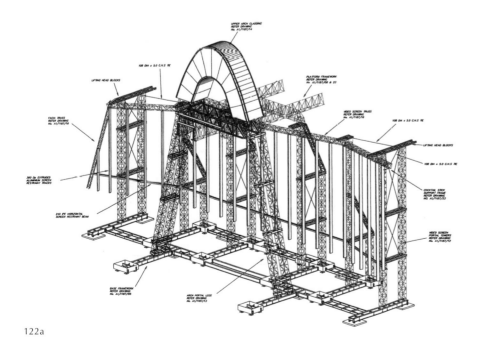

122a

122a Construction drawing for U2's 1997 tour stage set, *Popmart*, designed by Mark Fisher and Atelier One

CHAPTER VIII
SHELTER AFTER DISASTER

It can be said with some assurance that relief management in the fields of medicine, health, and nutrition has ... significantly improved over the last decade. The benefits of the lessons learned from major disasters during the 1970s and early 1980s are beginning to show. However, there remains one particular sector in which too little progress has been made, and in which many conservative and obsolescent attitudes survive, that is: emergency shelter, and shelter after disaster in a more general sense.[1]
United Nations Disaster Relief Coordinator (UNDRO), 1982

Once again, it should be pointed out that a suitable shelter concept to match, in particular, larger-scale emergency measures was not at hand. In addition, the lack of experienced agencies to deal with shelter issues was badly felt ... What is needed is a comprehensive shelter strategy with appropriately developed standards, supply methods, specifications for shelter units and industries to make the right products available in time ... [2]
United Nations High Commission for Refugees (UNHCR), 1993

These two statements, both made by UN organisations, though more than a decade apart, show that the development of a structured approach to the provision of shelter in post-disaster situations appears to have made little progress in recent years. Yet there can be no doubt that the potential of demountable and portable structures for use in these situations is perceived as a real avenue for development by those involved in the architectural design and construction world. There cannot be an architecture school in the developed world that has not at some time set its students to design a disaster relief shelter based on the premise that those without housing in a critical post-disaster situation require outside help to replace their destroyed homes. Experienced and respected architects have also devoted time and energy to the creation of new, innovative and sometimes ingenious prototypes for disaster relief situations, including, amongst many, Buckminster Fuller (see Chapter IV), Alvar Aalto, and more recently Future Systems.[3] Industry has also expressed interest in the problems of shelter manufacture and many prototypes of varying degrees of complexity have been produced, tested and in several cases deployed in post-disaster situations. Yet the scenes that are sought out by the media each time a disaster occurs are remarkably similar – people who are without adequate shelter, in obviously needy circumstances, surrounded by the destruction that was once their own homes. It is therefore clear, even from the selective images of television and the press, that despite the wide-ranging and diverse activity carried out into the problems of shelter after disaster, this work appears to have had minimal impact on the relief of human suffering on the ground. The reasons for this mismatch between the problems of disaster relief and the proposed solutions are complex, but are in the main related to a fundamental misunderstanding of the reasons why disasters occur and the nature of the circumstances that victims experience in a post-disaster situation. In recent years designers have been blamed by some agencies for the problems associated with their proposals, although in many cases it is not their design work which is at fault. Indeed, many products are inventive, ingenious and exciting, providing rational solutions to the problem as they perceive it.[4] The problem is that their understanding is based on fundamental misconceptions related to their own experience and not that of the actual victims. Ian Davis, the respected researcher in the field of post-disaster shelter situations, has identified these misunderstandings and labelled them as 'myths': incorrect yet striking images that have led relief agencies and their agents to gauge their

123 Demountable shelter prototype developed by students at Liverpool John Moores University, Centre for Architecture, 1993. The aim was to create a system capable of infinite repetition so that any size shelter could be made with the individual, independent unit costing less than £100 to manufacture. The tensegrity structure can be carried by one person and all components can be recycled into permanent reconstruction

124

125

response on seemingly potent concepts that are unfortunately based on an unverified and inaccurate understanding of the actual situation.

Many of these myths surround the response of victims to the disaster in which they are involved – myths often perpetuated, if not created, by the media. For example, it is a common and understandable misconception that disaster victims are dazed and helpless, simply waiting for outside aid. It is true there is a short period of shock at their misfortune, but very quickly, far more quickly than the authorities are usually able to react, they become actively involved in the task of saving lives and property.[5] Another is that people camped out in the wreckage of their home impede reconstruction efforts. In fact these are the first coherent acts of rebuilding property and community, inhabitants staying close to their belongings to protect them and maintain their personal geographical identity.[6]

In order to better understand how these myths have developed and how they influence the capabilities of designers to respond effectively, it is important to understand the nature of the disaster situation. Disaster relief situations can be roughly divided into three types: natural disasters that have as their source a phenomenon such as extreme weather conditions or geological disturbance; war-time or post-war disasters that occur as a by-product of human conflict; refugee situations which may occur as a result of natural or war-time disaster, escape from famine or plague, or migration for economic reasons. It is important, however, to acknowledge that regardless of the cause of a disaster, the severity of the problems it causes are inevitably and inextricably linked with mankind's ability to respond. UNDRO studies have shown that post-disaster problems are aggravated by human error and lack of foresight and that disaster relief can without doubt be made more effective through systematised planning and management carried out in the event of disaster rather than in response to it.[7]

Effective preparation has rarely been a part of disaster relief activities. If the first documented disaster was the Flood, Noah's remarkable act of disaster preparedness in building the Ark has yet to be repeated in as efficient a manner. In fact, disasters have been and will continue to be a regular feature in human history. Natural disasters such as floods, famine, tornadoes and earthquakes occur regularly, though organised response to human plight in these situations is a comparatively recent phenomenon. One of the earliest documented cases of a specific effort to provide temporary shelter after a disaster was in response to the earthquake that affected Concepción in Chile in 1835. Captain Robert Fitzroy of Darwin's ship *The Beagle* reported that: 'Much misery was alleviated by the good conduct and extreme hospitality of the inhabitants of Concepción.' The inhabitants built:

> straw-covered huts and temporary houses of board, living meanwhile in the open air under trees. Those who soonest obtained or contrived shelter, collected as many about them as they could assist, and in a very few days all had temporary shelter.[8]

After the San Francisco earthquake of 1906 much of the city was destroyed by a fire that levelled 250,000 homes. The authorities' response to this disaster is one that is still common today.[9] The people initially helped themselves, making rough shelters from whatever materials were to hand, or sought shelter with friends and relatives in a better situation. When the authorities responded it was first with the aid of the military, who by their efficient hierarchical organisation were able to act quickly, establishing tent camps that provided shelter but did not respond to community or social needs. The tents were replaced with two-roomed, wooden shelters, or 'cottages' as they were called by the relief committee, situated in camps adjacent to the city. As the people returned to their property in the city, many of the resourceful inhabitants jacked up their temporary dwellings, placed them on wheels and towed them to the site of their permanent home where some still exist to this day.

The destruction experienced during the Second World War elicited a variety of design responses to the refugee problem (the examples of Fuller and Aalto have already been mentioned) but as Ian Davies has noted, the dramatic disasters that occurred in terms of human casualties and destruction of homes were much larger than anything that has occurred before or since. These experiences still offer a valuable lesson in the way people respond to the problems of the destruction of

124 UNDHA photograph of tents erected in the ruins of a family home after the 1976 flood in the Pansear Valley, Afghanistan; **125** San Francisco, 1908. Temporary building being moved after 19 months on its original site

their homes, their displacement and subsequent requirements. Wherever possible, victims prefer to find alternative homes, staying with relatives and friends. When the limited amount of emergency accommodation eventually arrives, *if* it is of acceptable quality, it becomes a substitute for permanent housing. It is not used for housing the homeless but for those who have decided to leave other accommodation and make a new start. In some cases this emergency accommodation becomes part of the permanent dwelling pattern and continues to be occupied decades later (see Chapter V).

Contemporary disasters follow the repetitive pattern of those in history, though each is of course unique in its own way. However, since the Second World War, organised response to disaster has changed dramatically. A vast range of disaster relief agencies has been established by nations, groups of nations, and independent, sometimes international, organisations. These groups naturally have different perceptions of their role in disaster relief and are sometimes governed by strict regulations that control the nature of their intervention in a situation. A great deal of money and effort is now available to mitigate the problems of a post-disaster situation and there is no doubt that the benefits of this international responsibility for human suffering have been felt by many. Yet the effectiveness of these resources is now cast into doubt by recent reports based on careful case studies that have examined the actual events of relief operations. This research has led to a better understanding of the nature of some of the problems and why they continue to recur.

In the case of natural disasters, it is clear that certain geographic areas are prone to particular problems which are repeated at reasonably predictable intervals. Easily recognised examples are the cities of San Francisco, Los Angeles and Tokyo – cities that are located in areas of predictable seismic activity. Yet these cities have little use for disaster relief shelter assistance. When an earthquake occurs, as it did in Los Angeles on 17 January 1994, people are able to find shelter with friends and relatives. The tents and other temporary shelters erected by the authorities were a response to media demands to find out 'what the authorities are doing' rather than a response to what the victims required. The people who continued to occupy this makeshift accommodation were actually part of the city's existing housing problem, as were those who received the food and welfare handouts that followed in subsequent days.[10] The inhabitants of Los Angeles continue to live in the city for economic and social reasons, and because it is an accessible area in a rich country, they can be confident that help is at hand in the event of a disaster.

People who live in disaster prone areas in poor countries also remain for economic and social reasons. Day-to-day patterns of existence are more important to most people than the chance that some disaster may occur at an unknown future date; thus if a particular location is more suitable to providing a better way of life it will attract and retain inhabitants. This was the case with people affected by the Turkish earthquake near Lice in 1972, the Guatemala City earthquake of 1976, and the typhoon near Chittagong, Bangladesh in 1992 that made ten million people homeless and killed more than 125,000. Each location has its attraction: respectively, relatively fertile land for crops, an urban centre that held the promise of work, and a coastal region that supports port and fishing activities. In these situations a key factor in the casualty toll was the methods used in the buildings' construction. Surprisingly, vernacular housing is not generally designed to respond to a disaster situation, unless that disaster is a relatively frequent occurrence.[11] In the post-disaster situation there may be very few shelter alternatives for the victims. Because of their inappropriate construction even the buildings that are left undamaged may still pose a risk if re-inhabited. In these cases the value of effective emergency accommodation is in the provision of a practical, usable base which can be utilised to protect the inhabitants and their property in support of their efforts to rebuild their dwellings and community. Advice on safer methods of construction should be incorporated in a way which will make the buildings less vulnerable to future disaster.

War-time disasters pose special problems for disaster relief agencies. Is it appropriate to invest funds in providing shelter in areas where conflict is still underway, to risk wasted effort and worse, expose aid workers and inhabitants to the danger

126

126 OXFAM photograph of victim-made shelter after the Guatemala earthquake of 1976. Available materials have been used to create a base around which are stored personal belongings

127

128

127 Bayer Chemicals polyurethane foam shelter for the West German Red Cross at Chimbote, Peru, 1970; **128** Elcos emergency low-cost shelter by the British Aluminium Company Ltd., England. This UK manufactured shelter was developed by the Building Research Establishment and OXFAM in 1978

of becoming a target? In 1992 and 1993, the UNHCR attempted to help those made homeless by the conflict in Bosnia-Hercegovina, primarily by finding shelter for refugees in existing buildings repaired or reconstructed to provide temporary accommodation. The problems of setting up agreements with governments and local authorities in conflict led to uncertainty about the long term value of their efforts. Fundamental questions about the nature of shelter provision in such situations still remain to be resolved.[12]

The problems of housing refugees, resulting either from war-time situations or natural disasters, is quite different from housing those who maintain proximity to their existing homes. People who are either forced or decide to make a mass exodus to a new location pose quite a different problem from those who are at least familiar with their surroundings, even if they have gone through a cataclysmic change. Douglas Stafford, the Deputy High Commissioner for Refugees, states their case forcefully:

> Refugees are ripped up from everything they love and own. They are driven out of their homes. They are forced to cross borders, mainly women and children, exhausted by journeys that may have lasted for weeks, hungry, sick, and in despair. But they are strong people, they are the survivors. In order to survive, the first thing they do is build a house. Suddenly in the middle of nowhere, there are whole villages, or even small cities, that are refugee camps or communities, thriving with life. That is what being a refugee is all about – seeking shelter. Political shelter in the form of asylum; and physical shelter in the form of a place to live until they can go back to their real homes.[13]

Though refugees have indeed proven their resilience countless times, they face dramatic problems when arriving at their temporary camp. They are:

> displaced, even when it takes place in their own country. This situation has two consequences; the first is that they are invading someone else's territory and the second is that they may not always recognise the local conditions or at least evaluate them correctly.[14]

These refugees thus require assistance in many areas associated with their acclimatisation to a new environment, and not least in the provision of adequate shelter in a layout and organisational framework which they will find familiar. Refugee camps are frequently situated in tenuous situations on unwanted land which is either subject to dispute or reluctantly loaned by central or local authorities, without any economic basis to provide for the occupation and support of the inhabitants. It is unwise to treat the creation of the camp as a temporary expediency. Although it may be desirable to encourage the return of the refugees to their homes as soon as possible, and they may actually desire this themselves, it may be years before they can return, if indeed, at all, and resettlement in permanent new areas may be the only viable long term solution. This latter option inevitably takes a great deal of negotiation, and therefore time, to accomplish. Meanwhile, inadequate conditions will prevail for a group of people who have already suffered much.

It is clear that there is a place for portable and temporary shelter in disaster relief situations. In 1988 the General Assembly of the UN adopted a 'Global Strategy for Shelter to the year 2000' (GSS); its main objective is 'adequate shelter for all'. In 1992, UNHCR spent $45 million on shelter, second only to its budget for transportation.[15] However, it is also clear that most efforts that have been made have fallen far short of expectations, either for logistical reasons (for example, arriving too late or being appropriated for use by non-victims), or for design reasons (for example, being inappropriate on a functional, economic, or cultural level).[16] The reason for this is that virtually all designs manufactured and deployed so far have been donor-led in terms of their requirements – that is, the agency supplying the shelter has decided the parameters for its creation. One example of this, though there are many, is the polyurethane igloo made by the Bayer Chemical Company in collaboration with the West German Red Cross. These shelters were transported as a constructional system and were designed to be made *in situ* in only two hours to provide rapidly deployed, instantly usable shelters. After the 1972 earthquake in Masaya, Nicaragua, they were not occupied until 148 days after the disaster and only 30 per cent of the shelters were ever occupied despite being rent free.[17] In addition, a relatively high technology solution can bring high technological problems. In this case, the risk of fire in a culture that habitually uses an open fire was increased by the use of an extremely combustible building material that gives off toxic fumes when burning. This technology was clearly inappropriate. It required not only flown-in components, which added dramatically to the cost of deployment, but also skilled erection by non-local personnel.

Unfortunately, these problems have been the norm for imported design solutions, rather than the exception, yet they remain unrecognised by the majority of designers and manufacturers.[18] Even if such solutions could be seen to be effective in logistical and functional terms they also raise other, less easily quantifiable issues. The provision of complete imported solutions cannot be seen as an aid to long term problems as they increase the danger of foreign aid dependence, while the development of local confidence and economic growth and activity is hindered.[19]

In terms of design of refugee settlements, virtually all current solutions are based on a military type layout that puts expediency and perceived efficiency before sensitivity to the inhabitants' social, cultural and historic living patterns. This type of organisation can in fact hinder the recovery process of the people. UNDRO comments:

> Military organisations seek uniformity and conformity. This concern for order is simply too much to expect from a civilian population stricken by disaster. The period immediately after a disaster is a time when people need to get together and develop collective responses. A military hierarchy of decision-making inhibits this organic social process.[20]

Organisations which provide expert specialist help to the aid agencies in the provision of such camps naturally put their emphasis on the provision of adequate water and sanitation supplies in the effort to prevent disease. The issue of settlement planning is generally ignored. However, it has been established that the introduction of sensitive planning consultation at an early stage in the creation of the settlement proves valuable in the long term. The work of Fred Cuny has concentrated on the development of strategies that can lead to a much higher acceptance and involvement in the establishment of settlements by the refugees themselves.[21] Unfortunately, apart from a very few cases, the good work of both the technical workers in the field and the planners has not been sufficiently integrated to provide a concerted approach to the design of refugee settlements. As a result: 'Camps are usually designed according to crude engineering principles ... the product is imposed on a resistant refugee clientele.'[22]

For all these reasons, there are limited opportunities for the examination of appropriate examples of disaster relief structures, portable, demountable or permanent, or their layout into cohesive settlements for refugees. However, such is the body of research on the subject, based on firsthand knowledge of those in the field, that it is possible to formulate a pattern of design both in built form and in planning terms that could establish a pattern for successful response in post-disaster situations. These should be established for two distinct and separate cases: post-disaster relief associated with a stable population; and post-disaster refugee settlements. The logistical arrangements are quite different for each.

Post-disaster Relief for Stable Populations

When a disaster occurs, the immediate preoccupation of the population is to save life, then property. Suitable shelter can play a major role in preventing further distress, illness and death *if it is made available immediately*. Therefore, emergency shelter must be in use by the victims within the first few days of the post-disaster situation if it is to be at all effective. On the ground, operatives who understand the local situation and the victims themselves are in the best position to decide the nature, numbers and location of the shelter requirements and also to undertake its erection. Thus logistical problems are tackled in the most immediate and efficient manner while also reducing the feelings of helplessness and despair that these people might otherwise experience.[23] The shelter should be capable of supporting the efforts of the victims to rebuild their lives, economic and community activities, so its deployment should not divert resources from these areas. It should therefore be capable of being speedily erected with the minimum of effort, and of fulfilling its function for the duration of the emergency period without

129

129 Proprietary shelter systems displayed at the First International Workshop on Improved Shelter Response and Environment for Refugees, UNCHR, 1993

further maintenance. The shelter should also have a built-in life-span or obsolescence which will render it unattractive for diversion by unscrupulous parties for sale or use in non-relief situations. Any permanent components in the shelter's construction should be capable of recycling into permanent building stock.

The shelter should be designed and built as part of a coordinated disaster preparedness process dedicated to the location in which it is to be deployed. It should be designed with the benefit of local knowledge and constructed with materials of local origin, as part of a process of investment in local industry.[24] The provision of shelter should be simultaneously accompanied by expert advice, from sources acceptable to the recipients, regarding the rebuilding of their property in ways which will reduce or negate the possibility of future disasters. In some situations this may not only relate to building construction methods, but siting and layout. Relief money should then be channelled into these areas to encourage activities that will limit shelter-related problems if or when a similar disaster recurs. The aims of such a policy in relief operations are to improve the conditions of the inhabitants without eroding their cultural patterns, a positive outcome therefore being the surprising end result of a calamitous event.[25]

Post-disaster Refugee Settlements

The major problem for refugees is finding a place of political and physical shelter. This is also the major problem for the relief agencies who must negotiate with governments and local authorities to stabilise a volatile situation. If a place is found it is often one which has proven unsuitable for habitation in the past and can therefore provide profound problems in the establishment of a suitable settlement. However, in the midst of these immense logistical problems the pattern and layout of the settlement should be decided with care and sensitivity, with regard to both immediate concerns and the future. Instantly deployable shelter is once again required as the refugee will have the minimum of tools and materials and should be discouraged from denuding local supplies for short term expediency.[26] However, as soon as possible, the future inhabitants of the settlement should be involved in its design and erection. They should be consulted in organised groups about the layout, which should be based on their previous communal, social and family groups; they should be involved in the allocation of dwellings and they should be able to erect their own shelter. Special provision should be made for the young, the old and the ill. Investment should be high in the earliest stages, to save money and avoid problems through ill health later on. The buildings should be appropriate investments for their purpose and life-span, reusable and sufficiently

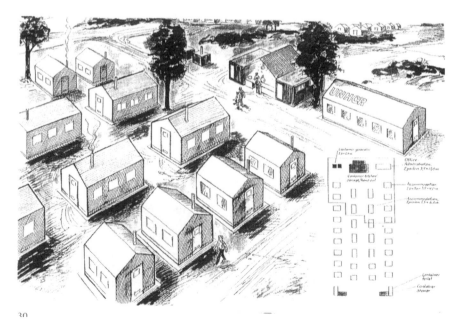

130 Refugee camp concept for UNCHR by ROFI Industrier AS, Norway, 1993

130

portable in order to be transported by the refugees themselves in the eventual move to a permanent home.[27]

Guidelines for the Design of a Shelter

In terms of appropriate shelter, it is first necessary to determine the functional, social and cultural demands that will be made on the building. These will be different for each situation and the determination of the actual parameters for form and construction should only be made after appropriate use of local knowledge.[28] However, it is possible to outline the purpose of such a shelter. It should: protect the inhabitants from harsh weather conditions, cold, heat, wind, rain, snow; establish an area of territory for the inhabitant, either of occupancy or ownership; support the activities of social and physical construction; provide a physical manifestation of personal identity, privacy and security; provide an address for the receipt of communication, services and aid and support the continuation or establishment of a form of income, either from business or by adjacency to previous or new employment. The shelter should also be capable of expansion to accommodate family members and be able to store and protect personal property.

These requirements may sound comprehensive and complex, but it must be remembered that the long term purpose of emergency shelter, which supports the re-establishment of the individual in his community, is also a complex issue and should be a key factor in its creation and deployment.

The Future

These ideas are by no means new, yet the idea that they can be met within existing resources can be considered innovative. The current recommendation of the major authorities on the subject of shelter provision after disaster is that, with the exception of the distribution of tents, plastic sheeting, and in some cases corrugated iron, all built responses are without value.[29] The reason for this assumption is clear – the aid agencies have been let down by the groups who advise them, not least by designers who have refused or been unable to become involved in this problem in a meaningful way.[30] Esoteric and inventive creations are interesting to others in the design professions, but of no value whatsoever to refugees and disaster victims. What is required in the future is a series of dedicated design responses to the clearly identified geographic locations where disasters are known to occur. These are well documented and, with some degree of certainty, many disasters can even be predicted. A global effort to provide a network of shelter after disaster planning, as part of a locally based, cohesive and integrated disaster strategy, is the logical and attainable solution.

131

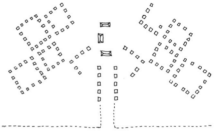

132

131 This Belgian Médecins Sans Frontières Project in Croatia in 1992 used Tepe Prefabrik prefabricated buildings made in Ankara, Turkey. 1,600 families were housed in 800 housing units; **132** Refugee camp tent layout designed by Fred Cuny

CHAPTER IX
PROTOTYPES AND PREDICTIONS

The city that had occupied Mesa Canaan now marched across the plain. Jeshua watched with binoculars from the cover of the jungle. It had disassembled just before dawn, walking on elephantine legs, tractor treads, and wheels, with living bulkheads upright, dismantled buttresses given new instructions to crawl instead of support; floors and ceilings, transports and smaller city parts, factories and resource centres, all unrecognisable now, like a slime mold soon to gather itself in its new country.
Greg Bear, 'Mandala', 1978[1]

Once, in Mexico, years before, Turner had chartered a portable vacation module, solar-powered and French built, its seven-metre body like a wingless housefly sculpted in polished alloy, its eyes twin hemispheres of tinted, photosensitive plastic; he sat behind them as an aged twin-prop Russian cargo-lifter lumbered down the coast with the module in its jaws, barely clearing the crowns of the tallest palms. Deposited on a remote beach of black sand, Turner spent three days of pampered solitude in the narrow, teak-lined cabin, microwaving food from the freezer and showering, frugally but regularly, in cool fresh water. The module's rectangular banks of cells would swivel, tracking the sun, and he'd learned to tell the time by their position.
William Gibson, *Count Zero*, 1986[2]

Science fiction can be looked upon as the history of the future. If it is not strictly accurate, at least in some ways it represents the hopes and fears of those who write it. The genre can also be seen as an extrapolation of present day science fact, so if it is a guess, it is at least an educated guess. Science fiction can also be described as experimental work, the role of which in all fields of creative endeavour is to challenge preconceptions about what might be, to avoid the obvious and seek out the alternative. Through these means the creator, whether a writer, a scientist, or a designer, asserts control over his or her environment, and consciously avoids the restrictions of conformity. This revolutionary behaviour has at least one benefit for the individual and for the group: the chance that something new and useful will come as a direct result or as a by-product of breaking new ground.

The two pieces of predictive prose here, Bear's description of a moving city beginning its journey to a new location and Gibson's self-sustainable vacation module do not, however, appear to be science fiction at all (though much of the work of both these authors clearly is), but accurate descriptions of actual projects designed by architects.[3] That they manifest themselves in some fictional far future is, depending on which way you look at it, either an encouraging sign of the level of advancement of the writer's ideas, or a miserable example of contemporary, conservative society which can only assimilate such ideas in an unrealistic 'entertainment' scenario.

The idea of the transient building is a powerful one in experimental architecture. The image of machinery, especially when associated with motion, has intrinsic connotations of power and speed. The innate propensity for movement is also associated with freedom, and creative freedom is at the heart of experimentation. In many ways, experimentation in architecture also means a rejection of tradition, in particular the static conventional building methods that could arguably be the cause of stiff, inflexible building designs. New materials have always encouraged experimentation – the exploitation of new structural systems has inevitably led to new architectural forms. In the nineteenth century it was cast iron, in the early twentieth century, reinforced concrete and after the Second World War, steel and glass. In their search for new materials and manufacturing techniques, contemporary experimental designers have most consistently explored the possibilities of

133 Lebbeus Woods, Aerial Paris, 1989. The ultimate in free-form structures

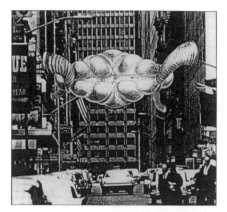

134

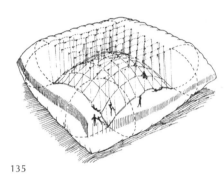

135

technology transfer and with constructional influences have come the associated formal influences of the objects that they were devised to make: aircraft, yachts, cars, spacecraft. The contemporary experimental designer therefore admits no boundaries in the search for new directions; everything is available, everything has possibilities.

Portable Architecture and the Experimental Tradition

A new sort of architectural practice first began to emerge simultaneously in the 1960s at different places in the world, though most notably in the UK – the generally accepted starting point for a new cult of youth, variously termed the permissive age, the counter-cultural revolution, or the Swinging Sixties. Jim Burns, who prepared a visual history of these groups' history in 1972, dubbed them 'Arthropods' and summarised their characteristics:

> The ability and the willingness to change, to become involved in process, to open up to experiences with the environment and with other people, to work directly with environmental creation on all levels – these are the objectives, the attitudes, the aspects of the new Arthropods.[4]

He saw these groups of anarchic environmental designers/activist/artists as having an interconnected purpose, yet existing in separate identities and segments. He also recognised the beginning of a whole world culture, crossing boundaries between differing experiences and disciplines:

> The separations between art, science, technology, architecture, and everyday life, are beginning to appear as artificial boundaries and hence to disintegrate … The infusion of a universality of cancers into the creation of art, architecture, and environment brings about a new ecumenicism of endeavour, where artists create with architects, architects with cyberneticians, sculptors with technologists, designers with ghetto-dwellers. It is possible to conceive of an entire recycling or feedback system of environmental creativity through which all the elements of a creative 'chain of evolution' might speak.[5]

These aspirations, though in some ways naive, are a direct development from the proclamations of Buckminster Fuller a decade or two earlier, though he has suggested that the designers might meet with industrialists rather than ghetto-dwellers! However, Fuller's influence must be acknowledged in the development of the anarchist/architects, as a result of his tireless lecture tours in the Fifties and Sixties and of his now grudging acknowledgement by the architectural establishment.[6] These groups of architects, designers and artists (rather than individuals) developed independently all over the world.

Missing Link, based in Vienna, produced ideas for disposable and transportable housing – *Fleder Housing*, a foldable structure of cloth and synthetics over a lightweight foldable frame, and *Children-Clouds*, soft inflatable bubbles that hung between hard-edged buildings to provide a flexible playground for children above the city streets, and the *Golden Viennese Heart*, a mobile, multi-use structure aimed at the alteration of the city neighbourhood.

Ant Farm was based in Sausalito on the West Coast of the USA: 'Mobile, self-transporting, nomadic, turned-on, information/media, inflatable, truckin'-down-the-highway freaks of the Seventies.'[7] The group produced a manual for lightweight transportable pneumatic structures called the *Inflatocookbook*, which was part alternative architecture manual, part comic-book.[8]

Other groups were Archizoom of Florence, EAT (Experiments in Art and Technology) of New York, Huas-Rucker Co of Vienna, and the Event Structures Research Group of Amsterdam, but undoubtedly the most famous and the most influential was Archigram of London.

134 Missing Link, Children-Clouds, Vienna, 1972. A PVC community play/communication facility that hung between buildings in urban sites; **135** Ant Farm, a lightweight transportable structure from *Inflatocookbook*; **136** Missing Link; Golden Viennese Heart mobile, multi-use structure

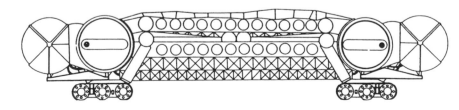

136

The Archigram group was formed in late 1960 by a group of recently graduated students (mostly architects) as a reaction 'to the boredom and obviousness of post-war English office blocks and local authority housing.'[9] The name was drawn from the ambition to publish more experimental architectural work which at that time had no official outlet. Instead of a journal, the concept was something more simple and urgent, like a telegram – archi(tecture)gram – Archigram. This idea for a publication is important in that it was through this that the group created a discipline for their organisation that reinforced their reasons for producing ideas, and also provided a means of communication which disseminated and perpetuated those ideas. In Archigram's case the 'media' acted as an instigator as well as a reporter. The initial members of the group were Peter Cook, David Greene and Mike Webb, but this soon expanded to include Dennis Crompton, Warren Chalk, and Ron Herron. Individual projects were produced under the group name but all members also collaborated on group themes while working in more conventional architectural practices in London.

137

The general pattern of the group's work was summarised by Peter Cook in 1970: 'We have been concerned successively with the notions of throw-away buildings, of buildings which can transfer from place to place, of environments which are not made up from the complex hardware of the built form at all.'[10]

The early publications by Archigram were concerned with comments on general issues, and though illustrated in a thought-provoking and interesting way, it was not until the group's own projects began to be published that the significance of their investigations into alternative architecture started to carry the added weight of actual, if futuristic, proposals.

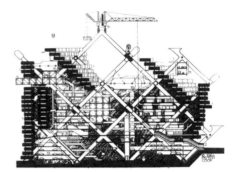

138

The first such project was a series of ideas around the concept of plug-in architecture, beginning with the cabin housing of 1962, which placed removable house elements into a concrete megastructure, and culminated with Plug-in City of 1964. This work paid homage to Buckminster Fuller's Dymaxion Bathroom and Dymaxion Deployment Unit, but extended the idea to include the whole infrastructure as part of the brief. It also saw the first full emergence of Peter Cook's seductive images of giant technological cities, megalopolises of constantly shifting components: 'a whole urban environment ... programmed and structured for change'.[11] These drawings showed convincing pictures of how this future city might work, ranging from maps of the UK showing the dispersal of the cities, to comprehensive elevations, sections, plans and details, that encompassed not only the buildings and infrastructure but the new type of logistical and servicing arrangements, which even specified the life-span of the various parts of the system. Despite this detail, it is clear that Archigram, at this time at least, was not interested in producing actual architectural solutions. Plug-in City looked like architecture, the 'taste' of its detail simulated architectural concerns, but was it architecture? Bryan Lawson describes the work as: 'more akin to the artistic than the design process' and also not intended to: 'solve any immediate problems ... it explored and expressed ideas, beliefs and values'.[12]

Other projects associated with Plug-in City such as Capsule Homes by Warren Chalk (1964) and Gasket Homes by Warren Chalk and Ron Herron (1965), investigated details of the interior spaces and image of the plug-in dwelling modules, futuristic, womb-like machines, inspired by the space programme and the early, prototype aviation industry homes by Fuller. Plug-in City was Archigram's first real exploitation of the technology of construction as a generator of architectural form. Mike Webb's student project, in a new style dubbed 'Bowelism', had displayed the services on the outside of the building, but their purpose and form was deliberately left obscure. In Plug-in City all the elements that make a building work were expressed in their full recognisable shape and celebrated as kinetic components that added to the movement and interest of the building, in an attempt to remove the anonymity and bureaucratic facelessness from the big building:

The essential physical operations are stressed; the craneways and the bad weather balloons, and the lift overruns are deliberately exaggerated. But overriding all this was the deliberate variety of each major building outcrop; whatever else it was to be, this city was not going to be a deadly piece of built mathematics.[13]

137 Walking City by Ron Herron of Archigram, 1964; **138** Plug-in City by Peter Cook of Archigram, 1964

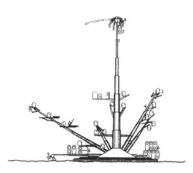

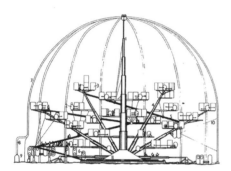

139

Walking City, created by Ron Herron in 1964, emerged in pictorial form only as an impressive collaged image of giant buildings with humanoid/animal/robotic characteristics strolling the world on telescopic legs. This may at first seem to be linked into the Plug-in City concept; however, it was the first example of a move away from the group's concern hitherto with the need to replace existing building types with their own updated versions. Walking City was a radical concept, one not envisaged by architects, engineers and builders in industry, though as Peter Blake pointed out in *Architectural Forum* in 1968: 'these engineers have designed and constructed a couple of dozen structures, some the height of forty-storey office buildings, that move serenely across the flat landscape.'[14]

Other projects followed in this category, the general trend being towards the negation of the building as a static, largely unchanging object. Blow-out Village (1966) by Peter Cook envisaged a hovercraft type structure that moved over the terrain to wherever it was required, then expanded at its chosen location: 'Mobile villages can be used everywhere to rehouse people hit by disaster, for workmen in remote areas, and as fun resorts sited permanently or seasonally at the seaside and near festivals.'[15] Ideas Circus and Instant City were proposals for travelling shows that moved from place to place containing interactive media presentations to introduce life and vitality into flagging communities. Their concept was almost non-buildings in that it was the ideas they communicated that were important, and after a time, the machinery left the locations to continue independently, but now tied into the network that had been created.

Ideas for personal living also developed into non-buildings, and instead of the giant resources wasting mega-cities proposed earlier, highly personal lifestyle models were investigated, though still made possible by the benefits of new technology. The Cushicle by Mike Webb (1966) was the first of these: 'an invention that enables a man to carry a complete environment on his back. It inflates-out when needed. It is a complete nomadic unit – and it is fully serviced'.[16] The Cushicle was a type of life support pack that could be taken to any location and opened out to contain all the facilities for survival in a small personalised space. Webb developed this idea further by reducing the same functions into the Suitaloon (1968) based on the space suit, but with the same availability as a production motor car. Webb captioned the Suitaloon: 'Clothing for living in – or if it wasn't for my Suitaloon I would have to buy a house.'[17]

Inevitably, Archigram as a group ceased to exist, as much from the intellectual pull of members' ideas moving in different directions, as anything else. The themes of the later work headed increasingly towards non-architecture, whilst paradoxically, as architects, many were actively involved in building. In 1970, Archigram won first prize in the Monte Carlo Entertainments Centre Project and it looked as if an Archigram project would actually be built, though without many of the transient and movable ideas associated with virtually all its theoretical work. Unfortunately, this did not happen, but with the publication of the *Archigram* book by Peter Cook in 1972 and the exhibition at the ICA, which appropriately then travelled around the world, the group seemed to have had sufficient influence anyway.

The individual members of Archigram have continued to influence architectural thought, particularly Peter Cook, through his writing and teaching. However, the

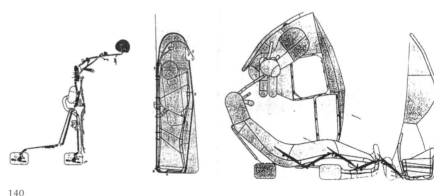

139 Blow-out Village by Peter Cook of Archigram, 1966; **140** Cushicle by Michael Webb of Archigram, 1966-67

140

buildings which have emerged from the former group members have not carried through the philosophies for which they became famous.[18] This work has been left to others. There is no doubt that the landmark building of the Pompidou Centre by Richard Rogers and Renzo Piano, and the work by the Metabolist group in Japan would not have taken place without the influence of Archigram. Peter Blake stated: 'without what they have done, the world of architecture in this century and the next will never be quite as projected.'[19]

Archigram produced a series of dramatic and thought-provoking images that seem to fit perfectly with the age in which they were made, although many of the ideas they produced were not new, but convincing illustrations of ideas that had already been stated before by others.[20] What is left is the realised buildings by groups actually involved in building, who in some cases (though not in the Pompidou Centre) followed the image and not the philosophy. Perhaps David Greene was hinting at the lack of significance of all the non-specific technical wizardry which had been implied, but not physically created, by Archigram when he heralded the cowboy as an icon of the transportable environment:

> Cowboy international nomad hero ... Cowboy was probably one of the most successful carriers of his own environment because his hardware needs were low (mug, saddle, bedroll, matches, and because his prime mover, horse, selected its own fuel and was a fairly efficient animal robot) the ranch was his oasis, his base. Modern nomad sophisticated needs servicing, Howard Johnson understands this.[21]

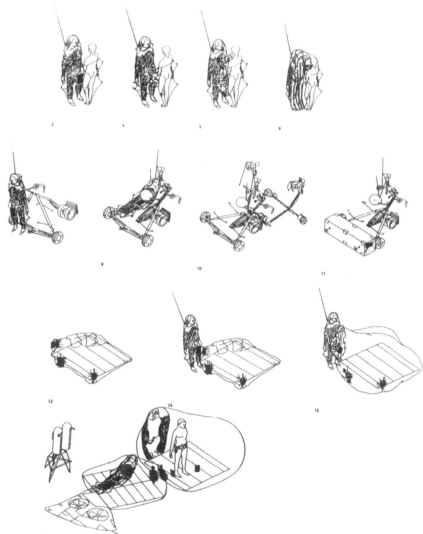

141

141 Suitaloon by Michael Webb of Archigram, 1968

113

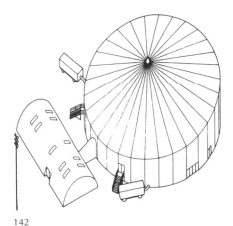

142

A contemporary of Archigram who has repeatedly managed to take innovative ideas into the built world is Cedric Price. In 1966, he stated that: 'The separation of the structure from the site has been a constant interest of this office, and in temporary projects; there is inherent uncertainty in the validity of any permanent site. This basic design premise thus activates the entire nature of the component parts.'[22]

This idea that kinetic and impermanent forms of architecture were particularly valid solutions to contemporary issues guided many of his responses to apparently conventional briefs: 'The value of permanence must be proven, not merely assumed'.[23] Price refuses to make an automatic response but seeks to prove the parameters of design for each individual problem: 'No-one should be interested in the design of bridges – they should be concerned with how to get to the other side.'[24]

Throughout the Sixties, Price not only contributed to Archigram but began to implement his own independent experimental ideas in actual projects. In 1969, he was asked to devise a mobile performance space in Rotterdam for the musical *Hair*. The circular structure utilised a tent covering by Stromeyer, the German circus tent manufacturers, and mobile heating and servicing units as used by the Dutch military. Its deployment and operation on site were supervised by an ex-road manager for the Rolling Stones. After six months in operation the performance tent had proven its worth, as had the show, which transferred to a permanent theatre.

The Fun Palace project, conceived in London in 1961, was for a sort of interactive 'people's workshop or university of the streets', a facility that was to be flexible in function, operation, and life span. Like the Archigram projects it proposed an instant catalytic environment that interacted with the community to bring about change, but unlike them it dwelt on how the building structure could deal with real issues of changing size and operation of spaces and services. Many of the ideas developed for the Fun Palace project were utilised in the Inter-Action Centre built in Kentish Town, London in 1972. Price created a framework that incorporated only a few fixed elements (to provide a determined three-dimen-

143

142 Cedric Price, *Hair* performance tent, Rotterdam, 1969; **143** Cedric Price, the Fun Palace project, London, 1961. Section showing the auditoria suspended within the framework with independent air conditioning and circulated bridges; **144** Cedric Price, Potteries Thinkbelt project, 1964. Collage showing one of the development nodes

144

sional route used for means of escape). Arranged within this was a series of small scale cell type units with a high degree of servicing: kitchens, workshops, lavatories and larger volume low service units; auditoria, cinema and meeting halls. These room-sized components, made from standard constructional systems and commercially available units, were able to be relocated at short notice with minimum effort by using a built-in, full span travelling crane. Price commented:

> The whole complex, in both the activity it enables and the resultant structure it provides, is in effect a short-term toy to enable people, for once, to use a building with the same degree of meaningful personal immediacy that they are forced normally to reserve for a limited range of traditional pleasures.[25]

The Fun Palace used movement within a defined structural grid to provide freedom for the building's users. Another project by Price envisaged that the entire organisation of the building be arranged around the movement of its components over an entire landscape, as a way of serving its function better. The 1964 Potteries Thinkbelt project for Staffordshire was for a kind of linear university that used as its base a railway line along which nodes of accommodation, workshops and meeting places could be established. At the nodes, temporary and permanent structures for housing and manufacturing would become established in response to the developing requirements of the linear infrastructural elements, the railway and road. In this way Price reversed the normal understanding of communication systems as a supporting element for nodal facilities. The route itself, as a symbol of energy and progress, now became the crucial factor, generating and communicating ideas for the sedentary bases to make into physical reality. Reyner Banham summarised the importance of Price's work in these two projects:

> In the Thinkbelt, and in the almost as blatantly architecture free Fun Palace that preceded it, as in practically everything he has designed since (though not always as obviously) he has demonstrated that buildings – quasi-permanent closed volumes – are not the only way of squaring away environmental maladjustments and that architecture is not the only way of designing such closed volumes as you discover you need.[26]

Two Futures

The London-based architectural practice, Future Systems' use of borrowed imagery from the transportation industries can be seen to continue the revolution which Price began with the Thinkbelt project, in that their work supports the idea that the journey itself, rather than the destination, can be the objective for ephemeral architectural projects. David Nixon stated in 1983:

> Future Systems believes that borrowing technology developed from structures designed to travel across land (automotive), or through water (marine), air (aviation) or vacuum (space) can help to give energy to the spirit of architecture by introducing a new generation of buildings which are efficient, versatile and exciting.[27]

Though Nixon formed a most effective voice for Future Systems while he was a partner, it is the design work of Jan Kaplicky which has created the image of the practice as an experimental studio concerned with utilising all that technology has to offer in the creation of architecture.[28] Kaplicky's series of wilderness retreats, beginning in 1975 with project 001, Cabin 380, explores the notion of a pre-manufactured and self-sustaining object settling into a wild and natural environment. Project 005, Weekend Retreat for Miss B; 015, House for a Helicopter Pilot; 016, The Cockpit; 018, Vehicle; 019, 45-degree House; 023, Une Petite Maison; 117, Bubble; and 124, Peanut – all exhibit similar characteristics. The collages used to illustrate these projects accentuate the technological aestheticism of the 'buildings' as a foil to the organic nature of their sites. They forecast a concern with minimum impact and ecological issues that has become the basis of their recent larger scale work. These minimal living pods must owe a lot in their initial conception to the earlier Archigram projects; however, as the designs developed, they seemed to revel far more in the technological aspects of their design, the manufacturing of the details having as much apparent interest for the designer as the philosophical concerns of technology as a liberator.

The Peanut House consists of a small pod dwelling, this time attached to the end of a hydraulic arm, the type used by maintenance and construction firms for the

145

146

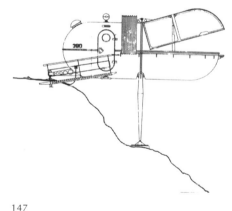

147

c

145 Future Systems, House for a Helicopter Pilot project, 1979; **146** Future Systems, Une Petite Maison, 1982; **147** Future Systems, Cabin 380, the first of the Wilderness projects, 1975

148

149

erection, repair and cleaning of buildings with minimal effort. This structure is located at the edge of a lake and its arm moves from its surface to the land, or to an elevated position, dependent on the whim of its occupier. The logistical siting of the house is therefore only established in general terms and its finite relationship with its site can be fine-tuned from day to day, hour to hour, minute to minute. These 'house' projects are Kaplicky's main expression of his interest in mobile architecture, although there are other Future Systems designs which have exploited the lightweight nature of engineered architecture to provide portability. Future Systems are one of the few British architects who have been commissioned by NASA to work on extraterrestrial design projects, producing designs for self-deployable space structures, a spaceship accommodation module and a pre-manufactured lunar base. They were also invited to create a modern caravan, a prototype of which was built in Australia.[29] Proposals such as this have been received with enthusiasm and interest by the architectural press; however, though the practice has now progressed to impressive permanently sited buildings such as Lord's Cricket Ground Media Centre, there have been very few built portable architecture projects and these are of a small scale. Perhaps the most interesting portable Future Systems building (designed with engineer Peter Rice) was the hospitality tent built for the Museum of the Moving Image, to be sited primarily on the South Bank of the Thames in London. The building was designed for repeated use, to be erected and dismantled in two days by six people, as an economic replacement for conventional hired marquees. The superstructure consisted of a translucent Tenara skin (a Teflon based, self-cleaning fabric of high translucency) supported on a series of inclined GRP wire-stiffened ribs, braced at each end by a steel arch. These ribs are called poltrusions and utilise the technology used to make fishing rods. This structure was supported on a steel and aluminium platform with a plywood deck that incorporated air handling and lighting services. Entry was through the gables which utilised a transparent flexible skin into which conventional glass doors were set. The image of the building changed from day to night. By day, natural lighting from outside illuminated the interior through the translucent skin and at night the building's external surface was illuminated by artificial lighting to create a mysterious, lightweight jewel of a building. Deyan Sudjic called the building 'an ethereal visitation from another universe, braced by a structure as delicate and fine as a web of fishbones.'[30] John Welsh, commenting on other areas of unused public space on the Thames' South Bank suggested: 'Enlightened architecture of the quality of this tent, either permanent or temporary, should re-inhabit some of that barren land. The tent shows a way forward; Momi must be complimented for its patronage.'[31]

Though some of Future Systems' work appears on the surface to be a blatant attempt to produce a controversial response to a conventional problem, this is not the case. The architects are simply single minded in their belief that the appropriate use of existing technology, in an innovative manner, will lead to a more efficient architectural response. The images of the wilderness retreats are not so shocking if one imagines the helicopter or off-road vehicle in those places for which they are, after all designed; self-powered, air-conditioned, radio-controlled, human enclosures that require no preparations before arrival at their destination and leave minimal effects (dependent on the sensitivity of their operator) on their departure. Whether Kaplicky has simply adopted these scenarios, or *adapted* them to become more radical, appears to be a subjective issue. However, as quoted at the beginning of this chapter, it is hard to refute the argument that

148, **149** Future Systems, Peanut House, 1984. The hydraulic arm can be manoeuvred from the surface of the lake to an elevated position and back to the land; **150** Future Systems, hospitality tent for the Museum of Moving Image, 1993

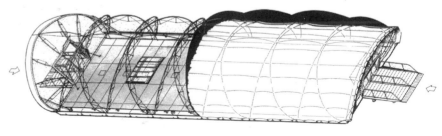

150

Gibson's vacation pod temporarily dropped into the wilderness would have less long term impact than a cabin made of conventional materials, which would forever alter its location, although it may be occupied for only a few weeks each year. Future Systems, provocative images have a place in the development of current architecture in that they can be seen to have prepared the ground for a truly technological architecture. Whether it is necessary for architecture to be so overtly machine-like to have the same pragmatic benefits remains to be seen.[32]

If the goal of experimental architecture is to seek freedom, then the ultimate architectural freedom fighter is Lebbeus Woods. Woods' aim is the creation of a suitable architecture to accentuate the freedom of the individual. The essence of his design work is the ambition to create a new form of architecture which to many may not be socially acceptable, but is to him individually necessary. His design principles are based on his belief that all architecture should be created for the individual and that any restrictions applied by the group are artificial and undesirable:

> The individual human being is *organically* autonomous, in fact an organism. Strictly speaking, a group of individuals is not an organism, however much philosophers and apologists of hierarchical structures might wish it to be, however much groups might behave like an organism in certain situations. *By nature, only the individual human being is autonomous.*[33]

The characteristics of an architecture which can respond to the individual's requirements are necessarily based on individualistic concepts, unique to each situation – instead of a hierarchical architecture which is based on existing traditions, Woods aims to create a heterarchical architecture which expresses the freedom of the individual. This architecture is characterised by its indeterminate nature, often seen in his images as a foil to the existing pattern of historic cities – recognisable organisational structures which have been developed by groups of people over time. He states:

> *actual* cities form the rationalised, over-determined matrix, while *free-zones* and *free-spaces* – as I have come to call an architecture of indeterminacy – form the matrix of unpredictable *possibilities* for cultural, social, and political transformation latent in human knowledge and invention.[34]

Yet this does not mean that Woods' architecture uses unrecognisable images that have no connection to contemporary ideas about built form. In fact his designs' construction and materials seem to be an intrinsic component in the message; their part-completed appearance of an assembly of mechanised, industrial components enhance the appearance of indeterminacy which is an intrinsic part of the desired image. It would seem that though Woods' designs show a utilisation of contemporary and futuristic technology, he does not believe it can really be relied upon to aid a solution without a revolution in the way architects approach its use:

> In the present technological society, innovation has already begun to race ahead of tradition. Technology cannot become a tradition. New knowledge, new conditions of living are developing faster than can be thoroughly assessed and tested, or their effects controlled. These conditions force changes in thinking and society, from which a new type of coherence must come ... Most architects today seem confused when they confront new technology, knowledge and conditions of living, preferring either to ignore them or fall back on stereotypes. Their confusion will end only when architects accept that the mandate for practising architecture today is not the control of change, but its *invention*.[35]

In a series of projects which he has undertaken since 1988, Woods has attempted to utilise this change as a seminal element in the creation of architecture. In the free-zone projects for Berlin in 1990 and Zagreb in 1991 interventions are made into the existing city structures that provide new, alternative spaces for the individual that overtly break with the traditions of city form. In the earlier Berlin project these forms sometimes appear cut into the heart of an existing structure as if positioned there by some form of advanced matter transporter device; in the later work they are obviously pre-manufactured, complete structures which are dropped into place by helicopter and are perched, in a temporary way, within the existing street pattern. In this case they are reminiscent of the event structures

151

151 Lebbeus Woods, Zagreb Free Zone, 1991. Helicopter deployed intervention into the existing city infrastructure

created by the German groups Missing Link and Coop Himmelbau, but they are also unmistakable 'real' portable structures that receive their powerful image as much from the deployment in a recognisable conventional situation as by their aggressive and deterministic character.

Perhaps the ultimate portable architecture created by Woods are the projects for Aerial Paris in 1989, and Anti-Gravity Houses in 1991. These structures are located in the atmosphere as a rejection of the 'arrogance' and 'tyranny' of gravity. Woods likens the inhabitants of these houses to the performers in a circus who have an admirable freedom of habitation and occupation. The drawings of these structures show constructed floating objects, each different from the other, designed to utilise four dimensions. As well as occupying three physical dimensions they also utilise the fourth, time, by shifting position over the ground below and also in relation to the movement of air in the sky. How different are these physical addresses in the sky from the notional ones which have existed for decades created by air traffic controllers to manoeuvre aircraft safely around the sky, or from the actual objects which the air lanes have been created to guide, the aircraft? In 1929, the *Graf Zeppelin* flew around the world in a flight that lasted 21 days with 20 passengers on board. The possibility of living in the sky existed more than 70 years ago. Woods has simply reinterpreted its meaning – from the manifestation of a technological society, to the instrument of its liberation:

> architecture that moves, slowly or quickly, delicately or violently, resisting the false assurance of stability and its death – architecture that comforts, but only those who ask for no comfort – architecture of gypsies, who are hounded from place to place, because they have no home – architecture of circuses, transient and unknown, but for the day and the night of their departure – architecture of migrants … architecture that moves, the better to gain its poise.[36]

Future Systems and Lebbeus Woods in many ways represent opposing values in architectural experimentation. Kaplicky's work exhibits an absolute faith in the value of technology as a source of improvement in the future condition of the built environment. Woods' work is more wary in that it acknowledges that technological development will undoubtedly affect the way we make buildings, but questions that it will have a completely positive effect, and thus seeks to find more fundamental factors upon which to base the direction of future architectural design and our approach to the utilisation of technology. Of course, both designers' work is driven by more complex motives than these simplistic black and white descriptions. There are also many other designers who are involved in experimental work, some of which has led to the investigation of movable architecture as a potential solution to the indeterminate nature of current sociological,

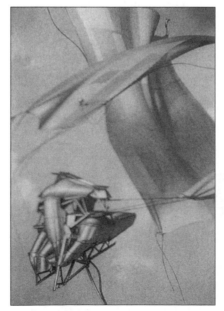

152 Aerial Paris, 1989

152

environmental and economic pressures. Though it is difficult to perceive a discrete architectural movement in such a diverse range of vibrant and exploratory design work, Kenneth Frampton has recognised a commonality of purpose that has led him to use the term 'new constructivists' whose purpose is 'to ground architecture once again in structure, craft and the poetics of construction, rather than in the gratuitous aestheticism of abstract form'. This of course includes predictive and theoretical architectural design that responds to real issues about the environment we inhabit, the ephemeral nature of contemporary society, and the problems of actually constructing a physical object that expresses these concerns.[37]

153

Alternative Movable Architecture

Experimental work in the field of portable architecture is not just the province of professional designers. Aspects of traditional architecture and contemporary mobile homes are grounded in vernacular creative responses, and this source of ideas is still active in the present century. The roots of North America's most common affordable building have already been traced to the home-built trailers of the Tin-Can tourists of the 1920s and 1930s (see Chapter VI). Contemporary versions of these personal mobile dwellings are still built, particularly in North America where road culture is very strong. Chip Lord uses the term 'nomadic truckitecture' to describe:

> the appearance of so many one-of-a-kind shelters attached to truck beds as to constitute a movement ... although mobility is primary and integral to the design of their vehicles, speed is of little consequence. They tend to travel slowly, usually avoiding freeways, sticking to rural roads. Theirs is a drive for individual freedom.[38]

Truckitecture is a highly personal form of design that takes into account a completely different lifestyle that is in itself an unplanned experiment. Truckitects devise dwellings that not only have to make use of invisible servicing and networking arrangements, but also deal with unreliable gravity (which shifts when the dwelling/vehicle turns a corner) and the utilisation of unpredictable and unreliable resources. Yet truckitects are enthusiastic about the infinite possibilities of their base material: 'Junk cars have been ignored too long. They have roofs, windows that open, and doors, all of which are most expensive in house buildings. Old trucks can be a semi-portable foundation for a house.'[39] Chip Lord describes the Ant Farm Media Van which was used as a mobile base to document the American landscape:

> The van resembled a quasi-military rig. It looked official with its antenna, its silver domes and TV window, and on the side, instead of a government logo or motor pool ID number, it said Ant Farm. It was our version of the ultimate nomad package, a complete life-support system worthy of NASA, including a kitchen built into a small trailer and two inflatables, one a shower stall, which could be inflated off the truck's twelve-volt current. A solar collector heated the shower and the other inflatable, Ice 9, could shelter five people from the elements.[40]

These dwelling/vehicles tune in to the traditional values of the open road which are particularly strong in the USA, but have also generated new myths:

> Surfers and hot-rodders, straights and freaks have gone over to vans as a symbol of freedom and independence. These vans have developed a mystique about them varying from 'love machine' to 'dope den'. The van's large interior gives room for mobile living with water bed, refrigerator and television; while its slab sides allow for unique expressions in graphics and graffiti, colour and protest. The van gives the owner a chance to be an artist; to create a personal statement out of a mobile metal box given to him from his sterile technological environment.[41]

However, because these conversions are carried out by people who have chosen a different lifestyle from those who normally control the built environment, and who are in fact generally rejected by all of conventional society, their response is not taken seriously.[42] Yet these dwellings are cheap, effective, economical in the use of manufacturing and running resources, and highly personal to the occupants.

Homeless people appear to be an intrinsic problem of contemporary urban life. The provision of conventional shelters does not seem to have provided a perma-

153 Ant Farm Media Van by Chip Lord and Ant Farm

154

155

156

154 School bus and Volkswagen camper van conversion; **155** Barbara Cole, Kansas State University student project, for providing employment and housing for homeless people utilising redundant industrial buildings; **156** Genesis 1 community dwellings in Los Angeles. Prefabricated mobile dome design by Craig Chamberlain

nent solution, partly because of insufficient funds to tackle this major problem, but also because of its unique nature. Two recent projects seek to address the problem in quite different ways. One is a simple act of recognition of the nature of these people's self-made homes, for they do make homes, though like New Age travellers they are not generally recognised as such by conventional society. Photographer Margaret Morton has chronicled the variety of homeless dwellings found on the streets of Manhattan over a four year period. The dwellings range in type from mobile structures built on a supermarket trolley to permanent buildings that have lasted for nineteen years. The design of these structures, largely built from 'free' building materials (consumer garbage) are sometimes based on complex issues of spatial and environmental understanding, but always carry the unique hallmark that is human shelter. Coupled with the statements of the inhabitant/builders, Morton hopes that 'an analysis of the particulars that transform a cardboard box into a home will provide useful insights for the development of more appropriate solutions.'[43]

One of Morton's findings is that many homeless people prefer building their own houses to staying in the city's shelter system. Ted Hayes is founder of Justiceville/Homeless USA which aims to provide a solution to the homeless problem yet avoids paternalism. The idea is to create small communities that not only provide accommodation but also a base for learning new skills, and seeking or making employment opportunities. After several false starts, Hayes has now founded Genesis, a community for about 30 people in downtown Los Angeles. The core of the project is its buildings: proprietary, polyester fibreglass domes, with lighting powered by solar energy.[44] They can be transported on the back of a truck and assembled by the residents using Teflon bolts. Though these buildings are single skin, which is acceptable for the mild South Californian climate, the components can also be supplied with bonded insulation and have been tested in an Alaskan winter. The community provides a supportive, self-operated environment for homeless people, in buildings that cost $6,500 each. The project has the backing of a real estate developer who understands the requirements of affordable housing, and Hamie Schneider, grandson of Buckminster Fuller. Plans have been made to extend the idea to other cities, beginning with San Francisco, using the insulated buildings. Because of the informal, self-build nature of these buildings and the communal image they create when assembled in a group, they provide a recognisable half-way situation for street dwellers between destitution and assimilation into permanent conventional lifestyles. The occupants take part in the creation of their homes and organisation of their communal activities, steps towards establishing a rejuvenated independence and self-responsibility.

Extraterrestrial Design
The field of extraterrestrial design possesses all the problems and restrictions of construction, deployment and maintenance that have led to the creation of portable architectural solutions on earth. Space architecture, whether destined for the surface of other planets or for orbit, must be prefabricated to a large degree, capable of transportation over vast distances in either dismantled or assembled form, and lightweight in order to be a viable proposition for lifting into orbit. In addition to these logistical characteristics it must have performance capabilities that are far superior to most earth buildings, even those created for the harshest of environments, and architectural qualities sensitive to the needs of its inhabitants who are required to endure remarkable extremes of physical and mental hardship. The demanding profile of successful extraterrestrial design makes it an excellent example for predicting the future of earth-bound portable architecture. This applies not only to the projects that have been completed but also to those that are planned.[45] Space architecture is probably the only form of building technology that has been, and is still, subject to a continuous programme of pure and applied research, developing concepts through prototypes into deployed solutions.

All space vehicles have some aspect of dwelling included in their design because they must contain their crew within a completely self-sustained environment that provides everything for their safety and comfort. Like ships, most have as their prime function transport, although journeys to the more distant planets will need to be much longer than any terrestrial voyage. It is with this in mind that the first space stations were established to find out how humans could live and work in space. The Soviet space station programme began in the late 1960s with the first successful space station, *Salyut 1* being launched on 19 April 1971. The *Salyut* programme was a long and generally successful one; *Salyut 6* stayed in orbit for five years whilst the *Salyut 7* set cosmonaut endurance records of more than 236 days. A new generation of Soviet space stations was launched in 1986 with the *Mir* which after more than 15 years in orbit as a base for a series of record-breaking missions by 104 astronauts, burnt up in the Earth's atmosphere when it was given the final thrust towards the Pacific Ocean on 22 March 2001.

Skylab, the USA's first space station was launched on 14 May 1973. Damage during lift-off led to a dramatic rescue attempt 11 days later when astronauts spent several days effecting repairs before occupying the station. *Skylab's* volume was 368 cubic metres and it contained 907 kilograms of prepared food, stored in freezers and lockers which could be heated as required. Water was available for personal hygiene, showers and drinking. Sixty changes of outer clothes were provided for the astronauts as well as 210 changes of underwear. There were specialised working, eating and sleeping areas and power came mainly from a compact solar array. After four successful missions the station was allowed to fall into a decayed orbit in 1979 and destroy itself on re-entry.[46]

In the 1970s NASA's funding fell by 20 per cent and successive presidents were more concerned with domestic issues and international affairs than space exploration. However, in recent times this policy has changed substantially. Now aware of the value of spin-offs from space technology and the commercial, and unfortunately, military, benefits to be gained from space research, a new commitment to ongoing research has been initiated.[47] This has resulted in many new research projects carried out by a wide range of experts: engineers, scientists, doctors, architects, and specialist contractors, which are aimed at solving the logistical, constructional, and psychological problems of living in space. There have been so many new ideas and projects originated that research has also been done into the creation of analytical methods for assessing their relative performance.[48] Most of this work is based on pragmatic problems, but research has also been carried out into the architectural issues generated by such constructional projects. Brent Sherwood of the NASA Goddard Space Flight Center comments:

> Leaving behind the sustenance and protection of Earth opens a level of interleaved technical problems quite beyond anything we have tackled so far… Yet, once those problems are solved, even primitively, they will cease to pose the dominant obstacle to space civilisation. We can safely assert that before multitudes of people begin living in space, more ancient architectural issues will have superseded the technical dilemmas of putting and keeping them there.[49]

This new research examines the issues that designing in space generates for architects but also the opportunities that have arisen: 'For the five millennia of its civilised history, architecture has worked within a fairly practical range of conditions. Space bursts those archaic boundaries substituting an unprecedented set of freedoms and restrictions'. The International Space Station *Freedom* is the most visible contemporary presence in space. Built in a consortium between the USA, Russia, Europe and Japan (though primarily funded by the USA), construction is behind schedule but still progressing steadily.[50]

Contemporary proposals for future extra-terrestrial construction fall into two categories; accommodation for orbiting or interplanetary platforms, and buildings that are to be based on the planets' surfaces. Because of the problems associated with the transport and assembly of building structures in space, research has been carried out into self-deploying building systems. These have significant advantages in that they take up very little space when being transported and also avoid the necessity for highly skilled astronauts to be involved in the dangerous and time-consuming assembly processes. Self-deployable structures take materials technology to the limit as new properties are sought to overcome logistical requirements which are simply not possible using conventional systems. A principle called 'Elastica' has led to the creation of linear structural masts such as the *Astro-mast* which was used for deploying equipment remote from the *Voyager* spacecraft. Elastica are elastic curves based around the twisting of a rod so that its centre line forms a helix. Planar Elastica is now being used to develop this prin-

157

158

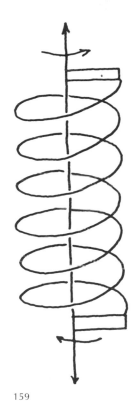

159

157 *Skylab*, NASA's orbital laboratory; **158** A deployed mast structure photographed from the Space Shuttle; **159** The principle of 'Elastica' used to create self-deploying mast structures

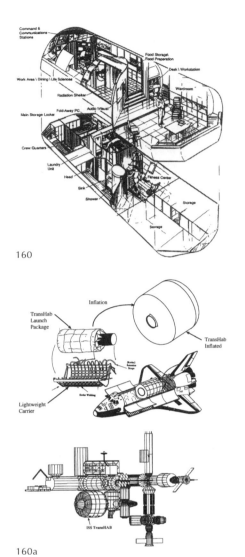

160

160a

ciple into self-deploying planar structures. Space engineers comment on the different ways in which they have to approach the design of these demountable structures compared to those who work in conventional terrestrial situations:

> Creating a rational structural concept should be the first step in the process of designing a structure and it precedes the practical design step. As far as earth-bound structures are concerned, however, designers often tend to skip over the conceptual design step. It is because there is a lot of information on structural concepts and, in many cases, the only thing they have to do is to select a concept among feasible concepts.[51]

Prototypes are currently being tested for inflatable structures in space. These structures consist of a membrane containing UV protection which is inflated within a reusable container of an appropriate shape (a sphere is suggested for early prototypes). A second skin is inflated within this for an inner leaf, the gap then being filled with expanded polyurethane. The building is therefore transported in a very compact state and able to form large protective volumes in space. The ISS TransHAB designed by NASA provides 342 cubic metres of pressurised volume on four 'floor' levels for use by a maximum 12 person crew. Full-size prototypes have been undergoing tests in vacuum conditions and if the system continues to work as expected the first deployment will be in 2004.[52] Other conventional ideas for space stations are also well advanced, including proposals by the European Space Agency using the *Ariane 5* launch vehicle.[53] The function of these stations will be to research all aspects of life in space: physiology, psychology, habitability, safety and survivability, as well as develop techniques associated with constructional assembly, proximity operations, robotics, and extra-vehicular activity. They may also form the platforms for the assembly and servicing of space vehicles, particularly those which will journey into deep space.

Building on the planets is a completely different problem, in some ways easier than space station construction, though without doubt more significant in architectural terms. Surface construction offers the opportunities of gravity and materials availability, both equating to earth situations. However, because the distance from the Earth is much greater (less than a week to the moon, but up to a year or more to Mars), these bases must be much more independent and be capable of long term habitation. Many proposals have been made for the construction of such buildings, ranging from a simple portable single module (a sort of extraterrestrial Portakabin) to large complexes made from indigenous materials. Prototype facilities have already been manufactured here on Earth to test the habitability of isolated, self-sustainable accommodations over long periods. The Space Habitat and Operations Module (SHOM) has been built at Martin Marietta Astronautics

160 Space Habitat and Operations Module, SHOM, manufactured by the Martin Marietta Astronautics Group in Denver, Colorado, USA; **160a** NASA's TransHAB deployment strategy via the Space Shuttle (top). The International Space Station *Freedom* indicating the location of the TransHAB module scheduled for deployment in 2004 (bottom); **161** NASA emergency survival bubble

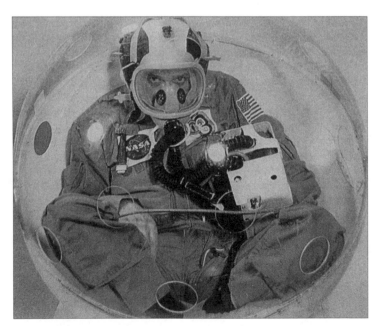

161

Group in Denver, Colorado, USA. Living, working, resting, exercising and storage facilities are contained in a compact tube. The designers state their concern over the habitability of such projects, yet in most cases little thought appears to have gone into the micro-design of the interior that would make it acceptable for long term occupation – their priorities are clearly to make an affordable project that responds to logistical, scientific and political agendas. The creation of a new form of architecture that will respond to human architectural requirements is only recently beginning to be recognised as a crucial part of the design process.[54] The construction methods for the more complex facilities that take these considerations into account have to be more ambitious than the simple transportable module method and a range of possible systems has been devised. At the core of most designs there is still the prefabricated module which is made on Earth and transported whole to the surface of the planet to be colonised. This provides not only a basic starter facility for the first inhabitants, but a place of safety if construction does not go according to plan. It can also provide a location for sophisticated communications and scientific equipment, air locks, and life support. In larger projects there are several of these prefabricated modules.

All designs envisage that some, if not all, of the building systems are also transported to the planet from Earth. In some cases, such as NASA's Inflatable Habitat, all the components are earth-manufactured. This project utilises a large inflatable tube which is deployed within a supporting spaceframe. Modular sleeping compartments are fitted into this when it is complete, though most of the area remains open plan to provide a pleasant working environment for the inhabitants. Projects like this are worked out in great detail in order to determine exact assembly and operational procedures that will result in maximum safety for the crew, but also define accurately transport and deployment requirements. This particular project encompassed a volume of 2,145 cubic metres and 547 square metres of floor space, its total mass being only 77,355 kilograms. The accommodation module would be the heart of a settlement, which would also include solar and nuclear power plants, an oxygen production unit, and a vehicle maintenance facility.[55] Other designs for Moon and Mars settlements utilise locally available materials to supplement imported construction systems. These take advantage of Lunar regolith (surface mineral material) or Martian lava to protect the relatively fragile imported membrane from the harsh external environment. These strategies require the use of more complex building equipment that could include roving building machines which may support self-sustainable, operator-protecting pods, or be remotely controlled robots.[56]

162

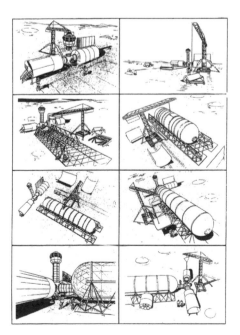

163

162 Lavapolis, a series of inflatable modules constructed in lava tubes in the Lunar regolith. Designed by the Department of Architecture, Texas A&M University, Texas, 1991; 163 NASA inflatable habitat by the Planet Systems Office at the Johnson Space Centre, Houston, Texas, USA

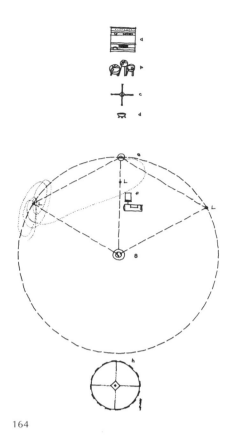

164

164 Hiroshi Hara, Extraterrestrial Architecture System: a) Lunar Base, b) Temporary Lunar Substation, c) Low Lunar Cross, d) Lunar Lander, e) Low Lunar Lunar Orbit, f) Orbital Transfer Vehicle, g) Lowest Earth Orbit, h) Low Earth Orbit Ring, i) Lagrange Point

The logistical and environmental problems of building in space have resulted in proposals that test the capabilities of portable architecture to the limit. The success of these proposals has yet to be tested in this most extreme of environments; however, parallels can be drawn with the most extreme conditions here on Earth. The similarities between the environment at the polar regions of this planet – extreme cold, months of darkness and inaccessibility, and the lack of local resources – equate closely to those found on the Moon. Indeed, the political and scientific reasons for being in these two places are also similar. The first over-winter expedition to Antarctica began in March 1889. Led by the Norwegian born Australian, Carsten E Borchgrevink, they prepared and shipped two prefabricated huts, assembled them over a ten day period, and made them their home for ten months until relief arrived on 28 January 1900. Proposals have been developed by the Sasakawa International Center for Space Architecture to create the Antarctic Planetary Testbed (APT), an Antarctic facility which will mimic the requirements of a similar extraterrestrial building and will utilise similar modular construction methods, closed-loop life support systems, automatic/robotic assembly and maintenance systems. The benefits will not only be the scientific exploration of the Antarctic, but the development of advanced construction techniques for use in related situations – in effect a dry run for space exploration that is a physical example of its viability.[57] This project is one which has seen close collaboration between architects and other disciplines in the creation of space architecture. Architects not only have an opportunity to help engineers create more habitable human environments, but also to learn from the possibilities of remotely deployed projects that depend for their viability on the efficient use of materials, construction techniques and servicing arrangements.[58]

One architect who has seriously attempted to utilise the opportunities of designing in space to create a new form of architecture is Hiroshi Hara. Hara states that his work in this area is guided by physical, phenomenological and social aspects, and that design in space is not entirely new but a development of existing intuitive responses to architecture, though altered by new technological capabilities. He believes that the same intuition that guides the design of earth-bound building must be used in the creation of this new architecture.[59] He has devised a range of related projects that together form an organised approach to human development in outer space, based on predictive technology and observable architectural principles. These projects not only relate to the logistical and environmental conditions of space, but also to human understanding of architecture as it has been developed on the Earth. Some of these projects (such as the Space Square, a lunar based city) are permanent structures and groups of structures assembled partly from imported components, but also from locally obtainable materials. Others depend wholly on the kinetic aspects of space habitation: moving facilities built in one situation, assembled in another, and once complete, forever changing position in relation to the planets they link. The LEO (Lowest Earth Orbit) ring is a space station 10 kilometres in diameter, situated 300 kilometres from the earth's surface, yet so large it can be observed with the naked eye. It provides a base with artificial gravity for transition between the home world and the other planets, and its form and position are intended to represent a gateway to space – a specific place (though of course moving all the time) where space travel begins. The LLO (Low Lunar Orbit) cross provides a similar facility in orbit around the Earth's closest neighbour, though significantly different in form as befits its location – an arrival rather than a departure point. The Lagrange Point is a location of stability in space due to the counteracting forces of lunar and earth gravity. This gives it a particular advantage in becoming a zero-gravity manufacturing location for the assembly of objects. In this completely three-dimensional space factory, the organisation of construction projects will be based around a facility constructed from reconstituted lunar regolith, used because the Moon's relatively low gravity will make it more economic to transport into space. Hara has not only designed the architecture, he has also created detailed scenarios that envisage how these facilities will be used and how they relate to earth-based architecture. He sees this work as not only being influenced by, but also an influence on terrestrial architecture and has produced ideas for new earth cities that take into account the different perceptions of Earth's inhabitants once the experience of space travel is commonplace.

Extraterrestrial architecture is unique in that it is based on a wide range of experimental ideas that attempt to synthesise completely new practical and humanistic issues. There can be little doubt that this architecture will be built, though for the foreseeable future its physical impact will be on relatively few people. However, the significance of the manned missions to the Moon, though especially relevant to the few who were directly involved, had immense repercussions in scientific, technological and psychological terms for a whole generation. It has changed human perception of the world and its relationship with the universe. The technological spin-offs have had an equally dramatic impact, though in such a widespread manner that they are less easily recognisable. The current development of dramatically higher performance portable structures should also be seen as a spin-off resource for the development of earth-based architecture which has remarkably similar design parameters.

Expo Architecture

The mounting of an exposition on an international scale is a prodigious feat. The historic derivation – from travelling show to international exposition – is unquestionable, and the concept of a temporary circus that descends on an empty site, sets up for a short period and then departs would undoubtedly be the most economical way to mount an expo. The actual fact of the modern expo is, however, far more complex. Plans are laid years before – 1989, in the case of Seville '92, 1994 for Hanover 2000[©], although even these lead-in times are seen by many as too short a time in which to make proper preparations.[60] Despite this planning, the master strategy can never be seen as definitive, for even at a late stage it cannot be certain which countries will provide an exhibition building, or quite what the form and scale of that building will be.

The infrastructure associated with an expo site is huge and complex – roads, drainage, power, telecommunications, landscaping – all of which must be done well in advance. Even so, the site works themselves are one of the more simple factors in the preparations, because the infrastructure that provides access to the site for millions of international visitors must be extensive and coordinated within the existing city and regional systems. New motorways and circulation roads need to be built, and in the case of Seville, eight new bridges, a new airport and railway station, and ten new hotels.

In a relatively short amount of time, a wide range of new projects, created by different architects, designers and construction teams and funded by different organisations with different aspirations, are built on sometimes difficult sites in the city and the adjacent expo site. Such a dramatic environmental event has a significant place in the evolution of architectural thought. The 1951 Festival of Britain exhibition celebrated the centennial of the 1851 Great Exhibition, and to mark the emergence of the country into a new post-war era. The editors of the *Architectural Review* saw the exhibition as a symbol of a new beginning in architecture:

> It is clear to all those who have followed the development of the modern movement in architecture, and who comprehend the ideas for the future still only implicit in it, that at the South Bank exhibition we have not only a major architectural event but a work of art which – like the Crystal Palace before it – has potential world-wide influence.[61]

However, in one aspect at least the 1951 exhibition was inferior to the 1851 exhibition. Paxton's Crystal Palace was a structure that had been designed to be inherently capable of being relocated to an alternative site for reuse once the exhibition was over – this was not a part of the concept of the Festival of Britain buildings, and significantly, this fact is not commented on in the architectural criticism of the exhibition.[62] The economic and ecological ramifications of destroying the vast majority of the buildings built for a temporary exhibition were not considered to be of great relevance by the architectural press at this time. However, by the time of Expo '67, the work of innovative designers like Fuller and Otto had begun to make an impact, and the US and West German Pavilions, designed by them, were recognised as amongst the most impressive for their logistical approach to the problems of exhibition design as well as the architectural forms that were generated (see Chapter IV).

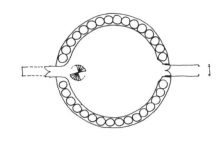

165

By the time that Expo '70 was complete, the journalists now questioned the relevance of creating such ostentatious impermanent, yet permanently constructed, structures, which in many cases appeared to make contradictory architectural statements. JM Richards stated in his editorial for *The Architectural Review*:

This should be the last Expo – anyhow the last to follow the pattern we have become familiar with during the past half-century ... the pattern itself is becoming more and more pointless and its ambiguities more confusing – ambiguity of purpose between trade promotion and cultural exposition, ambiguity of design-objective between the serious contribution to architecture and display technique and the attention-catching gimmick and, above all, ambiguity of conception between international cooperation in creating a world exhibition ... and national rivalry in the shape of separate buildings for each country, competing for attention and each trying to shout louder than its neighbour.[63]

However, Osaka did contain, perhaps for the first time, serious experiments in the creation of large scale demountable buildings, perhaps because of its location in Japan, where the Metabolist architects (greatly influenced by Archigram) were able to construct 'Instant City' and 'Plug-in City'. Kisho Kurokawa's Takara Pavilion consisted of a modular steel pipe framework capable of 'unusually rapid erection, transport and dismantling for re-erection elsewhere.'[64] The Expo version was erected in a single week, utilising a bolt-together structural system that provided the framework for modules containing the exhibition elements and services. The building was described as: 'by far the most imaginative ... its exhibitionism is related to exhibiting and to a feasible future for construction.'[65] The largest pneumatic structure up until that time was also erected at Osaka, designed by Yutaka Murata for the Fuji Group. The building was devised in the shape of a 'covered wagon' with 16 PVA tubes 4.8 metres wide by 79 metres long. This structure used a high pressure pneumatic system that allowed ready access for the thousands of visitors to the audio-visual display it contained.[66] Renzo Piano also created the Italian Industry Pavilion, a lightweight steel framed structure with roof and walls of tensioned translucent polyester fabric. This relatively low key building failed to attract as much attention as the dramatic futuristic and now, in many cases, anachronistic designs, and yet its careful attention to detail and economic response to shelter using contemporary materials can now be seen as one of the most appropriate forward-looking designs at Expo '70. It was not a great *tour de force* of dramatic future science, but a considered examination and application of state-of-the-art materials and construction techniques, utilising prefabrication to reduce the logistical problems of limited assembly time, and reuse of the structure after its initial purpose was fulfilled.[67]

JM Richard's plea for Osaka to be the last to follow the pattern of the intermingled commercial and cultural show has not been met, the two major expos in the last decade of the twentieth century, Seville, Spain and Hanover, Germany (there was also a considerably smaller event at Lisbon, Portugal in 1998) being based on an apparently identical formula. The enormous investment in infrastructural and site development has the ambition of attracting the attention of the world to the host city for just a few months in a single year to promote: 'cultural exchange, understanding, cooperation and optimism.'[68]

If the exhibitions at these events were intended to be a microcosm of the world's nations, the world appears to be a very strange place indeed. The exhibitions formed an intriguing, if disconcerting, array of contemporary architecture: from countries which commendably decided to show their capability of building to high standards of quality, technological advancement and ecological awareness, to others which resorted to the easiest pastiche of their most recognisable national characteristics. After the party was over, the host city could hope to benefit from the physical improvements which had been brought about: roads, infrastructure, restoration of ancient monuments, a brief though important place on the world stage. However, the other countries taking part could generally only look to less physical benefits, though the substantial investment in their pavilion should still reap tangible rewards: a boost in national pride, the hope of increased trade, marketing of goods and services, increased tourism, a way of placing a small part of your country's culture in one place where millions of potential travellers

165 Fuji Group Pavilion at Japan Expo '70; architect, Yutaka Murata and engineer, Mamoru Kawaguchi. The building was 50 metres in diameter and contained an internal projection screen also of pneumatic design

would see it. For most of the buildings, 'pavilion' is not an appropriate description. They were large, expensive, sophisticated buildings, with commensurate capital investment in materials, manufacture, and erection. If this investment was not simply to remain as a gift to the host city (which may even be unacceptable as part of the long term strategy for the site after the exposition finished), reuse of part or all of the building would seem a logical concept.

There are other reasons for creating a building which can be taken apart and reassembled elsewhere. One important factor is that it can be remotely manufactured, built in the country of origin and thereby provide a more genuine exhibition of that country's skills. This also maintains manufacture costs and quality control under immediate supervision. Making a building that can be relocated also means that a greater initial investment can be justified by its continued use, perhaps for many years into the future. A higher level of investment will also produce a higher quality exhibition building for the expo and, therefore, a better showcase for the country.

The range of exhibition buildings at Expo '92 and 2000 can be generally placed within defined categories based on the strategic decision made during their preliminary design stage. These categories are: low expenditure for a permanent structure of affordable build quality; expenditure commensurate with a permanent structure of high build quality and high expenditure for a part or wholly demountable building of high quality. One other category, most noticeable at Hanover, was for a building constructed from primarily easily recyclable materials that might be reused for a completely new building project at a later date.

It is not surprising that the first of these categories generally resulted in buildings that represented a poor public relations exercise for both the country and the Expo. Many less affluent countries invested in buildings limited by the funds that could be made available, and not surprisingly, this accentuated the considerable problems that exist in financing such an investment and their level of experience in this design area.

However, a notable exception at Seville was Chile's Pavilion, whose architects, German Del Sol and Jose Cruz, created a superb, simple exhibition building of high design quality. This building was constructed largely from radiata pine from South Chile, in a simple yet effective manner that used the material appropriately, dividing the architectural form and the spaces it contained into areas and volumes that varied in size and shape according to use. During Expo '92 this building contained a genuine South Atlantic iceberg as an exhibit which provided a unique cooling system for relief from the harsh Andalusian climate. Rather surprisingly, the USA's pavilion organisers at this event, in spite of having access to a wealth of expertise and resources, produced a pavilion that cast into doubt its commitment to the Expo. It comprised a simple frame structure that attempted to unify the exhibits within. These consisted primarily of two small proprietary geodesic domes each containing a short film show, a basketball court and a small stage. There was also a car exhibit, a house that supposedly portrayed the image of the American home (but was in fact a speculative builder's show house, with matching interiors) and an ice-cream stand.

Minimum investment resulted in an exhibition of a value hardly commensurate with the country's achievements, particularly in an expo that simultaneously commemorated the discovery of the Americas.[69]

Permanent buildings that can be placed into the second category can result in good public relations for the country of origin and Expo, but their investment must generally be written off after the show unless they can remain as a permanent gift to the host organisation or be utilised on their original site for a new purpose. Relatively rich countries such as France, selected this design strategy in 1992 and produced dramatic and popular pavilions that were good envoys for the duration of the expo event. At Hanover 2000 the wonderfully eccentric Netherlands Pavillion designed by architects MRDV as a layer cake containing different representations of the Dutch landscape must surely have paid back its budget many times over in public relations value with the thousands who queued for hours to get in.

Opportunity and enlightenment did, however, prevail sufficiently at Seville for there to be several excellent buildings that can be placed in the third category: high quality demountable structures – buildings that not only provided a quality

166

166 The Chile Pavilion at Seville, Spain, Expo '92 by architects German Del Sol and Jose Cruz

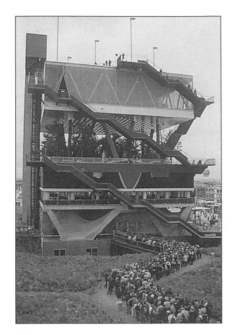

167

167a

167 The Netherlands Pavilion at Expo 2000, Hanover, designed by architects MRDV; **167a** The Danish Pavilion at Expo '92 by architects KHRAS; **168** The British Pavilion at night. The character of the building changed completely under artificial light and yet its construction seemed to be a main component in its drama. Architects, Nicholas Grimshaw and Partners; engineers, Ove Arup

showcase for their country of origin, but had the potential to continue in an extended life on a new site after the show. The Danish Pavilion, designed by architects KHRAS, was built entirely in Denmark and shipped in containers to the site. The design was in two main parts: a thin modular support block that comprised 24 prefabricated units containing offices, conference rooms, and services, stacked eight storeys high, and an open exhibition space created inside large sail-like glass reinforced plastic panels. A multimedia exhibition was projected onto screens, again reminiscent of sails but this time of a square-rigged ship. Water was used to cool the structure by evaporation as it flowed over the external sail walls. The building's demountability has been utilised for its resiting as a landmark building in the Denmark Park in Tamba, near Kyoto, Japan. Despite its demountable design, the Denmark Pavilion did not express its portability as a major part of its character, though its geometric form and simple modular detailing produced a confident modern building that reinforced the image of good Scandinavian design.[70]

The British Pavilion was, however, a structure that displayed its demountable nature from every visible detail, both inside and out. The design was the result of a limited competition which was fortunately funded with an appropriate £15 million budget. This enlightened proposition by the British Government led, after a limited competition, to the appointment of architects Nicholas Grimshaw and Partners and engineers Ove Arup, and involved exhibition partners from industry, such as British Steel and British Petroleum, which made important contributions to the design concept. The building was manufactured in the UK to a high specification and was designed to be capable of being demounted when the exhibition had ended for reuse at a different location.[71]

Parts of the building could also be used elsewhere if the climate of the new site, in the UK for example, did not require the energy systems incorporated for the extreme heat of the Andalusian summer. Forty independent solar powered heat pumps were incorporated in the building as part of the energy strategy and each, if redeployed, had sufficient capacity to provide the power for a complete village in the Third World.[72] The building was also designed to follow a logical erection sequence that braced each end frame as it was put together to simplify the dismantling process. The British Pavilion was one of high quality, appearing finely tuned to its purpose and presenting an impressive example of the British building industry's capabilities. The building's overtly high-tech image made: 'a statement about a certain British belief in technology which … [conveyed] … a clear message to its visitors.'[73] The architects state that the design was firmly established in British engineering traditions and that a great influence on their early design studies

168

was Paxton's Crystal Palace, which they perceived as an established prototype of the expo pattern. The building was sold on after Expo '92, dismantled without problems in reverse order to its assembly, and shipped home in containers at a total cost of £1 million with the intention of being reassembled as part of a major development in London.[74]

Besides the national and theme pavilions in Expo '92 there were a large number of other exhibition buildings that served a variety of functions associated with group exhibitions, hospitality, and servicing. Many of these buildings were of a temporary nature and built from proprietary demountable systems. Most were relatively small and of a familiar pattern; however, the Pavilion des Artes and the Marbella VIP Pavilion were representative of the more ambitious structures. Both these buildings used a waterproof, translucent, synthetic weather membrane, though it was supported by a different method in each case. The Marbella Pavilion utilised a lightweight metal frame consisting of a series of arched ribs. The membrane was stretched between these ribs and therefore contributed substantially to the rigidity of the system. Lighting and other servicing systems could be suspended from the internal frame. Internal walls were provided by the incorporation of a proprietary partitioning system which continued around the internal perimeter of the building, using potentially valuable floor space, but also providing a more permanent quality to the space it contained.

The Pavilion des Artes was a much larger structure and required higher standards of environmental control due to the nature of its exhibits: paintings, sculptures, and drawings. This building had a geodesic type exoskeleton with the fabric skin suspended from special connections at regular junctions in the frame. Entrance was via special environmental air-lock units that incorporated revolving doors. At ceiling level there was a continuous space frame separate from the main structure, that carried the high degree of servicing necessary for this type of building. It also acted as a brace for the internal wall system upon which most of the works of art were displayed. The building was placed on an *in situ* concrete pad which also contained services below a paved surface. Air conditioning was provided by proprietary units which were mounted at ground level outside the building. The external appearance of the building, though interesting in itself due to the exoskeleton structure, was given further coherence by the addition of sculptural art installations on an architectural scale to define the entrances and the perimeter of the building.

Both these buildings provided high quality temporary environments that were able to cope with the extreme weather conditions of Seville, where summer temperatures reach up to 40 degrees centigrade, and dramatic torrential rain storms

169

170

169 The British Pavilion's use of the British Steel yacht, not only as an exhibit but as part of the architectural composition; **170** The Marbella VIP Pavilion at Expo '92. The tent structure is a series of lightweight arches; the interior walls maintain their rigidity with a secondary space frame type structure that also supports lighting

171

171a

171b

in the autumn. Their superstructures and most of their services were fully demountable for reuse elsewhere, though ground preparations utilised permanent construction methods. The buildings can, however, be defined as 'loose-fit', specific requirements associated with their location and purpose being accommodated by the use of relatively high energy, expensive servicing plant rather than a dedicated architectural response that takes into account building form and function.

Were there any really innovative portable building systems used at these most recent major international expos? The answer has to be no (though there was innovation in the recyclable buildings at Hanover, most notably the paper structured Japan Pavilion by Shigeru Ban and the stacked timber walls of Peter Zumpthor's Swiss Pavilion). If comparison is made with the 1967 Montreal Expo, Frei Otto's dramatic tented tension structure for the German Pavilion paved the way for a series of larger and more sophisticated lightweight buildings in different applications throughout the world.[75] Since then, tension structures, though now generally utilising fabric skins designed by computer and incorporating new synthetic materials, have been used extensively and were commonly found at Seville.

If anything is significant about the use of demountable systems for the larger buildings in Seville, it is the way designers utilised a variety of solutions to produce quite different, architecturally impressive buildings. This meant that the building designs, instead of simply having to express the nations' achievements by means of a modern, even futuristic building, were also able to express other notions which were more closely associated with that country's historic and technological achievements. The Danish Pavilion accomplished this in a simple and powerful manner. Its appearance expressed visual associations with the country's and the sponsor's concern for contemporary carefully designed products, and also a more romantic association with the Danish landscape: 'like a sailing boat floating on the water.'[76]

The British Pavilion was more complex in its message. It was a more aggressively modern building, yet in its complexity could be seen a strong image of the traditional exhibition buildings of the nineteenth century. The large imposing facade of Alfred Waterhouse's Natural History Museum in South Kensington contains many messages to the visitor about what he may find within, and the potent power of the Empire that can build such a building. The British Pavilion, with its sails, water cooled walls flowing to a symbolic moat, while addressing the building's energy requirements admirably, also characterised the maritime history of its island nation. The building, though complex in detail, was simple in form, with a grand, almost classical facade that contained a great hall-like space that flowed from the basement to the roof. The internal exhibition was unfortunately nondescript; however, the external siting of the British Steel yacht to one side of the building to continue (or perhaps begin) the rhythm of the structural bays was a masterly gesture. It made clear the sponsor's and designers' intention to link tradition and innovation, and the opportunities of technology transfer utilised in the building's construction.[77]

On examination, the buildings that were erected at Seville with planned reuse in mind have very little in common. There are no standard structural formats, or commonalities of materials. Even those buildings which used proprietary manufacturers did not use the same or even similar systems. Two features were common to all and are worthy of comment. All the buildings, no matter how their superstructure was constructed, were built onto prepared concrete bases (many incorporating sophisticated services), most of which were abandoned when the buildings were disassembled. There are several reasons for this: the large volume of visitors the buildings had to accommodate and the substantial, if temporary, nature of the exhibition period (from April to October). However, it was more probably related to the scale of the buildings. Large buildings require firm foundations and as this was an active building site, conventional concrete foundations were easily installed. The other common factor was that all of the buildings incorporated conventional fitting-out systems: proprietary partitioning, services, furnishings and furniture. All these items were long term, normal building products, which would either have to be shipped to the building's new site (where a possible change in the building's function would render the fixtures and fittings unsuitable) or be sold on or be scrapped. Except in a few cases, this appears to be because the building designers were not in control of fitting-out, and the exhibition designers were not able or willing to continue the reusable design philosophy.

Expos '92 and 2000 resulted in the design and erection of many excellent buildings, several of which can be categorised as those that have been designed to seek a more effective role in the use of resources, and have further useful life after the exhibition. Yet, it is quite difficult to find appropriate criteria to examine the nature of these buildings in relation to the rest of the world's architecture devised in more usual situations. As the character of the exposition event is one where public relations and publicity are of paramount importance, the nature of these structures generally stresses appearance and image, rather than function and the appropriate constructional systems. The expo buildings, cannot even be examined on the basis that they were a gathering of the world's best exhibition buildings, as more important site-specific permanent structures of this nature have been built elsewhere, before and since. The expo can best be seen as a convenient marking point in architectural development, in that it provides a survey (though by no means exhaustive or comprehensive) of the stage of development that this field of design had attained at a particular point in time. In 1967, the editors of *The Architectural Review* felt confident enough about the history of exposition architecture and the quality of individual buildings at the current Montreal event to state that:

172

> The architecture of successive international exhibitions is part of the history of modern architecture itself. They have been a laboratory for architectural experiment, a proving ground and a shop-window in which ideas, structures, styles and personalities have first been presented to the world. Landmarks in architectural history identified with such exhibitions are too many to be listed.[78]

By 1992, enthusiasm had become more qualified:

> There is no doubt that Expos are still fruitful catalysts for visionary architecture ... freedom from the usual constraints can inspire sophisticated and memorable expressions of a nation's cultural identity ... But if future Expos are to fend off increasingly unflattering comparisons with Uncle Walt [Disney] and have any greater relevance to humanity than being just colourful marketing binges, there must be some reassessment of their values and agendas. Anything else is simply rearranging the deckchairs on the *Titanic*.[79]

In the intervening period, the world has discovered that industry and technology are not the complete solution to human progress, and that ecology and efficiency should be part of the new world development strategy. Therefore, reuse of the two-thirds of buildings that are of a temporary nature at these expos was obviously a reasonable proposition. It is disappointing that relatively few design teams appreciated this important point. Is it too ambitious a hope that the new millennium could bring a more rigorous response to the specific constructional issues of this building type so that they really do form a model for efficient and environmentally aware architecture in general?

171 The Pavilion des Artes, Expo '92; 171a The Japan Pavilion at Expo 2000, Hanover, by architect Shigeru Ban. The building is structured primarily with paper tubes and clad with a paper-based roof membrane (though the German building authorities forced the use of an additional plastic layer for fire protection), with other components made of timber, metal and stone aggregates capable of easy recycling; 171b The Swiss Pavilion at Expo 2000, Hanover, by architect Peter Zumpthor. The entire structure is made from standard timber lengths which are connected without holes to allow for easy recycling after the exhibition ended; 172 The Pavilion des Artes, Expo '92 interior; a highly serviced flexible space contained within a commercial demountable building

173

CHAPTER X
THE IMAGE AND IDENTITY OF PORTABLE ARCHITECTURE

... modern self-conscious design has tended to result in places which are single-purpose, functionally efficient, often in a style independent of the physical setting, reflecting mass values and contrived fashions. The present trend appears to be away from a variety of authentically created places which reflect an interaction of diverse intentions and values with a respect for physical settings and landscapes, toward non-place urban realms, international landscapes and place-lessness.[1]
Edward Relph

This was a peaceful place, this camp – a Garden of Eden on wheels, capable of picking its own latitudes and following the gentle weather round the year, a haven in which every occupant had brought his life into focus by compressing it into the minimum space, a miracle of internal arrangement plus mobility.[2]
EB White

Identity

The sense of identity associated with a specific place is intimately linked with the human consciousness. Heidegger states that: '"place" places man in such a way that it reveals the external bonds of his existence and at the same time the depths of his freedom and reality.'[3] In the creative field, the usual assumption of how this sense of place is achieved is by the establishment of some permanent artifact that, with the passing of time, acquires a 'history' of activities and events associated with its location that lend it significance. It is also assumed that this acquisition of 'history' is somehow accelerated by the adoption of a recognisable architectural form, neoclassical for instance, which already has a place in human understanding. In fact, such achievement of a sense of place is artificial. The adoption of stereotypes and their repeated use has rendered them less and less meaningful in the general world: common in many places, unique in none. It is this placeless-ness to which Edward Relph refers in the extract above.

Much of recent architectural theory has focused on a phenomenological approach in which all aspects of human existence relate to actual physical objects and events. This philosophy identifies all the components as human conscious-ness with concrete meaning. The inarguable presence of a physical object is important in human understanding of that object but not less than the personal subjective feelings it may generate, though these may be more difficult to quantify. In architectural terms this means that the human relationship with places and buildings is defined by a complex matrix of observations that stem from the psyche as much as the conscious mind. Many traditional societies exhibit an understanding of even the smallest environmental details and their implications. This indi-cates the intrinsic ability that humankind has to synthesise these complex issues into an appropriate built response when the issues have not been confused by external factors. Christian Norberg-Schulz has defined the phenomenological responses to the environment which humankind makes as visualising (under-standing what can be seen to occur in nature), complementing (adding what is felt to be lacking in the natural environment) and symbolising (translating the meaning of the environment into another medium and thereby utilising this under-standing in the manufacture of a cultural object). These responses are what define the character of man-made spaces and make space into *place*. 'The making of places we call architectural. Through building man gives meanings concrete presence, and he gathers buildings to visualise and symbolise his form of life as a totality. Thus his everyday life world becomes a meaningful home where he can dwell. There are many kinds of buildings and settlements. What they gather varies according to the building forms and situations.'[4]

173 'This was a peaceful place, this camp'. The contemporary camper in some cases requires an equipment level not matched in many sedentary homes

174

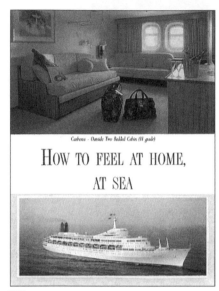

175

An important and perhaps unique aspect of portable building, recognised by White and his fellow campers, is the concept that place can exist anywhere, free from the topographical or geographical attributes of a particular location. The significance of place is that which is determined by the builders of that architecture, not by the permanence of the artifacts which express that significance. We are accustomed to identifying the symbols of civilisation in architectural terms as large permanent structures. In fact, the ideas and philosophies that are embodied in that form are no different from those that exist in the most transient of our built structures, and even in our understanding of a sense of place, where no structure exists at all. Permanent architecture that is intimately connected with its location is in fact very rare indeed, and only a handful of buildings from any age are truly site-specific. Much of the architecture which civilisation has identified as important could in fact exist anywhere, its location a mere accident of economic and social factors contemporary to its construction. This is not just true of individual buildings but of whole cities. All the coastal cities of the USA are situated in places that in the past were convenient for the landing of a small sailing ship. In an age of instantaneous, remote communication, what relevance has that to the meaning of those cities today, except perhaps as of historical interest? Susanne Langer in her book *Feeling and Form* argues that places are culturally defined and that location, in the geographic and topographic sense, is merely an incidental factor in the identification of place:

> A ship constantly changing its location is none the less a self-contained place, and so is a gypsy camp, an Indian camp, or a circus camp, however often it shifts its geodetic bearings. Literally, we say a camp is *in* a place, but culturally it *is* a place. A gypsy camp is a different place from an Indian camp though it may be geographically where the Indian camp used to be.[5]

This is not to say that certain distinct geographical places do not have significance for man. The chance occurrences of nature in moulding the landscape has resulted in features, or relationships of features, that humans have associated with their own beliefs, to which they have then attached special significance. The organisation of stone circles by prehistoric man, whether for astronomical reasons or otherwise, shows a sensitivity to siting in order to emphasise the effect of their construction. The stone circle at Castlerigg in Cumbria, England, is one example of a prehistoric site at the centre of a natural bowl of surrounding hills that utilises the natural 'architecture' to emphasise the man-made. In these circumstances the builders have used their creative skills to utilise the natural elements for their own purposes and have added significance to the place with

174 Tropical motor home by National Recreational Vehicles, Perris, California. The cost of one of these vehicles is more than a permanent house in many parts of the USA; **175** Advertisement for the P&O cruise ship *Canberra* from the 1994 brochure; **176** A Bedouin camp layout, specific repeated relationships between dwellings defined in response to each other and the topography

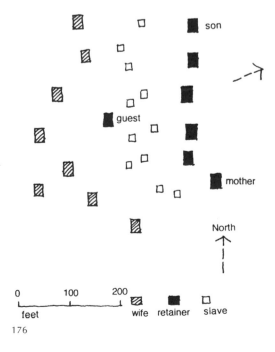

176

the erection of their architecture. The architecture is the catalyst which makes the significance of the place identifiable.

This example of early man's decision-making when selecting sites for the erection of symbolic architecture serves to reinforce the fact that the same process can be undertaken with the erection of all types of architecture, regardless of the intention for it to be permanent or temporary. In the case of a migratory Bedouin tribe that transports the entire community from place to place, each encampment leads to an identical erection of the village's buildings. The leader's tent has a significant position that relates to close family members, the followers and the hangers-on. The hierarchy of the arrangement of the dwellings is established regardless of the location of the encampment. The interior of the tents is also identical, the beds, the social area, the storage compartments being re-erected in identical positions at each new camp. The food will come from the same containers and be cooked in the same kitchen area and even the water, which will come from a different source, will still be drunk from the same cups and be poured from the same vessel. The sense of place is finite, determined, and continuous but the geographical location is infinite, undetermined and transitory.

These people live the same way today as they have done for centuries, and are resistant to the inevitable pressures for change – they look down on the sedentary dweller living in a solid house, and pity their tenuous and dangerous existence. Tenuous because they must rely upon external, uncontrollable factors for their existence; the continuous supply of water in a single place and delivery of food to them rather than finding their own; dangerous because of the investment of resources in a single heavy architectural form that could fall on the owner while sleeping. The users of this temporary architecture go through exactly the same process every time it is erected, using important organisational criteria to determine the place, orientation, and site arrangement, creating a 'sense of place' no matter where that place is. Because the main components of the architecture remain unchanged each time it is recreated, in effect there is also a recreation of place.

Examples of this non-geographically based sense of place in the developed world are not hard to find. Lévi-Strauss describes his first voyage to Latin America as: 'the opposite of travel; in that the ship seemed to us not so much a means of transport as a place of residence – a home, in fact, before which Nature put on a new show every morning.'[6]

Parallels can be drawn between the transitory lifestyle developed by the settlers of the great mid-west of the USA, based on the nineteenth century Conestoga Wagon, which can be said to continue in the refined recreational vehicle and mobile home culture that exists today. Twenty-five percent of all new homes in the USA are provided by mobile home manufacturers and it is estimated that every American family, no matter which type of dwelling it inhabits, will move house on average once every three years. Even more significant is the motor-home culture that has evolved, in which the retired community constantly tour the continent equipped with dishwashers and VCRs – the view out of the picture window might be different each evening but home is still the same. These facts about our modern, transitory society have led observers to conclude that 'location or position is neither a necessary nor a sufficient condition of place, even if it is a very common condition. This is of considerable importance for it demonstrates that mobility or nomadism do not preclude an attachment to place.'[7] In fact, the place is reconstituted each time a new camp is established as it always contains sufficient identifiable features to enable the resident to feel the essential attributes of home which Martin Heidegger describes as to be protected and at peace.

A human-made sense of place (which could also be described as architecture) can even exist without the presence of any buildings. Some Aborigine communities of Australia still follow a nomadic lifestyle that is based on a complex understanding of the nature and form of the Australian bush. Each individual has an inherent perception of the sense of place that is not defined by a single object in a specific location, but the journey between locations; a constantly moving 'place', not a route or highway as defined in other cultures by names such as the Appian Way, or Route 66, but a historical and mythical (but still pragmatic) organisation of space that extends over many miles and

177

178

177 Tropical motor home interior. There is a multitude of choices in interior layout and finishes; 178 This Walibiri Aboriginal diagram represents a cave surrounded by an oval camp. The converging lines and semi-circles represent four kangaroos that arrived at the camp from different directions. The drawing depicts an architectural 'place' based on events rather than objects

180

180

very different sorts of territory. In each case, the individual may make use of some naturally occurring topographical features in the organisation of the route, but the crucial identifying elements are the events in the story or song that describes the journey. The journey is not a conventional one that can be undertaken at speed in order to be completed as soon as possible, or more slowly for leisure, but in a predetermined way that includes specific rituals and processes at defined points. The ways in which rest and shelter occur during this journey can also be significant. The Aborigine builds his architecture with his own actions and movements through space and time, determining the significance of place in relation to his personal requirements, simultaneously identifying the territory associated with his community. To the Aborigine, the importance attached to these forms is no less significant than the local town hall is to a Western city dweller. Indeed it carries more significance as the Aborigine is personally involved in determining the continuation of his community's existence and territorial rights.

The significance of the realisation that the architectural 'sense of place' is not related to a specific geographic location is that it enables designers to contemplate new criteria when devising architectural forms. Certain structures devised for specific functions may be determined with a greater awareness of the economic, social and ecological factors that are available to generate their form. The lightweight temporary building type, if designed correctly, can be created in such a way that it leaves behind its cheap and impermanent image, resulting in the creation of a transitory form that may still be associated with a permanent identity, regardless of geographical location. The notion that the symbolic nature of the form then remains permanent can lead to a greater level of investment in this type of building and results in a higher quality artifact which eradicates the image of a throw-away architecture. The concept of a flexible and reusable architecture has obvious benefits in terms of economical use of available resources.

This concept of an identifiable architecture (that contains the elements of transience that appear to have become a necessity, albeit a temporary one, in our society) has been the subject of investigative design projects by several experimental architects. The temporary nature of these buildings means that they can have access to sensitive sites that would normally not be suitable for permanent structures. Speedy erection on temporary sites transforms the erection process from one associated with conventional building to an event to be watched and admired. The building's departure can leave a memory of the site, perceived in a different way from that in which it was seen before – a new possibility for that location, an addition to its history. The building, however, maintains its own history, which is transposed to its next geographic situation. Though the location is different, the building's history remains the same; its function, contents, personnel remain unchanged, its message intact.

These projects have dealt with a varied range of issues and problems touching on many of the purposes that contemporary architecture must fulfil: education, commerce, industry, shelter. Each of these may be solved with a building that has a definitive form, yet leaves its traces in its users' memory rather than rubble, when its use is no longer required. Buildings are an essential cultural requirement of society that form a physical manifestation of the way we live in the world – a transient architecture does not denote a transient society, just one that may be more in tune with the requirements of an appropriate, thoughtful, economical existence.

Moving buildings have maintained their relevance in nomadic societies for centuries in that they not only form a vital part of these people's physical utilisation of the environments which they inhabit, but also deliver a solution in a culturally appropriate way. This persisting relevance is also apparent in the portable products of the developed world; vehicles that are home to definitive groups of people exist in many forms, from the mobile home 'parks' and recreational vehicle gatherings of North America to the giant floating cities of the world's navies. The fact that these unusual settlements manage to create a 'sense of place' is significant in that it challenges the view that in order to be relevant, architecture must be established and permanent.

179 Takashima-Cho Gate by Riken Yamamoto and Field Shop, 1989; **180** Circus Bouglione, the temporary building as event

Image

Portable architecture will never be more than a part of the entire output of the construction industry. Permanent buildings are an intrinsic part of the aspirations and requirements of society as a whole and a replacement form of architecture is neither required nor desired. However, an examination of the history and development of portable architecture does reveal that this significant part of constructional design has been largely ignored both in terms of the opportunities it presents for appropriate solutions to specific problems and as a source of theoretical, formal and technological inspiration in the creation of architecture in general. The form of early transportable buildings undoubtedly influenced the first permanent architectural examples – new lightweight architectural forms such as the MOMI tent and the Swiss Centennial Pavilion, utilise innovative yet appropriate construction techniques that can today provide a valid source of influence in the same way. The way our cities, towns and buildings are being made is clearly subject to change. Richard Rogers forecasts:

181

> Present-day concerns for single objects will be replaced by concern for relationships. Shelters will no longer be static objects but dynamic objects sheltering and enhancing human events. Accommodation will be responsive, everchanging and ever-adjusting. Cities of the future will no longer be zoned as today in isolated ghettos of like activities; rather organisationally they will resemble the more richly layered cities of the past, living, work, shopping, learning and leisure will be housed in continuous, varied, and changing structures.[8]

Now, more than at any time in history, an appropriate response to changing external influences is clearly necessary. If portable architecture is to have a significant place in design strategies for the future, there are a number of specific tasks that need to be undertaken to develop the understanding and communication of its potential.

182

Research

The search for new building types is also a search for new applications for existing technology and new technologies to fulfil requirements which cannot be met by utilising existing methods. Recent studies of the value of technology in the development of the design process have shown that experimentation in this area is essential. Robin Spence, Chairman of Cambridge Architectural Research Ltd. comments:

> we need to strive for a new understanding of the possibilities implicit in building technology. Not as a process of gradual indoctrination into 'the way we build now'; but as a process of invention and selection from among an infinite variety of options, some already in existence, some easily achievable, others still awaiting discovery or invention. New materials, new structural forms, new approaches to energy conversion, new ways to build.[9]

Though many educational establishments (primarily courses in architecture, but also in engineering, product and three-dimensional design) currently run individual projects related to portable buildings, it is normal for these assignments to start from scratch as if the problem they are dealing with is a completely new one. The students undoubtedly gain valuable design experience and an understanding of the advantages of lightweight and kinetic construction; however, because the work is not part of a correlated continuum of experimentation it does not generally result in the overall development of the building type. It can be said that this experience is largely the same in industry. Research, where it is carried out at all, is generally in response to specific legislative requirements rather than a desire to increase the overall quality of the product. Genuine investigative work needs to be coordinated and published in order to pool knowledge and information, transfer ideas and foster the identification of legitimate research aims.[10] Furthermore, this research should not cease at building completion, but should continue onto the logistical problems that surround the implementation of promising ideas to the prototype and eventually, to the manufacturing stage.[11] The active pursuit of these research ambitions is particularly important for the portable and prefabricated building industry if its products and range of deployment opportunities are to achieve their full potential.

183

181 Turtle House, a project for a prefabricated apartment building, built in a shipyard at Portland, Oregon and floated down the river to its site. Student project by Jeff Fountain, Kansas State University, 1994; **182** Renzo Piano Building Workshop, IBM Pavilion. A portable building with a high quality image; **183** Greenhouse in Dresden, Germany. The structure is used to protect a fragile tree in winter and is moved aside in more clement weather

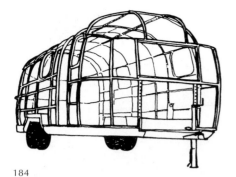

184

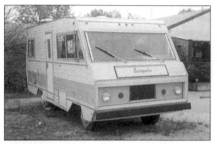

184a

185

186

In this research, use should be made of design, manufacturing and materials expertise in other industries, though it is important that this should be carried out in a way that adapts new techniques in a sensitive manner. New technologies can be seen as a double-edged sword that should be used only in response to established requirements – they are not a universal panacea. Without careful investigation and analysis of specific issues, the result of which is a realistic understanding of the design situation, the application of new technology may lead to alienation and the development of unforeseen sociological and environmental problems. Remote decision making in the field of shelter after disaster is a significant example of this problem (see Chapter VIII).

The potential for such careful and considered research would appear hopeful. There are already many interesting and innovative solutions that are proof of the existence of a viable and relevant contemporary portable architecture. The value of these good ideas should not be seen as one-off phenomena but as precedents which others might use in the development of similar, though unique, solutions.

Perceptions of Portable Architecture

The portable building generally has the image of a poor quality product. Unfortunately, in many cases this image can be seen as accurate, as economy has been high on the agenda for clients who will simply discard the building when it is no longer required. Therefore, an important factor in the development of the role of portable architecture is to make clear that in this case, temporary does not necessarily mean disposable. When a movable building is successful it is not generally recognised that its portability has been a factor in its success. In functional terms, as long as the building is effective in use, it is not important to the user if it is temporary or not. Many of the most successful portable buildings have been specifically designed, relatively high-cost projects, the result of enlightened clients and their designer's search for an appropriate solution. The success of these buildings is not, however, linked to the low-cost but high-volume end of the market where the value of good design and enlightened patronage has yet to be of significance. It is important to transfer both image and experience between these two if perceptions of the building type as a cheap, loose-fit product are to be discarded.[12] A greater understanding of the value of the building type will result in a willingness by the client to seek greater performance and a higher quality product. Like permanent architecture, portable building design should be seen

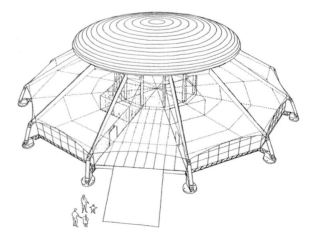

184 The structure of an Airstream trailer. A design that fulfils and expresses its purpose with beauty; **184a** Escapade Motor Home, the purpose remains … **185** Mobile classroom by Wernick Buildings, Essex, England; **186** Future Systems, 45 Degree House, 1981. Portable architecture does not consist solely of the Portakabin; **187** Robert Kronenburg, Gary Seed, Neil Clarke, Eisteddford Mobile Arts Pavilion project, 1991

187

as the creation of specific solutions to specific problems, not as the expedient provision of loose-fit, low-cost projects with minimal satisfaction thresholds.

In general, portable architecture has not achieved its potential as a building type that portrays a functional aesthetic associated with symbolic content. There are certain iconic precedents, such as the Airstream trailer, which display both purpose and beauty admirably, but this characteristic, which could be a major advantage in the success of these buildings, remains relatively unexplored. In general, manufacturers' products look like poor quality buildings rather than high quality architecture. This is another area where the automotive, boat and aircraft manufacturing industries could present a powerful lesson for portable building designers and manufacturers. Reyner Banham describes the inhabitants of conventional architecture as: 'trapped with our forebears under a rock or roof' and sought a 'domestic revolution beside which modern architecture would look like Kiddibrix'.[13] The transport industries already market their products based on issues of safety, efficiency, beauty, ecology (though in some cases imagined rather than real), and the adaptation of advanced technologies in the service of the human race. Movable architecture has a similar, inherent kinetic quality that makes it feasible to borrow the principles they use.[14]

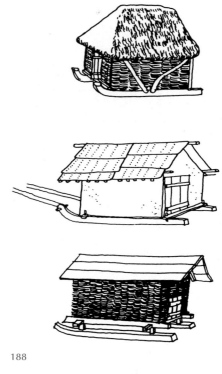

Communication

Once real, coherent advances have been made in the purpose, image, design and manufacture of portable architecture, effective communication of the advantages afforded by the type can begin.[15] This will not be easy. Due to the limited way in which the opportunities of the type have been exploited, most users of portable buildings wrongly believe that they already understand the products' failures and successes. It is important that people discover that portable architecture does not consist solely of the Portakabin and the mobile home. This understandable prejudice must be overcome not only in the minds of the users but also in those of clients, designers, manufacturers, and legislators.

188

The advantages of a well designed portable building can be briefly summarised as the provision of an appropriate solution in an ecological manner at an affordable cost. To be appropriate means that the building functions well, is beautiful, and is sensitive to social considerations. An ecological approach is possible because it is designed to be recyclable, has a low site impact, and is buildable with materials and construction methods that utilise renewable resources. It is affordable because it is adaptable to change, can make use of contemporary production methods, and avoids waste in manufacture and deployment. Many of these attributes can also be applied to well designed conventional buildings. However, the relatively instant response, remote manufacture, and possibility of reuse in a changing situation are virtually unique to demountable buildings.

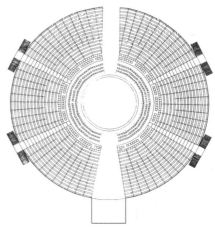

Portable architecture will never replace permanent architecture. Nor should it, as the requirements for specific building types are tuned to their purpose, and permanence is a performance requirement in many cases. However, it should be recognised that portable buildings have many advantages that have resulted in their successful utilisation in traditional, historic, and vernacular circumstances. In contemporary design, portable architecture has provided many appropriate and exciting buildings, usually in situations where necessity, imaginative thinking and a consummate understanding of the issues have been factors in the generation of the solution. These buildings should therefore be seen as part of the mainstream architectural tradition. They possess a long and interesting pedigree of their own that cannot be ignored as an influence on the generation of future architectural solutions. In a world that seeks to find new ecologically aware design routes in the creation of all our manufactured artifacts, the study of the nature of building types that leave little, if any, impact on the environment, and yet still convey the necessary impressions of established society, may reveal a valuable resource.

189

188 Nomad shepherds' huts, Bulgaria –
recyclable and adaptable to change;
189 The plan of Circus Mikkenie, 1953. The form
of this 4,000-seat portable auditorium is an
explicit expression of its function and purpose,
characteristics of mainstrean architectural design

139

Fig.CXI. Fig.CX.

CHAPTER XI
ARCHITECTURE AND CHANGE

It would appear, therefore, that the first care of an architect, when he is about to design any building, should be to consider the full destination and purpose of the edifice, from thence to determine the character which is proper and suitable thereto, and then to compose the building in such a manner as to be expressive of such character ... The destination of a building is divisible into three heads: as, for example, the use it is to serve, the place in which it is to be situated, and the person for whose use it is intended: each should be considered in determining the character of the building.
W. Newton, preface to *The Architecture of M. Vitruvius Pollio*, 1771[1]

This powerful statement of architectural intent reinforces the continuity of human ideas, for the ambitions the author describes, though they were written in the context of a Renaissance review of classical forms, still ring true today in an age when contemporary architecture is very different. Human ideas persist despite the fact that permanence is a state of relativity – the only constant in human existence is change. Perhaps it is this paradox that underlies our reverence for the apparently 'unchanging'. As American architect Wes Jones states, '... architecture ... provides the 'storia' or shelf upon which history's trophies are arranged (as well as being a trophy itself) ... the endurance of such structure is magical, because all of our other experience tells us that time flows, that things change, we die.'[2] The old and historic, that which has had a lengthy physical existence, appears to have some special value not related to the quality of what it is, but of what it has been (i.e., itself) for a long time. Permanency is an attribute which many people perceive as desirable in all our worthy institutions, be they cultural, economic, political, or spiritual. Though the new may be of passing interest, it is commonly felt that what is of real value will have 'passed the test of time' – though time is a peculiarly shifting measure by which to test anything.

It is not easy to comprehend that humankind's presence on the Earth has only been in the very last few moments of its existence. If the Earth has existed for 4.5 billion years, for most of that time the continents have been shifting, seas forming and dissolving. Many species have evolved, been the dominant life form for a time and then become extinct. The genus *Homo* has existed for about two million years. The most ancient signs of significant permanent buildings are only about 10,000 years old as it was only when more geographically settled patterns of agriculture were adopted that permanent buildings became feasible at all. Before that time, temporary or transportable shelters were the homes and workshops of the human race, and of these, only minimal fragments remain. The developmental history of these portable structures lasted for up to a hundred times longer than the 'permanent' structures that have formed the majority of our buildings since.

How permanent are permanent buildings? Durham Cathedral is not yet 1,000 years old, a long time in terms of the typical mediaeval human lifespan of forty years. The Pantheon in Rome is nearly 2,000 years old and the Temple of Ammon in Karnak dates from 4,000 years ago.[3] There are not many buildings of this vintage, and what examples do exist are usually preserved not for their continued usefulness but for their unique age and their meaning in historic terms – important reasons for preservation, but ones which have understandably been insufficient to preserve the countless other lesser structures which were built alongside them but have long since been destroyed.[4] If we were just to count the buildings that were over 100 years old, we could make a much longer list of 'permanent' buildings that are still in existence, though in terms of the entire building stock of the world, they would still form a very small percentage – less than half of one per cent. In the whole history of human construction the vast majority of buildings in use today have been built just yesterday, and what is more, they will be demolished tomorrow.

191

190 Mobile wheeled siege towers from the *The Architecture of M. Vitruvius Pollio*, translated by W. Newton, 1771; **191** Developing technology forces change: the epitome of the late 20th century built environment – Tokyo neon. What will the 21st century be like?

Though buildings, like any other manufactured product, do eventually wear out, this is not the primary reason for most new construction. Continuity in building use is less important than other factors, such as suitability to function, economy, operational efficiency, and fashion. So-called 'permanent' building hardly exists at all – buildings, like all tools, are made for a specific task that has a time limit on its value and when a better way of performing that task emerges, the vast majority of existing outmoded tools will usually be junked.

Despite the vast majority of buildings in the world being static (if not permanent) for 99 per cent of human history, it has been a part of our genealogy to be mobile. The temporary and transportable buildings that have supported complex human activities for hundreds of generations no longer remain. However, like the genes we retain in our bodies from our human ancestors, these architectural precedents can still be clearly seen in the tents, yurts, and igloos which are still being manufactured and used today in much the same form as they have been for thousands of years. The ancestors of these buildings were once a vital part of the human-made tool kit that enabled our species to survive and develop during the catastrophic changes in climate that swept our prehistoric planet. Movement was imperative to humankind's survival. That these simple yet sophisticated structures were the prototypes for the permanent buildings we have today is undeniable. That they still hold valuable lessons for contemporary designers whose aim is to make adaptable, affordable, easily transportable buildings is also true. In the great droughts and ice ages of the past, the circumstances of existence made a mobile life a necessary part of human continuity and development. Today, it would seem that equally momentous changes are taking place in technology, society, and the environment that will lead to similar upheavals.

The presence of technology in most people's daily lives is now ubiquitous; it affects every aspect of the way we live – education, commerce, industry, medicine, entertainment are all dependent on a range of technological innovations, many of which have only appeared in the last decade. Communications are at the centre of this shift and though people and objects are now able to physically move around the world at speed and at affordable cost, the most important development is in the non-physical movement afforded by information technology. The world wide web, personal computing, mobile phones and e-commerce have all fundamentally changed the way the world operates. These changes have created genuine communities of people who work together, socialise, do business and create art but who will never actually meet.[5] The technology that makes this possible has shifted the focus of many aspects of society away from the group to the individual.

Freedom has always been a key factor in human identity. Work is frequently perceived as the activity that ties you down – the liberation at retirement to live life the way you want it is something to be yearned for. The North American retired person reborn as a 'snowbird' is a vivid example of how people can and do break away from the sedentary life (see Chapter X). Information technology is the new tool that can set you free while you are still involved in that working life. There is little doubt that we are just at the beginning of enormous changes in the way work will be undertaken. John Worthington, in the introduction to his book *Rethinking the Workplace,* states: 'The changing workplace requires a reappraisal of the way we work, the space we occupy, the technology required and the work group settings. For architects it is a challenge not to be blinkered by well-established models, but rather to be prepared to reconsider the nature of work, and to rethink the physical consequences from first principles. The physical expression of the workplace may be very different from the stereotypes we currently recognise.'[6] With a mobile phone and a laptop the working person can communicate with colleagues and clients instantaneously from any place at any time. It enables the farmer to be at his office in the fields and it is beginning to liberate the control of manufacture and production, by instructing the actual machines that make the product direct from another location, perhaps many miles away. Gary Brown has coined an evocative term for the newly emerged IT-equipped roaming worker: 'Technology is now aimed at the provision of machine enhancements for individuals of a mass culture, creating mobile machines through which individuals become techno-nomads.'[7] These techno-nomads have little interest in the topography they roam, and primarily use it to reach new feeding/working bases – the physical jumping-off points that are necessary for all mobile activities. They expect to browse 'free' space as the traditional nomad expects to graze 'free' land. Time is escalated as communication becomes almost instantaneous and real space becomes 'facility' space allowing virtual activities to take place instead of real ones.

An important guideline for the introduction of new technology might be to ask: 'what problem does it solve?' and perhaps even more importantly: 'whose problem does it solve?' because a new solution to help the élite might actually form a new problem for the rest. We are just beginning to assess the potential of the information age, and also to come to terms with the difficult issues it presents – global markets closing down industries in one area as products are imported from abroad, homogenisation of the built environment due to internationally marketed products and services, and the threat to cities as the apparent need for commercial centres decreases. These are the signs of an enormous shift in the way the world operates and it would be impossible at this point to predict exactly how all these changes will impact on the future built environment.[8]

It is certain, however, that to keep abreast of the situation we must monitor change and gain as much information as we can in order to make good decisions. An increasingly crucial issue in the decisions made about building architecture is how its performance is appraised. The UK government has introduced a range of initiatives that focus on the attempt to improve the delivery of buildings. Unfortunately, many of these initiatives have been criticised from all sides of the industry for their focus on 'value for money' considerations rather than quality, and it has proven especially hard to determine methods to evaluate design quality. The 'Private Finance Initiative', 'Rethinking Construction' and the 'Key Performance Indicators' devised by Movement for Innovation focus on measurable construction processes such as materials selection and programming implications, though even those who have initiated these programmes are concerned that they may simply become another tier of bureaucratic control.[9] As well as these industry-wide initiatives there are more dedicated tools that are probably of more immediate quantifiable value. New design techniques are now available that enable engineers and architects to accurately predict energy and material use for a proposed building and to consequently adjust the balance between manufacturing costs and running costs, in both financial terms but also, more importantly, in terms of the total energy used and pollution saved over its predicted life.[10]

The decisions to be made are complex. In evaluating the potential for a portable building solution, it can be calculated that the proposal will save on materials and labour transportation costs as it is made close to the source of these items – but then it will have to be transported to its place of use. It may use less total material in construction if steel is adopted for a light, minimal structural frame – but steel is ten times less energy efficient to manufacture than brick. However, steel can be more easily made from recycled materials! When reliable appraisal techniques are developed, despite the risk of adding further complexity to our already burdensome legislation system, it is hard to see how they will be implemented without the support and involvement of national and international governments. Though some commercial organisations actively seek more efficient and more sustainable building solutions, voluntary adherence to such a design philosophy will not lead to a radical rethink throughout the entire construction industry where competitive pressures are generally paramount.

Despite these complexities, it is not unrealistic to speculate that a changing, newly mobilised social and commercial environment will require buildings that are as flexible and adaptable as the changing situation, and it is interesting to see that as these changes make themselves felt new examples of mobile architecture are being made – increasingly in situations where there are other options besides a portable one. Where previously the typical response to the need for a transient function would be to build a temporary structure which would be demolished after its period of use was over, with all the attendant waste of energy and materials, there are now more and more examples of enlightened clients commissioning portable buildings which have a life after their initial use, sometimes in quite diverse locations and occasionally for quite different purposes.

Some of these new buildings make use of traditional formal patterns such as the

191a

191a Mobility with connectivity - advertisement for LG products mobile phone connection to household appliances

192

193

tent and the dome with lightweight frames and membrane skins. The Radha Soamy Satsang Beas (RSSB) shelter is a demountable tent structure remarkable not for any specific technological advances used in its construction but, rather like Paxton's Crystal Palace, for the logistical systems that have made it possible – in this case to allow repeated seasonal deployment of a vast structure by an army of untrained helpers. The RSSB is a religious organisation that has annual gatherings of up to 25,000 people at its centre in Bedfordshire, England. Engineers Buro Happold were commissioned to design a temporary shelter that could be reerected for this event each summer. It was important that this was a portable structure because, not only would it be far more economical to create a building that would not be redundant for the rest of the year, but also there would be no permanent impact on its rural location. The building consists of a membrane enclosed space of 20,000 square metres. Its roof is supported primarily on triangulated columns, with a column-free central space provided by a tensegrity structure that incorporates a central elevated compression member. Once complete, all rainwater is directed away from the 8 metre high apex to the perimeter. No special expertise or equipment is required for erection of the building, which takes just three days, and all the components can be disassembled for transportation and storage.[11]

194

192 The RSSB shelter designed by engineers Buro Happold; 193 Erection of the RSSB shelter is carried out each summer entirely by members of the religious community who will use it;
194, 195 The AT&T Global Olympic Pavilion, designed by FTL Happold, being erected in Atlanta, USA. The pavilion provided a focus for the entertainment events during the 1996 games

195

The AT&T Global Olympic Village designed by FTL Happold for first use at the 1996 Olympic games in Atlanta is also a tented building but is very different in both form and use. The Global Olympic Village was a multi-purpose commercial building containing meeting areas, restaurants, and a public international communications facility that allowed athletes and visitors to phone, fax and e-mail home. At the Olympics it was also the backdrop to a stage that would entertain up to 100,000 people each night, though reaching a far greater 'global' audience through world-wide television broadcasts. The 25 metre high building was also designed to be reutilised in a range of different public relations functions on other sites once the two week Olympic event was over.

The building consists of two shell-like pavilions that face end to end with the stage in between. Each shell is made from five prefabricated steel portal frames which are assembled on the ground and erected by crane. Cables brace the frames longitudinally prior to a series of inter-linked membranes being tensioned above and between them. The facility is completed to a high specification with two storey high rigid demountable walls, stairs and even a relocatable lift to reach the upper floor. The building and its environs also featured a large kit of parts that delivered the 'look of the games', flags, lighting, signs etc., structured primarily with standard rented components such as scaffolding. The translucent membrane skin of the building became a remarkable entertainment feature at night when images from the games and live concerts were projected onto it, the distortions generated by the curved surfaces being adjusted by a computer-controlled projector so that they appeared visually correct to the audience.

Perhaps the ultimate reinvention of a traditional portable form is the giant 'teepee' designed by Philippe Chaix of Jean-Paul Morel and Partners initially for

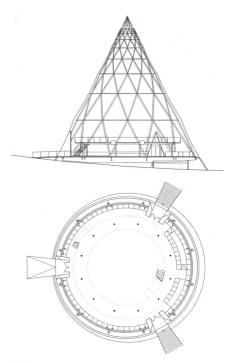

196

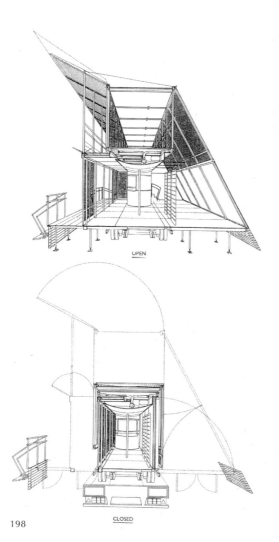

197

196 'Teepee' section and plan; 197 'Teepee' temporary exhibition tent designed by Philippe Chaix, Jean-Paul Morel and Partners, being erected in the courtyard of the Grand Palais, Paris; 198 The Trustee Savings Bank (TSB) mobile bank and hospitality pavilion designed by Apicella Associates

198

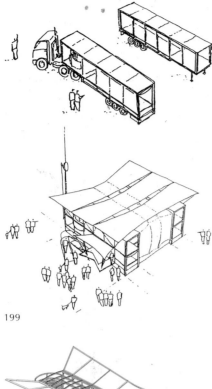

199

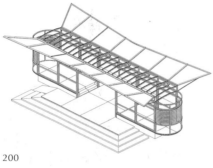

200

201

199 The Hong Kong Tourist Association building utilises two vehicle trailers and a componentised connecting floor and roof system; **200** One version of the Volvo Car Mobile Marketing Unit which is part of a family of similar facilities that can operate together or separately; **201, 202** The ECO LAB mobile classroom designed by Jennifer Siegal, Office for Mobile Design, Los Angeles. Interior fittings unfold into a learning route that weaves in and out of the building

the Grand Palais in Paris but since reused several times at the Bibliothèque de France and the Georges Pompidou Centre. The building's primary function is as a reception and information centre, though this remarkable 30 metre high translucent cone, usually erected on a sensitive historic site, obviously fulfils another important role as a highly visual sign for the event it supports. The building structure consists of a prefabricated steel base upon which rest twelve triangulated, steel frames that diminish in size towards the peak. Like the traditional teepee the membrane is non-load bearing and is simply dropped over the top of the cone by a crane before being tensioned by adjustable domed plates positioned at each of the frames' triangular nodes. The building is most impressive at night when the steel structure shows through the skin, bringing added articulation to the platonic form.[12]

Another familiar strategy for relocatable structures is the use of wheeled platforms. The articulated lorry trailer-based mobile 'building' facility has now become a common object. Often designed and built by specialist coach building firms, they incorporate many ingenious, high quality design features. Such facilities have many uses as exhibition spaces, catering facilities, shops, offices, etc. One of the most glamorous is the hospitality and relaxation trailers for the stars of mobile events such as Grand Prix motor races and pop music. However, the vast majority of these facilities are not greatly separated from their roots in vehicle design. London-based architect Lorenzo Apicella has gained considerable expertise designing wheeled commercial facilities and has specifically set out to break down the boundary between vehicle and building, taking advantage of the ease of transport that a conventionally sized trailer brings, though extending beyond its limitations to create distinctive, high quality, modern architectural statements.

Apicella's projects for the TSB bank, the Hong Kong Tourist Association (HKTA) and Volvo UK utilise the standard steel trailer platform as a base and, although this foundation is recognisable as a vehicle in transit, once the facility arrives at its site it is transformed into a completely different object. Typically, the wheeled base is hidden with removable skirts, entrance stairs and ramps. Walls fold out and floors fold down to create new spaces that extend from the limited width and length necessary for easy transportation. Extra floors and roofs extend upwards, in the case of the TSB using hydraulic power. The HKTA pavilion utilises two trailers positioned some distance from each other with a separate floor and membrane roof between that creates a whole new double-height atrium space. In the case of the Volvo project, rather than a single unit, the intention was to create a family of buildings that could be used independently but could also be brought together for larger events. Though these facilities are intended to travel to many different events each year (up to 250 separate deployments in the case of the Volvo project), once erected, the image they convey is not of a recently arrived and soon to depart vehicle, but of a high quality building somehow magically erected in a few hours.

Los Angeles based architect Jennifer Siegal also focuses on wheel-based mobile architecture, and although, like Apicella, she utilises building-like components and construction techniques, the result is much more craft-orientated with simple, affordable materials such as timber, plastic sheet, and wire mesh, composed into an artistic aesthetic that is simultaneously distinctly architectural. The ECO LAB is a mobile classroom used to communicate environmental issues to school children in the Hollywood area of Los Angeles. Built on a standard 10 metre long cargo trailer with recycled and donated materials, the structure is designed for ease of transportation and deployment. On arrival at the site, stairways, platforms and ramps unfold from the main volume creating an 'in and out' route that the children follow, on the way taking part in a range of activities and experiences before gathering inside a sun-dappled, woven wooden discussion space. The Portable Construction Training Centre (PCTC) is also an educational facility, although this time it is for adults. It has been conceived by the Venice Community Housing Corporation to provide construction training for disadvantaged and low-income people who, after training, support the development and maintenance of affordable housing. Built on a 20 metre long trailer, the structure contains workshops for plastering, painting, plumbing, carpentry and electrics plus a 4.5 metre square meeting and display area. When the facility arrives at its site, woodworking power tools roll out from the end of the structure, and one entire side unfolds to provide a 'porch' that allows access to each workshop zone. The informal, flexible nature of the PCTC is a symbol for the alternative, self-help approach to housing provision the Venice Corporation promotes.[13]

In a similar way to wheeled 'buildings', floating facilities are usually designed and built by shipyards and therefore primarily refer to the image of the boat. However, like the 'Teatro del Monde' by Aldo Rossi (see Chapter VI), the Japanese architect Fumihiko Maki completely abandoned the conventional image of the boat in designing a stage to be used in the city of Groningen in the Netherlands. The intention was to create a floating theatre that could be towed to different locations around the city via its ancient canal network which is still in commercial use. The structure consists of a 25 by 6 metre concrete raft that contains toilets and the normal back of house activities (in this case below the water line!) such as dressing rooms and props/costume stores. The roof of the raft forms the stage which is surmounted by a spiralling, membrane clad, steel frame inspired by ideas of movement, dreams and surprise. On either side of the stage is a row of 2.5 metre high, profiled, perforated steel forms that can either be used as seats for an intimate performance with a small audience, or, when folded down, enable a large crowd positioned on the bank to view the stage.[14]

Portable buildings that have utilised familiar or traditional formal strategies often make use of new materials and constructional strategies to great effect. However, new technology is also creating new architectural possibilities. Structures that incorporate pneumatics and air-support, ultra-lightweight tensegrity systems, and kinetic elements are making possible completely new constructional strategies resulting in new architectural forms. Building systems are also changing. The first intelligent building components are here now but the potential for future development is enormous.

Computer-controlled intelligent sub-systems in buildings can be programmed to respond to the users' needs and to external changes in climate, fire control, security, communication systems and even to react to geological disturbance. These semi-automatic response mechanisms are seen as marketing features in

202

203

204

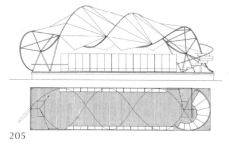

205

203, **204** The Portable Construction Training Centre (PCTC) designed for the Venice Community Housing Corporation, Los Angeles; **205**, **206** The Floating Pavilion designed by Fumihiko Maki for the city of Groningen in the Netherlands. The building can be used as a music stage, event space or for more formal theatrical events. The double-helical canopy is intended to evoke the ephemeral presence of a cloud

206

147

207

208

209

210

207, 208, 209 Festo's Airtecture hall, erected in Esslingen, Germany; **210** Variomatic internet house project created by Oosterhuis.nl

contemporary buildings and because of advances in design and competition they need to be upgraded and improved on a regular basis – for this reason they can be seen as independent systems. Intelligent materials are something different. The typical method for developing the new range of intelligent materials which will become available to the building industry over the next few decades is by the creation of composite materials – different elements (which may even have been altered at a sub-atomic level) matched together to complement each other's characterics thereby creating new and unprecedented levels of passive performance, or even active response to the changing physical conditions in which they are used. One current example is photo-reactive glass which changes opacity dependent on the level of light. A future development could be the 'living' façade that emulates the seasonal changes found in nature, 'growing' shading in summer and insulation in winter. Another aspect of intelligent materials is the potential for integrating sensory components into the fabric of a building, leading to the speculation that some day it may become unethical to build a building that does not automatically protect, or at least warn, its occupants of impending failure.[15]

One of the major research trends of robotics designers has been the search to create autonomous intelligence. This has many useful aspects for mechanical, task-orientated machines, particularly where that task must be completed in remote or dangerous situations such as exploring a planet surface which radio signals may take hours or days to reach, or searching for survivors in post-disaster scenarios. Autonomous intelligence is more than computing the correct response to a specific situation; it is about learning from the situation and altering future responses to take account of this. Simple robots are already used in the maintenance of buildings for repetitive tasks such as window cleaning. It is not difficult to surmise how such robots could not only be used to carry out the most dangerous or unpleasant construction tasks, but also to dismantle, erect and deploy building systems or to learn about a remote location from telemetric sensors in order to navigate to that location and prepare it for human habitation. In a range of ways, from simple subtle unnoticed environmental control monitoring to physical alteration of actual occupied spaces, it is becoming possible to design buildings that will be able automatically to take care of their occupants. Buildings that wake up to your presence and respond to your needs are here now; ones that follow you around and deploy for use when required are possibly not that far away.

In technological terms, perhaps the most interesting portable building so far built is Festo KG's 'Airtecture' hall, first erected at Esslingen in Germany. Festo is a multi-national, high-tech manufacturing company specialising in the hydraulic and pneumatic systems that are used in industrial robot design. Their corporate design division is headed by Axel Thallemer, who has the task of creating innovative new applications that build on their core area of expertise. Amongst his prototype products have been a micro-light flying wing, an inflatable balloon basket, and a hyper-efficient pump without moving parts. The company's most impressive new product is the 'Airtecture' exhibition and meeting hall, an air-supported building built purely for experimental purposes to test out a range of innovative concepts.

The main structure of the building consists of several inflatable, high pressure Hypalon elastomer coated, polyamide fabric elements – a 'Y' shaped column, roof beams, and flat wall panels. The walls are particularly interesting – 200 mm thick, flat, skinned, inflated elements interconnected by 72,000 threads per square metre that utilise technology developed from carpet manufacture. The opaque structural parts of the building are connected together by flexible translucent sections which not only allow natural light to enter but accommodate marginal movements between the different structural components. Although high pressure inflated buildings have been built before, they have been passive structures – the 'Airtecture' hall is different in that the whole structure of the building is operating under constantly changing levels of stress manipulated by varying air pressure. The tension cables that keep the building rigid are connected to pneumatic muscles, long pressurised tubes which can be continuously flexed or released. The structure is 'operated' automatically by a computer which gauges the pressure being exerted at any given moment by the wind, rain or snow loads and then stresses the structure to resist it. The current state of the building's structure can be monitored from anywhere in the world via its dedicated web site. Catastrophic failure, a common problem with high pressure inflatables that must usually be constantly topped up by air pumps, is not an issue in this case. In an experiment, all the monitoring and air pressure systems were turned off and by the end of a week the building had begun to sag ... a bit.

The 'Airtecture' hall is a complex experimental test bed for materials, structures and control systems and is the first attempt to make an entirely self-monitored and self-controlled active building structure – in essence, 'fly-by-wire' architecture. If relocated it can be shipped in its entirety in a single ISO container for assembly of the main elements in four days. Originally built to tour as an exhibition building, the 'Airtecture' hall has instead found a role at Festo's headquarters as a meeting space, exhibition hall, and permanent exhibit of the company's technical prowess. A second, simpler version of the building has been built for touring and was commissioned at Expo 2000 in Hanover. Lessons learnt from the experimental 'Airtecture' hall are now finding their way back into static architectural design as they have been used to develop a new translucent air-supported roof structure for the company's new building under construction in 2001.

211

The latest portable building from Festo is called the Airquarium. Air-supported structures are the most common form of pneumatic building but Airquarium sets new standards in performance, environmental awareness and portability. The building consists of an 8 metre high and 32 metre span membrane dome utilising a new material, Vitroflex, which is not only more translucent than any other that is capable of such large spans but also breaks down into a non-toxic vapour of water and vinegar in the case of fire. The foundation for the dome is a water-filled membrane in the shape of a torus that encircles its perimeter. The entire structure is transported in two standard 6 metre long containers, one holding the building's membrane, the other holding the foundation ring, air-lock entrance tunnel, and all the equipment for erection as well as air-conditioning plant, electrical supply, fuel and supplies for 48 hours' independent operation.

Where might the development of such intelligent, active-structure construction lead? In terms of portable buildings it could be to an architecture that is more easily deployable, more lightweight, more economical in materials, more adaptable to different users. In terms of static buildings, it is likely that the technology will be less visible and yet paradoxically have a much greater impact on the building's performance and efficiency. Take the example of the skyscraper – a building structure designed primarily to withstand the peculiar environmental pressures exerted on tall buildings by wind load. An intelligent, active building system that tenses and strains to withstand pressures where and when they occur will result in a much lighter structure, saving frame materials and foundations.[16]

212

The new relevance of mobile architecture is exhibited by the fact that the exploratory designs described here are not just ideas but have been built. Up until recently, the concept of investing large sums of money into the creation of a building without it being attached to a specific site was extremely rare. Buildings are investments and have been traditionally seen as something fixed against which their success can be gauged in capital returns. The traditional portable building was always seen by those who built and used it as something quite different, the land upon which it rested could not be owned and therefore the building was seen for the value it afforded in its own right. Portable buildings are investments, but the value they have is in the ability to enable activities to be carried out more effectively, more efficiently, more economically and more profitably. Sometimes it is the only way in which the activities can be accomplished at all. The success of contemporary portable architecture parallels the rise of the service industry, which is increasingly challenging manufacturing's traditional commercial dominance. In a world that is coming to terms with e-shops that have no physical shop front, libraries that exist within a computer hard disk, and meetings which take place without meeting rooms via web cams and ISDN links, the concept that a building may have no site is not that difficult to appreciate. Can the building do the job? If the answer is yes ... let's build it.[17] The responsive, adaptable nature of the portable building is synonymous with the rapidly changing environment of the virtual world that is dominant in the information age. The virtual environment we see through our computer screens (and increasingly in gaming, on television and at the cinema) challenges the physical world to keep up. In fact, some believe that the virtual

213

211 Airquarium multi-function, air-supported, mobile building; **212** Airquarium interior during inflation process; **213** A mobile dwelling can still be a significant place and form a permanent memory

149

world has now become the 'real' world because it is one that can be fully controlled – not only by the few who are specially trained but, because interfaces are designed to be so user-friendly, by everyone. Companies have been set up specifically to make it possible to design a house without any specialist experience, from those created around a kit of parts which use familiar domestic wall/roof/door/window elements like the US based Acorn house, to the more intuitive space/material/colour Variomatic housing system developed by *Oosterhuis.nl*.[18] These processes are the beginning of a new design opportunity for millions of non-professionals who will now be able to design their own home. Will these people, drawn by a personal desire to create their own environment, have the same conservative attitude to design as the commercial volume house builders whose preoccupation is not to find the best architectural solution but the one most likely to be inoffensive to a mass market? That remains to be seen, but it is certain that as long as we are confident that we are in control of our own destiny, human beings have a natural propensity to explore. Without this characteristic, civilisation would stagnate.

The concept that portable architecture is a viable mainstream alternative, is not just increasing in popularity, is because the industry's prejudices are being set aside. It is also because, this form of architecture appears to address newly recognised environmental issues such as ecological awareness and sustainability. Portable buildings can be comparatively low-impact in operation compared to permanent buildings. Because they are transported they need to be lightweight – using less materials for a given enclosure. They are also responsive to changing situations ensuring continued use in a fluctuating commercial environment. They can be built to leave sensitive sites unmarked by their transient presence (though as discussed earlier, transportation costs, both financial and environmental, must be offset against this). In all these ways they can be seen as experimental prototypes for more permanent structures. As they draw inspiration and influence from other related industries – primarily aviation, maritime and land transport – permanent construction techniques can, in turn, be inspired by newly developed portable systems.

Portable buildings are a link with the way we once were, nomads who used the earth as a resource in a sensitive manner, allowing the land to renew itself when we moved on. It would appear that mobile architecture may now be a sign of the way we want to be – more aware of the effect our activities have on the natural environment and more flexible in the way we operate in the world. To build is perhaps the most significant way in which human beings manipulate their environment. It is the way in which we define our existence.[19] Buildings define the places we make and form the setting for the events that make up our lives. Portable architecture, though it may not be located at a particular geographical place, does retain a particular place in our memories that is as permanent and meaningful as any other. It is a potent example of the way in which we are able to approach the creation of architectural space – space that is shaped by the application of innovative technology to not only keep pace with the changing world, but to provide for the newly emerging, flexible activities that are its focus.

Footnotes

PAGE 1

1 From 'Designing a New Industry', 1948 in *The Buckminster Fuller Reader*, James Meller (ed), (London) 1970, p209.

2 From the Talking Heads' song 'Houses in Motion', © Index Music, Inc/ Bleu Disque Music Co, Inc/EG Music Ltd.

CHAPTER I

1 Bernard Rudofsky, *Architecture Without Architects*, New York, 1965, from the preface.

2 In Sir Banister Fletcher, *A History of Architecture on the Comparative Method*, 16th Edition, London, 1954, p1, there was at least some mention of the antecedents of modern architecture: 'Hunters and fishermen in primeval times naturally sought shelter in rock caves and these were manifestly the earliest form of human dwellings: tillers of the soil took cover under the arbours of trees, and from them fashioned huts of wattle and daub: coverings of skins which only had to be raised on posts to form tents', even though this is chronologically inaccurate (nomadic hunter-gatherers with their access to animal hides emerged as the first recognisable humans). This was removed from later editions by subsequent editors.

3 For a detailed description of the finds at Olduvai Gorge see MD Leakey, *Olduvai Gorge: Vol 3, Excavation in Beds I and II 1960–63*, Cambridge, 1971. For a summary see *Past Worlds: The Times Atlas of Archaeology* (London) 1988, p56.

4 Ibid, p58.

5 '... only here is found working areas, shelters, and wooden tools found in a sufficiently well-preserved state to offer a rare glimpse into the details of early hominid life.' Ibid, p63.

6 Ibid, p30.

7 Ibid, p51.

8 See TO Dillehey, 'A Late Ice Age Settlement in Southern Chile', *Scientific American*, 251.4, 1984, pp106–13.

9 *Times Past*, p73.

10 Ibid, p32.

11 William Zuk and Roger H Clark draw attention to the relationship between adaptability and survival outlined by the naturalist Charles Darwin: 'Charles Darwin has suggested that the problem of survival always depends upon the capability of an object to adapt in a changing environment. This theory holds true for architecture.' William Zuk and Roger H Clark, *Kinetic Architecture* (New York) 1970, p4.

12 Ibid.

13 Torvald Faegre, in the introduction to his book, *Tents: Architecture of the Nomads* (London) 1979, p1, states: 'The tents of the nomads provide a unique look into the origins of human shelter and its subsequent evolution, since nomads occupy the marginal areas of the world, they have been less subject to change than many settled peoples; because of their ability to move they have remained a free people.'

14 Paul Oliver (ed), *Shelter in Africa* (London) 1971, p22.

15 Barry Biermann, 'Indlu: The Domed Dwelling of the Zulu', in Oliver, *Shelter in Africa*, p96.

16 Enrico Guidoni, *Primitive Architecture*, History of World Architecture series (London) 1987, p7.

17 It might be observed that the boat house is linked so closely with the water that it is not architecture; however, its specific role in relation to this study is as a dwelling or a function that supports the inhabitants of associated dwellings, so that as a group they may take on more the function of building than transport. The peculiar nature of water-based dwellings has been frequently referred to; for example, the Canton water roads have been described as: 'nothing less than a floating city'. See GAG Worcester, *Sail and Sweep in China* (London) 1966, p66.

18 This is borne out by some of the Earth Lodge patterns which appear to have developed from a structure related to that of the tipi. Ibid, p19.

19 Faegre, *Tents*, p153. Note: the tipi is often referred to as a tent; however, as its built pattern is that of a framework clad with a skin which has no structural element in its design, as a structural system it is more comparable with the yurt.

20 Ibid, p152.

21 Ibid, p153.

22 Ibid, p152.

23 Fritz Morgenthaler, 'Reflex-Modernization in Tribal Societies', in Paul Oliver, *Shelter, Sign and Symbol* (London) 1975, p152. Morgenthaler describes instances were nomads who have been settled in towns with permanent houses still erect a tent in their yard area in which to welcome guests.

24 Guidoni, p40.

25 Paul Verity, 'Kababish Nomads of Northern Sudan', in Oliver, *Shelter in Africa*, p34.

26 Faegre, p15.

27 Ibid.

28 *Shelter*, p13.

29 Ibid, p18.

30 For an excellent description of the Tekna tent see Peter Alford Andrews, 'Tents of the Tekna, Southwest Morocco', in Oliver, *Shelter in Africa*, pp124–36.

31 For a detailed study of the Tuareg see Johannes Nicolaisen, *Ecology and Culture of the Pastoral Tuareg* (Copenhagen) 1963. For a summary see *Shelter*, p12.

32 Faegre, p1.

33 Ibid, p62. As the tent preceded the masonry hut, the earliest model must therefore be the tent.

34 Guidoni, p39.

35 *Times Past*, p182. For a more complete description of the early nomads of the Steppe see M Zuelebil, 'The Rise of the Nomads in Central Asia', in AG Sherret (ed), *Cambridge Encyclopaedia of Archaeology*, pp252–56.

36 *Shelter*, p16.

37 Faegre, p90.

38 The reluctance of the Mongols to relinquish their traditional building type is shown by this example retold by Torvald Faegre: 'When Czarist Russia attempted to control nomads they built small castles for the tribal Khans to induce them to settle, they put cattle in the buildings and pitched their yurts nearby.' Ibid, p79.

39 Biermann, 'Indlu', p100.

40 Rudofsky, no page number.

41 Rudofsky, no page number. Rudofsky is here describing the houseboats in Shanghai's Soochow Creek.

42 The Canton Roads as described by GAG Worcester, p66.

43 Ronald Lewcock and Gerard Brans, 'The Boat as an Architectural Symbol', in Oliver, *Shelter, Sign and Symbol*, p107.

44 As quoted in Harry Hanson, *The Canal Boatmen 1760–1914* (Manchester) 1975, p125.

45 AL Stevenson, *An Inland Voyage*, 1919, p76. He also notes: 'There should be many contented spirits on board, for such a life is both to travel and to stay at home', p10.

46 See WM Whiteman, *The History of the Caravan* (London) 1973, p13. The vehicle was destroyed by fire in 1955.

47 The word comes from the Persian *karwan*, meaning a group of merchants or pilgrims travelling together for security or company.

48 Tim Rayment, 'Totally Beyond the Pale', *The Independent*, 17 Oct 1993, pp18–19.

49 Hasan-Uddin Khan, 'Mobile Shelter in Pakistan', in Oliver, *Shelter, Sign and Symbol*, p93.

50 Ibid, p196.

51 Guidoni, p28.

52 They have even developed a technique where planks can be prepared without cutting down the tree so that it remains *in situ* after as much as half of its trunk has been utilised. Ibid. p116.

CHAPTER II

1 Oliver, *Shelter, Sign and Symbol*, p8.

2 Ibid, p8.

3 This was discovered by the Swiss engineer Professor Culmann in 1866 after a visit to the dissecting room of anatomist Herman Meyer. See Philip Drew, *Frei Otto* (London) 1976, p22.

4 Built in Jena, Germany in 1922 on the roof of the Carl Zeiss optical works. See Chapter IV.

5 Oliver, *Shelter, Sign and Symbol*, p36. Sir Hugh Casson in his introduction to David Hancocks' book, *Animals and Architecture* (London) 1971, p7, enthusiastically commends animal building: 'Let us freely admit that birds and animals are better at architecture than we are. For elegance and precision, for structural ingenuity and powers of improvisation they are unbeatable, making even the best human examples … seem comparatively clumsy or contrived.'

6 For a description of primate constructions see Hancocks, pp16–17.

7 Ibid, p18.

8 Leonardo da Vinci carried out extensive research into the method of flight achieved by birds and the structure of their wings which he published in 1505 in a small codex entitled *Flight of Birds* now in the Royal Library in Turin. See Marco Cianchi, *Leonardo's Machines*, Florence, nd, p13.

9 Peter Rice undertook a study of the structural principles of spiders' webs in collaboration with Dr Fritz Vollrath of the Department of Zoology at Oxford University. See Peter Rice, *Exploring Materials: The Work of Peter Rice*, catalogue to the exhibition at the RIBA, London, June 30 to 25 Aug, 1992, p23.

10 Le Corbusier, *Towards a New Architecture*, translated by Frederick Etchells, London, 1927, p86.

11 John Maxtone-Graham, Epilogue to *Olympic and Titanic*, a reprint of *The Shipbuilder*, Vol VI, Midsummer, 1911, p151. Maxtone-Graham describes the *Aquitania* as follows: 'Overall, the *Aquitania*'s superstructure appeared too large and burdensome for her hull, a state of imbalance that Carlisle's *Olympic* design avoided completely. [The *Aquitania* had a] … boxy somewhat clumsy look', p155. These subjective descriptions are remarkably similar to those used by architects when assessing the appearance of buildings.

12 The *Titanic*'s tragic maiden voyage was on 2 April 1912 – on Sunday 14 April at 11.40pm she struck an iceberg and was breached below the water line along her length, and subsequently sank at 2.00am the next morning. Of the 1,308 passengers and 898 crew, only 703 survived. The *Britannic* was never delivered to White Star but became a hospital ship during the First World War.

13 Maxtone-Graham, *Olympic and Titanic*, p108.

14 Ibid, p184.

15 For a detailed description of the Nimitz class aircraft carriers see Rojer Chesnau, *Aircraft Carriers to the World, 1914 to Present* (London) 1984, pp280–81.

16 Equinox, *Fly Navy*, Channel 4, Sun 17 Oct, 1993. A sailor on board *USS Theodore Roosevelt* said: 'You have to think of it as just a piece of movable real-estate.'

17 Leonardo eventually abandoned his work with ornithopters and began to examine fixed wing aircraft – if appropriate materials and a more powerful engine than man (who only produces about 300 watts of useful power) had been available, Leonardo's experiments could have stood a better chance of success. For an interesting study of Leonardo's studies in flight and related engineering areas see Cianchi, pp45–61.

18 Le Corbusier, *Towards a New Architecture*, p100.

19 As quoted in Drew, *Frei Otto*, p24.

20 The R101 was the Government built airship, the R100 was built and designed by private contractors to Government specifications. The former crashed with the loss of many lives on its maiden voyage. The latter made many successful flights all over the world. Airships are still built today, now using helium, a non-combustible gas, as the lifting element; however, the scale of the great 1930s machines has never been matched.

21 The *Hindenberg* was larger than most buildings of the day, 803 feet long by 146 feet wide. The buildings built to accommodate these airborne structures also had to respond to new structural and logistical issues that resulted in some cases in innovative solutions. See Chapter V.

22 A remarkable testimony for this phenomenon is Humphrey Jennings' collection of images and texts that span the years 1660 to 1886 and bind together a continuous thread of human thought during the development of the industrial age. See Humphrey Jennings, *Pandaemonium: The coming of the machine as seen by contemporary observers*, edited by Mary-Lou Jennings and Charles Madge (London) 1987.

CHAPTER III

1 Sir Banister Fletcher, *A History of Architecture*, revised by JC Palmes, 18th Edition, London, 1975.

2 This description is by the Bishop of Suzdal as quoted in Eugenio Battisti, *Brunelleschi, the Complete Works*, translated by Robert Erich Wolf (London) 1981, p301.

3 The first effective use of linear perspective in architectural work dates from 1468.

4 Vasari, as quoted in Nikolaus Pevsner, *A History of Building Types*, London, 1976, p65.

5 Aldo Rossi created a contemporary response to these sixteenth century floating pavilions for the 1979 Venice Biennale; see Chapter VI.

6 The author is grateful to Mrs Margaret Fitzgibbon for access to the research work into Henry Tudor's temporary banqueting houses by her late husband, Mr James Fitzgibbon, director of Synergetics Inc and a professor of architecture at Washington University, St Louis, Missouri, USA.

7 A definitive study of the circus building is Christian Dupavillon, *Architectures du Cirque*, Paris, 1982.

8 Ibid, p205.

9 Ibid, p207.

10 An early example is a tent made by John Bill Ricketts in Philadelphia, USA, in 1792. Ibid, p229.

11 The German company Stromeyer, which was established in the nineteenth century, is one of the most famous tent manufacturers. Peter Stromeyer collaborated with Frei Otto on research that led to the development of tension structures for permanent buildings. See Dr Frei Otto and Peter Stromeyer, 'Tents', *AIA Journal*, February 1961, pp77–86.

12 Gilbert Herbert, *Pioneers of Prefabrication: The British Contribution in the Nineteenth Century*, Baltimore, 1978, p25. Herbert's book is a thorough analysis of the early development of the prefabricated building type.

13 These buildings were 12 ft by 83 ft and were eventually shipped to Sydney, Australia in 1790. Wyatt said: 'I exhibited the movable hospitals to the King… by taking down one of the buildings and putting it up again in one hour, which gave general satisfaction.' Samuel Wyatt to Matthew Boulton, April 1788, Birmingham Assay Office as quoted in Herbert, *Pioneers*, p5.

14 Ibid, p9.

15 A quote taken from Geffrey Dutton, *Founder of a City* (London) 1960, p218.

16 This building was illustrated in *The Illustrated London News*, 7 Sept 1844, p156.

17 For a comprehensive summary of the Sears building phenomenon see Katherine Cole Stevenson and H Ward Jandl, *Houses by Mail: A Guide to Houses by Sears, Roebuck and Company* (Washington, DC) 1986.

18 Fletcher, p1123.

19 Colin Davies, *High Tech Architecture* (London) 1988, p15.

20 In 1833, William Fairbairn built the *Minerva* which was transported in parts from Manchester to Hull, and reconstructed to make the crossing to Rotterdam. It then steamed up the Rhine before being dismantled for transportation to its place of work on Lake Zurich. For more details of this and other early prefabricated steamships see Herbert, *Pioneers*, p31.

21 Martin Pawley, *Theory and Design in the Second Machine Age* (Oxford) 1990, p72. The house is described fully in D Dex Harrison, 'An Outline of Prefabrication', in John Madge (ed), *Tomorrow's Houses*, 1946.

22 Innovation took place in North America as well. In 1848, James Bogardus built a five storey cast iron factory. He later wrote the influential book *Cast Iron Buildings: their Construction and Advantages* (New York) 1856.

23 Ibid, p72. See also Pevsner, *A History of Building Types*, p241.

24 As quoted in Pevsner, *A History of Building Types*, p241.

25 Turner tendered for a structure designed by Burton, four times the weight of the one he eventually built. It was Turner, the manufacturer, who introduced all the innovations utilised in its construction. See Pawley, *Theory and Design*, p75.

26 The continuous pneumatic bubble, as observed in soap bubble models, forms the most economical natural structural shape. See Chapter IV.

27 Pevsner, *A History of Building Types*, p244.

28 Pawley, *Theory and Design*, p74.

29 Fletcher, p1l31.

30 Pevsner states that: 'In usable area the Sydenham building far surpassed the Original Crystal Palace.' *A History of Building Types*, p245. The original north wing of the building was destroyed by fire in 1866 and in 1936 the whole building was burnt down. At the time, molten glass ran in the gutters and is still to be found in fist-sized chunks on the site. See John Windsor, 'Relics of a Lost Theme Park', *The Independent*, 16 Oct 1993, p32.

31 Martin Pawley, 'PS', *RIBA Journal*, April 1991, p97.

32 Ibid.

CHAPTER IV

1 Pawley, 'PS', p97.

2 Reyner Banham, *Theory and Design in the First Machine Age* (London) 1960, p329.

3 Sant 'Elia, *Citta Nuova*, 1913, as quoted in B Appleyard, *Richard Rogers* (London) 1986, p179.

4 Pawley, *Theory and Design*, p28. This quote refers to 'architectural thinkers', a dig at Pawley's fellow critics but it can equally apply to their protégés.

5 Reyner Banham draws attention to an anonymous writer in the *Architectural Review* of July 1905 who stated: 'if we could only think of our building as an entirely modern problem without precedent.' See Banham, *Theory and Design*, p47.

6 WR Lethaby, 'The Architecture of Adventure', lecture at the RIBA, London, 1910. See WR Lethaby, *Architecture*, London, 1911. If it were not made two years earlier this could almost be a reply to Sant 'Elia's quote regarding Citta Nuova!

7 'Be it resolved that the American Institute of Architects establishes itself on record as inherently opposed to any such peas-in-the-pod-like reproducible designs' was included in the minutes of the meeting that discussed the issue. As quoted in Pawley, *Buckminster Fuller*, p30.

8 Davies, *High Tech Architecture*, pp16–17.

9 Buckminster Fuller, 'Influences on My Work', *The Buckminster Fuller Reader*, edited by James Meller (London) 1970, p44.

10 This was a proprietary building block made from compressed material manufactured by a family company directed by Fuller.

11 Fuller's daughter died at an early age, and he put this down to the limited circumstances in which he could afford to house his family at the time.

12 Fuller created concepts for various Dymaxion products including the Dymaxion Car which was produced with yacht designer Stirling Burgess whom he met in a New York hotel in August 1932. Burgess went on to work on the mast based, ten-storey, Dymaxion dwelling. See Martin Pawley, *Buckminster Fuller* (London) 1990, p52.

13 Buckminster Fuller, *The Buckminster Fuller Reader*, edited by James Meller, p30.

14 Buckminster Fuller, 'Designing a New Industry', ibid, p169. This and the subsequent quotes are from a talk given to the new engineers who had recently joined the production engineering activities at Beechcraft in Wichita, Kansas, 26 Jan, 1946. All the new employees had come from leading US aircraft companies. Fuller obviously believed his conception of a 'house' to far exceed the demands previously made on it and therefore perhaps he considered the term outdated.

15 Ibid.

16 Ibid, p148.

17 There were other factory-made dwellings under development in the USA at this time, for example the Lustron House which is examined in Chapter VI.

18 Buckminster Fuller, in Meller, p83.

19 The great circle principle is defined by the line resulting from the intersection of a plane through a sphere; such a line will form a circle which is the shortest distance between two points on the sphere's surface. A geodesic is the shortest line between two points on a mathematically derived surface.

20 See 'The Wonder of Jena', in *Shelter*, 1973, pp110–11. See Chapter II for the 1930s work of Barnes Wallis, the British engineer who designed the geodetic framework for the R100 airship and the Wellington bomber.

21 Peter Cook, *Experimental Architecture*, London, 1970, p63. This aptly mirrors Fuller's own axiom 'More for Less' borrowed from the Bauhaus, 'Less is More'. Pawley, *Buckminster Fuller*, p122.

22 Buckminster Fuller, 'Continuous Man', in Meller, p335.

23 The other was Frei Otto's cable-net structure German pavilion. 'Expo '67 Special Issue', *The Architectural Review*, no 846, Aug 1967, p126.

24 Pawley, *Buckminster Fuller*, p14.

25 Ibid, p174.

26 Buckminster Fuller, 'Earth Inc', 1947, in Meller, p231.

27 One indication of the respect they gained from the architectural establishment is their award of the RIBA Gold Medal in 1979.

28 Ibid.

29 Derek Walker, 'Eames House, Pacific Palisades, 1949, Charles and Ray Eames', *Architectural Design*, Profile 'Los Angeles', 1981, p76.

30 Ian McCallum in a section on the work of Charles and Ray Eames. The full reference reads: 'Though emphasis may shift between film-making … and toy-making, between new ideas in audio-visual education and new ways of supporting the human frame, the Eames' refuse to dissociate any of these activities from that of architecture, and we can expect their work to continue as an embodiment of the belief … etc.', *Architecture USA* (London) 1959, p127.

31 The house first appeared in a different form to that completed in the March 1948 issue of *Art and Architecture*.

32 Michael Brawne, 'The Wit of Technology', *Architectural Design*, Sept, 1966, p449.

33 Ibid, p457.

34 Ibid.

35 Ibid.

36 Buckminster Fuller in Meller, p154. Peter Cook assessed their respective roles succinctly as: 'the operator and the Guru'. Peter Cook, *Experimental Architecture*, p81.

37 As quoted by McCallum, p127.

38 Faegre, p1.

39 Frei Otto and Peter Stromeyer, 'Tents', *AIA Journal*, 1961, 2, p81.

40 Frei Otto, 'Das Hangende Dach', Doctoral Thesis, Berlin University of Technology, 1954.

41 Philip Drew, *Frei Otto: Form and Structure* (London) 1976, p17.

42 JM Richards, 'Expo '67', *The Architectural Review*, No 846, Aug 1967, p156.

43 As quoted in Robin Boyd, 'Germany', ibid. p135, a comprehensive critical appraisal of the German Pavilion at Expo '67.

44 Ibid, p130.

45 Ibid, p129.

46 The Munich Stadium is not discussed in detail in this study due to its permanent nature.

47 Ibid, p130 and p135, respectively.

48 Otto has produced numerous designs for demountable buildings though not on the same scale as at Montreal. For examples see open-air theatre roofs at Killesberg, Stuttgart, Germany, 1954, Heppenheim, Germany, 1964, Masque de Fer, Cannes, 1965, Bad Hersfeld, Germany 1967; swimming pool roots at Boulevard Carnot, Paris, 1966, Davos (Switzerland) 1966, Regensberg-West, 1970.

49 Philip Drew asserts that: 'the dissection of his work for stylistic influences – indeed the very notion of his work for style – is alien'. Drew, p6.

50 Ibid, p12.

51 Boyd, 'Germany', p135.

CHAPTER V

1 Herbert, *Pioneers of Prefabrication*, 1978, p76.

2 Appendix to a report by EA Parkes, Superintendent of the Hospital at Renkioi, addressed to the Secretary State for War, 1 Dec 1856, as quoted in Herbert, p87.

3 Keith Mallory and Arvid Ottar, *Architecture of Aggression* (London) 1973, p281.

4 GP Neumann states that: 'during the four years of war, beneath the pressure of dire necessity, more technical improvements were effected in airship design than would otherwise have been accomplished in ten years.' GP Neumann, *The German Airforce in the Great War*, London, 1921, this edition (London) 1969, p8.

5 Aircraft were not initially used in combat with other aircraft but in a ground attack role. Relocating the base of Zeppelins and heavier-than-air machines was an effective way of avoiding air raids from opposing forces.

6 Richthofen's squadron, Jagdstaffeln 1, was taken over by Oberleutnant Hermann Goring at the end of the First World War, who it can be surmised, recognised the advantage of mobility and implemented it when he became Air Minister in Nazi Germany.

7 'These War Buildings were Significant', *Engineering News-Record*, New York. 19 Oct, 1944, p111.

8 On the 16 Jan 1993, during the Gulf War, seven B-52 bombers flew non-stop from Louisiana, USA, to Iraq and back releasing 39 cruise missiles, the longest air combat mission in history. Giles Whittel, 'Bombers Away', *The Times Magazine*, 17 Sept 1994, p23.

9 The US Army are still seeking a solution to this problem and have defined their requirements as a 'large air-beam supported maintenance shelter … of modular design …' that has 'flame resistance, quick erection/strike capability, and low visible signature.' Stephen A Rei, *Projected Performance Characteristics for Large Quickly Erectable Maintenance Shelters*, US Army (Natick, Massachusetts) 1993, p30.

10 'Concrete vessels can perhaps be made to carry a complete heavy gun turret, and these, on the admission of water to their outer chambers, would sit on the sea floor … other sinkable structures could be made to contain store rooms, oil tanks, or living chambers.' Winston S Churchill, 'Their Finest Hour', *The Second World War*, Vol II (London) 1949, p216,

11 Eventually this type of fort was also deployed on Red Sands in the Thames estuary.

12 Ron Herron was inspired by the Army forts at Red Sands in the Thames estuary in the creation of his 'Walking City' project in 1965 (see Chapter IX).

13 Mallory and Ottar, *Architecture of Aggression*, p203. For a detailed description of the Mulberry harbours project see *The Civil Engineer in War: a symposium of papers on War-Time Engineering Problems*, Institute of Civil Engineers (London) 1948.

14 For example, a Chieftain Mark 5 tank weighs more than 54 tonnes.

15 The bridge is built by Thomson Defence Projects, a division of the Rolls Royce Industrial Rower Group. See Mike Winney, 'On Active Service', *New Civil Engineer*, 10 March 1994, pp20–21.

16 Loads are classified up to Load Class 60 capable of carrying a 63.5 tonne articulated lorry. A Land Rover is Load Class 4. For a clear explanation of the logistical and engineering issues associated with portable and demountable military bridging see the Royal Military College of Science publication IFB Tytler, NH Thompson, BE Jones, PJH Wormell, CES Riley, *Vehicles and Bridging* (London) 1985.

17 The importance of fine-tuning cultural and social requirements in the provision of temporary shelter is examined in detail in Chapter VIII.

18 Mallory and Ottar, p77.

19 Pawley, *Theory and Design in the Second Machine Age*, p78. Pawley also calls this: 'the first mass-produced complete building' though it is also possible to bestow this accolade on Manning's Portable Cottage of the 1830s.

20 As quoted in 'The Nissen Hut on the Western Front', *The Architects and Builders Journal*, 14 Feb 1917, p92.

21 Mallory and Ottar, p81.

22 'War-Time Buildings. The Stancon System', *The Architect and Building News*, 3 May 1940, p92. as quoted in Mallory and Ottar, p187.

23 *Survey of Buildings of Prefabricated, Expandable, Inflatable, or Chemically Rigidised Types Suitable for Military Use*, US Army, Aug 1968, p11.

24 As quoted by A Jackson in *The Politics of Architecture* (London) 1970, p164.

25 Buckminster Fuller, 'Chronofiles', 1966, *The Buckminster Fuller Reader*, edited by James Meller, p30. Buckminster Fuller, *Utopia or Oblivion* (London) 1970, p291.

CHAPTER VI

1 Le Corbusier, *L'Esprit Nouveau*, No 2, p211. As quoted in Reyner Banham, *Theory and Design in the First Machine Age* (London) 1960, p221.

2 Le Corbusier, *Towards a New Architecture*, translated by Frederick Etchells (London) 1927, this edition 1946, p210.

3 The venture tailed due to excessive start-up time, high production costs, and organisational problems with labour, local building codes and financing. See Konrad Wachsmann, *Turning Point of Building*, New York, 1960 and Gilbert Herbert, *The Dream of the Factory Made House: Walter Gropius and Konrad Wachsmann* (Cambridge, Massachusetts) 1984.

4 Strandlund had previously run a company making vitreous enamel panels used as cladding for petrol stations where an easily maintained inflammable surface was required.

5 Koch was responsible for the Acorn house (with Huson Jack and John Callender), a fully demountable building that was designed in 1945. The building was transported as a narrow unit containing the kitchen and bathroom but once it reached its destination, panels at the sides folded out to form living areas and bedrooms, The building could be erected by four workers in a single day, and demounted for transportation to an alternative site in the same time. It was, however, unsuccessful in obtaining funding and was therefore not manufactured in bulk. See H Ward Jandl, *Yesterday's House of Tomorrow* (Washington, DC) 1991, p203.

6 For a thorough history of the Lustron Company see Jandl, *Yesterday's House of Tomorrow*, pp183–99.

7 While the war was still in progress it had been predicted that production line buildings would be of use in the years to follow for peacetime housing. See Chapter VI.

8 Others were the ARCON, Uni-Seco, Tarran, Aluminium Bungalow. For a detailed description of post-war industrial housing in the UK see RB White, *Prefabrication*, National Building Joint Special Study Report 36 (London) 1965.

9 'Popularity equals permanency' appears to be the normal destiny for popular portable buildings, for example the Crystal Palace or more recently the Cardiff Bay Visitors' Centre (see Chapter VII).

10 Joseph Carreiro *et al*, *The New Building Block: A Report on the Factory-Produced Dwelling Module*, Cornell University, Ithaca (New York) 1968, p16.

11 Edgar Kaufmann Jr, 'Design, sans peur and sans ressources', *Architectural Forum*, Sept 1966. As quoted in Pawley, *Theory and Design in the Second Machine Age*, p124.

12 Robert T Ratay, 'Building Around a Building', *Civil Engineering*, April 1987. Vol 57, No 4, pp58–61.

13 JR Illingworth quotes an example where 62 per cent of the total cost was ascribed to the temporary structure required to manufacture the permanent one. *Temporary Works: Their Role in the Construction Industry* (London) 1987, p6.

14 Tadao Ando, 'Karaza Theatre', *Japan Architect*, April 1988, No 372, pp35–9. See also the Takashima-cho Gate Area, a 5,300 m^2 temporary building and entrance structure designed by architects Riken Yamamoto and Field Shop to be a series of 'Instantaneous art forms'. Riken Yamamoto, 'Takashima-cho Gate Area', *Japan Architect*, Aug 1989, No 388, pp64–7.

15 The total cost for the project built by Dick Corporation was $32.4 million of which $0.5 million was for the temporary air-supported structure. See Daniel J McConville, 'When Winter Comes: Coping With Cold Weather Construction', *The Construction Specifier*, Oct 1988, pp42–9.

16 A 300-bed 'portable' prison was built near Boston, USA including cells recreation and work facilities. The portable solution was selected to allow for fluctuation in prison population but also to allow the entire building to be relocated in a future development programme. See 'State gets into portable cells', *Engineering News Record*, 26 April 1990, Vol 224, p20.

17 Flat-pack buildings can save a remarkable amount of on-site work compared to conventional construction processes. The system developed by the Heidrich Corporation of Edinboro, Pennsylvania, USA, claims that the building is 90 per cent complete when it leaves the factory and that a crew of three can erect a 150 m^2 building in a single day. Prefabrication saves 25 per cent of material costs by reducing on-site material waste. See 'Prefab building unfolds at site', *Engineering News Record*, Vol 204, No 23, 5 June 1980, p32.

18 Domestic commercially available tents, whilst using interesting and effective structural patterns to obtain lightness and strength, are unsuitable for more complex functions than basic protection from hostile environmental conditions, and cannot be therefore considered as true portable architecture.

19 Cannobio of Milan is worthy of mention as a manufacturer which stresses the innovative aspects of its products, covering a range of tension structures, geodetic based skin structures and pneumatic structures. Its sales material reads: 'Cannobio has been engaged in a process of continuous design evolution since 1926. Today we are leaders in technologically advanced structural design'. Cannobio sales leaflet (Milan, Italy) nd, c1993.

20 In a lecture to a joint meeting of the British Group of the International Association for Bridge and Structural Engineering on 2 September 1993, Ian Liddell of Buro Happold engineers stated: 'Nature would invariably find out the air structure in which design was compromised and where proper erection techniques were skimped.' Peter Harris, 'Air-supported structures', *The Structural Engineer*, Vol 71, No 18, 21 Sept 1993, p2.

21 One example of the systems approach is the temporary training base comprising reception, conference and restaurant facilities made for Mercury Communications at Birmingham National Exhibition Centre in 1993. The main spaces structural system consisted of several linked geodesic domes which were then covered with a thin skin membrane. Module type sanitary and service facilities were incorporated into the layout which therefore used every type of portable building system except pneumatic. Helena Russell, 'Dome Base', *New Builder*, No 196, 19 Nov 1993, pp18–19.

22 A selection of relevant British Standards is listed in the Bibliography.

23 Portakabin is the only other company to have this certificate, not necessarily because it produces the only products that meet the standards, but because the cost of contracting for testing is £12,000.00.

24 One interesting example is RB Farquhar, who initially began building accommodation units for North Sea oil platforms. Initially made from timber, these were upgraded to steel as regulations became more strict. As the oil rig work has declined the company has searched for new markets where its expertise can be used and has recently completed a 125-bed hotel at Loughborough where complete bedroom/bathroom units are built into a conventional frame. John Rawson, 'Buying Buildings off the Shelf', *Architects' Journal*, Vol 198, No 9, 8 Sept 1993, pp25–7.

25 The Building Research Establishment has produced several BRE Digests which refer specifically to the construction of portable buildings but these are really aimed at the manufacturing industry and do not help the user to 'identify a particularly appropriate product for his needs. See the Bibliography for a selected list of current BRE Digests.

26 'Antarctic Survey rapped over budget overruns on research station and airstrip', *Building*, 8 April 1993, p6.

27 See 'Instant housing feeds Japanese needs', *New Civil Engineer*, 14 Oct 1993, pp32–3. Toyota are also involved in this revolution; see 'Toyota Goes on Sale: The Western-Style House As Cars', *Business Japan*, 31 May 1986, p18.

28 Allan D Wallis, *Wheel Estate* (New York) 1991, pv.

29 Arizona, North America is a Mecca to retired people because of its equitable climate in winter and relatively inexpensive living costs. The area between Mesa and Apache Junction is: 'one mobile home and trailer park after another. The winter population is estimated at 150,000–180,000 and the year round population at 70,000. This is in 65 square miles of parks, each averaging 40 acres; each acre accommodates ten to 12 parking spaces for mobile homes and around 15 to 18 spaces for travel trailers.' Esther McCoy, '17 Miles Between Mesa and Apache Junction', *Lotus International*, No 8, Sept 1974, p212.

30 It has been suggested that earlier descendants can be identified in the simple, quickly built timber buildings that the emigrant used to establish his new home throughout the new world (see JB Jackson, 'The Mobile Home and how it came to America', *Discovering the Vernacular Landscape*). However, it is hard to separate these buildings from the general pattern of timber housing in North America, from the balloon frame to the craftsman house. The Conestoga Wagon, a mass-produced object built with transportation in mind, has a more readily identifiable link.

31 David Neuman states: 'we have in the Conestoga wagon not only an example of the first long distance moving van in America but also primary examples of convertibility and cultural influence.' David J Neuman, 'The American Courtship of House and Car', *Popular Architecture*, edited by Marshall Fishwick and J Meredith Neil (Bowling Green, Ohio) 1974, p58.

32 Publicity brochure, Auto-Kamp Trailer Company (Saginaw, Michigan) nd, c1923, as quoted in Wallis, p36.

33 Wally Byam, *Automobile and Trailer Travel*, Vol 1 No 2, Feb 1936, p20, as quoted in Watts, p54.

34 See Charles Jencks, *Architecture 2000: predictions and methods* (New York) 1971, p58.

35 Corwin Wilison, 'Mobile House', *Architectural Record*, July 1936, pp64–5.

36 In 1974, the US Government sponsored a major research project into housing after disaster which concluded that for North America, the manufactured/mobile housing industry was still best placed to respond with new housing in such situations. Abeles, Schwartz Associates and Beyer-Blinder-Belle, *Cost Effective Housing Systems for Disaster Relief*, US Department of Housing and Urban Development, Sept 1974.

37 See Wallis, pp83–95 for a more detailed history of post-Second World War government use of the trailer for temporary housing.

38 Alison and Peter Smithson, *Ordinariness and Light* (Cambridge, Mass) 1970, p117.

39 Arthur D Bernhardt, *Building Tomorrow: The Mobile/Manufactured Building Industry*, MIT Press, 1980, as quoted in Grant Burn, *Affordable Housing*, Jefferson (N Carolina) 1989, p68.

40 Wallis, p254.

41 Bryan Irwin, David Pollak, Anne Tate, 'The P/A House', *Progressive Architecture*, August 1992, p45. 'As in the auto industry... the technology is sophisticated, but it is used to produce a schmaltzy product because these companies think that is what people want.' Bryan Irwin

of Abacus Architects as quoted in Thomas Fisher, 'Industrialized Housing: Changing a Commodity', *Progressive Architecture*, Dec 1991, p47.

42 National Homes commissioned the Frank Lloyd Wright Foundation in 1970 to advise on the design of the mobile home. The result was a 'prairie' type design based on a typical linear plan format. The building, pictured in a highly hard and soft landscaped site, showed little understanding of the personal relationship mobile home occupiers have with their property or the nature of their siting in communal parks. The prototype was never put into production. See Wallis, p147. Paul Rudolph saw the potential of the mobile home and called it: 'the brick of the twentieth century'. In 1965 he produced designs for student housing in Charlottesville, Virginia. The design was based around a central kitchen/bathroom core with fold-out sections that formed living spaces. The project was not built. See Carreiro *et al*, *The New Building Block*, pp99–101.

43 Fisher, 'Industrialized Housing: Changing a Commodity', p47.

44 So called because in theory you could fire a shot-gun straight through the circulation areas from front to back without touching the building fabric!

45 The project was designed in collaboration with YRM and Anthony Hunt Associates. See 'News', *Building Design*, 9 April 1993, p4.

46 See 'First City Heliport', *Building Design*, 12 Feb 1993, p6. The project was, however, refused planning permission in Jan 1995.

47 See 'Prefab power plant floats into place', *ENR*, Vol 207, 10 Sept 1981, p14.

48 Both platforms were built by the Mitsui Engineering and Shipbuilding Company though the client, Rasmussen Offshore A/S is Scandinavian. See Hajime Okada, '*Polycastle* and *Polyconfidence*', *Process: Architecture*, No 96, June 1991, pp106–7.

49 The building was originally intended to stay on site at the reef permanently with just a periodic visit to its home port for refurbishment; however, a year after its deployment a more profitable site was found in the harbour at Ho Chi Minh City, Vietnam and it was consequently moved there. It can, of course, be moved again if required. See David Hutton, 'Barrier Reef Floating Hotel', *Process: Architecture*, No 96, June 1991, pp82–7.

50 See Eiichi Yanagida, 'Floating Island', *Process: Architecture*, No 96, June 1991, pp88–93.

51 Frederick H Fisher, 'Flip II', *IEEE Journal of Oceanic Engineering*, Vol 13, No 4, Oct 1988, pp174–85. Dr Fisher notes that one unexpected but welcome aspect of the craft's stability was that it enabled alfresco barbecues on deck, a welcome respite from the otherwise primitive crew facilities.

52 The contemporary descendants of the transatlantic liners are cruise ships which compete on the basis of standards of service and accommodation. These are seen as destinations in themselves; the places they actually visit is just 'scenery'. An advertisement for Silversea cruise liners states: 'Whilst on board Silver Cloud and Silver Wind you will enjoy a lifestyle normally reserved for guests of the finest five star hotels. … Imagine, sitting on your private veranda sipping champagne, as you cruise effortlessly up the Amazon river to Manaus', Silversea advertisement, nd, c1994.

53 The structures would also be self-sufficient by the use of wave power and solar energy. A Tetrahedronal City was also proposed for Tokyo Bay. See Pawley, *Buckminster Fuller*, pp158–61.

54 CH Waddington, *The Man-Made Future* (London) 1978, p173.

CHAPTER VII

1 Sir Richard Rogers in the catalogue to the RIBA Gallery Exhibition; *Exploring Materials: The Work of Peter Rice*, catalogue of the exhibition held at the RIBA, London, 30 June to 25 Aug, 1992 (London) 1992, p41.

2 Peter Rice has worked with Renzo Piano and Richard Rogers, Tony Hunt has worked with Richard Horden and Ian Ritchie. Atelier One has worked with Mark Fisher.

3 Other examples are the experimental houses by Charles and Ray Eames and Paul Rudolph. More recent examples are Eagle Rock House, Sussex,

1982 by Ian Ritchie and Michael and Patty Hopkins' house in Hampstead (London) 1977.

4 John Winter, 'Ship to Shore', *The Architects' Journal*, Vol 182, No 30, 24 July 1985, p38. John Winter also states: 'I cannot think of any modern house that has broken so much new ground, explored another technology so thoroughly and which convinces one that the world is getting better.' p42.

5 Description by Martin Pawley. He also calls the building a: 'light post-Miesian architecture of serendipitously chosen industrial products.' Pawley, *Theory and Design*, pp153–4.

6 Alan J Brookes and Chris Grech, *The Building Envelope* (Oxford) 1990, p113.

7 Horden's projects seem to get smaller and lighter. 'Point Look Out' designed in 1993 is a portable lifeguard's look-out post which can be packed up and carried from place to place. Though the prototype was heavier, the manufactured model will only weigh 70 kilograms. The structure can also serve as a shaded resting space and a sleeping enclosure. See Deborah Singmaster, 'Horden's infinitely flexible, lightweight ideas frame', *The Architect's Journal*, Vol 198, No 18, 10 Nov 1993, p15.

8 See Peter Buchanan, 'Barely There', *Architectural Review*, Vol 182, No 1087, Sept 1987, pp81–4 and Alan J Brookes and Chris Grech, *Connections*, pp105–8.

9 Deborah Singmaster, 'Summer themes welcome visitors to the Palace', *The Architects' Journal*, 8 Sept, 1994, p26. Hopkins' practice is well known for high quality buildings that approach each problem with a sensitive and appropriate touch. Michael and Patty Hopkins' own house, built in Hampstead in 1977 of commercially available industrial products, has been compared to the Eames house, both for its architectural aspirations and influence on other designers. Their interest in the assembly of buildings as a driving force in their design is also expressed in his creation of the Patera system, launched in 1982 as a flexible steel building method that enabled the erection of a building in 12 days using four men and a fork-lift truck.

10 As quoted in Paut Goldberger, *Renzo Piano and Building Workshop Buildings and Projects 1971–1989* (New York) 1989, p238.

11 Piano's understanding of the importance of local knowledge and interaction in the process of building led to one of the very few instances where Western architects have developed appropriate strategies for solving housing problems in the developing world. For further details, see the 1978 UNESCO mobile construction unit for Senegal Dakar in Chapter IX.

12 Chris Wilkinson comments that: 'The concept was so fresh and exciting that it appealed to a much wider range of people than most modern buildings' and quoted Reyner Banham: 'This object is a work of architectural art in its own right, the complexity of its functions and connections is an architectural composition richer than many complete buildings.' Chris Wilkinson, *Supersheds* (Oxford) 1991, pp62–4.

13 Callum Murray, 'Visitor Centre', *The Architects' Journal*, 24 April 1991, p42.

14 Kenneth Powell in his introduction to Rowan Moore (ed), *Structure, Space and Skin: The Work of Nicholas Grimshaw and Partners*, London, 1993, p9. However, Grimshaw also personally acknowledges a debt to Buckminster Fuller (he has described him as a 'staggering philosopher'), whom he met in 1967 when Fuller came to see Grimshaw's service tower project in Sussex Gardens (London), Ibid, p12.

15 Ibid, p148.

16 Ibid, p162.

17 Kenneth Powell describes the exhibition pavilion as: 'a building type always at the leading edge of architectural progress.' Ibid, p10.

18 The specific influence of exposition architecture is discussed in Chapter IX which, because of its grouping together of a particularly wide range of building types at a single site, can form a mirror on the future of architectural design, if a distorted one.

19 For a more detailed description of this building see Alan J Brookes and Chris Grech, *Connections* (Oxford) 1992, pp121–4.

20 As quoted in 'Tent's Moment', *The Architects' Journal*, Vol 193, No 7,13 Feb 1991, p13.

21 Luca Gazzaniga, 'Mario Botta: Tenda per il 700°b della Confederzione Elvetica', *Domus*, No 725, March 1991, p3. Gazzaniga also notes that proposals had been made to return the building to the site permanently after its tour was complete.

22 A building with a very similar function to Botta's was the competition winning design by Daryl Jackson for Australia's 1988 Bicentennial. Designed to travel from town to town during the celebration year, the building was announced by a series of transient media events, from laser shows to airships. This was followed by the arrival of 20 pantechnicons containing modular exhibition spaces and a single larger Bicentennial Theatre of 30 m span. See Peter Buchanan, 'Big Top Down Under', *Architectural Review*, May 1987, pp64–7.

23 For a more detailed description of this project see Jonathan Glancey and Tudi Sammartini, 'Piano + Novo, Temporary auditorium, Venice', *Architectural Review*, Dec 1984, pp53–7.

24 Nicholas Goldsmith, 'The Peripatetic Pavilion', *Design Quarterly*, No 15, Summer 1992, pp30–2. FTL have since designed other demountable music venues for the cities of Boston and Baltimore but the New York pavilion is still the most mobile.

25 As the investment has now been made ($3.4 million) it has been proposed that the trucks drive to a more equitable climate in the Southern United States for some winter touring shows.

26 The first tour by the Beatles of North America in 1965 was modelled on the circus theme.

27 The Pink Floyd Potsdamer Platz show was simultaneously broadcast to 35 countries.

28 Luca Gazzaniga, 'Marco Botto', p2.

CHAPTER VIII

1 Office of the United Nations Disaster Relief Co-ordinator (UNDRO), *Shelter After Disaster*, UN (Geneva) 1982, piii.

2 Statement from the United Nations High Commission for Refugees, documents of the First International Workshop on Improved Shelter Response and Environment for Refugees, 29, 30, June/1 July 1993, Geneva, part III, p4, commenting on shelter aspects of the relief work in Bosnia-Herzegovina during 1991/92.

3 In 1942, Alvar Aalto designed a wooden mobile shelter that could be used in clusters of four and in the post-disaster situation be reorganised to form a family dwelling. It was never built. In 1985, Future Systems' design for an air-deliverable shelter received considerable exposure in the architectural press. However, it failed to receive backing from the UN perhaps because this well-meaning response was clearly inappropriate for the reasons discussed in this text.

4 This fact has been clearly stated by various commentators in the field. For example: 'Emergency housing is often seen by designers, architects, engineers, and in some cases the relief agencies, as an opportunity for generating innovative designs impossible to implement', Alcira Kreimer, 'Emergency, temporary and permanent housing after disasters in developing countries', *Ekistics*, No 279, Nov/Dec 1979, p362.

5 For a full list of these myths and their factual counterparts see Ian Davies, *Shelter After Disaster* (Oxford) 1978, pp25–31.

6 Authorities' misunderstanding of this situation has led to forced evacuation of inhabitants to remote camps without facilities while the sites of their homes are bulldozed, destroying reclaimable belongings and reusable building materials. Ibid, p25.

7 UNDRO, *Shelter After Disaster*, piii.

8 RD Keynes (ed), *The Beagle Record*, selections from the original accounts of the voyage of *HMS Beagle*, 1979, pp255–7 as quoted in UNDRO, *Shelter After Disaster*, piii.

9 'The makeshift shelters of blankets and rags which helped shelter two hundred thousand from the rain after the fire didn't last for long. Tents issued by the military replaced them, and the beginnings of the permanent camps which were to dot the City's parks and reservations for more than a year were established.' William Bronson, *The San Francisco Earthquake: the earth shook, the sky burned* (New York) 1959, p118.

10 Because of the mild weather, some people preferred to sleep out in Los Angeles immediately after the earthquake as they were afraid to return to their undamaged houses. When the weather became less clement they returned. In Florida, after Hurricane Andrew, the tent cities were occupied by opportunistic builders who had travelled to the area to take advantage of the large amount of repair work that needed to be done, and the long term homeless who were reluctant to leave the tents when the state of emergency was deemed to be over. These issues were raised by Dr Frederick Krimgold of the National Science Foundation, Virginia Polytechnic Institute, Alexandria. Washington, DC in a conversation with the author, 4 March 1994.

11 1992, p13. Traditional earthquake resistant detailing in Turkish dwellings lapsed after a gap in seismic activity for several generations. In Vietnam, ties used in traditional roof construction intended to brace against high winds were omitted after a generation of calm, leading to mass destruction of buildings by Cyclone Irving in 1989.

12 The Swiss Disaster Relief Unit (SDR) was involved on the ground in these efforts. In 1992 it found 90,000 people staying in 'totally inadequate accommodation' and about 55,000 in shelter which was 'unsuitable for the winter' or lacked basic facilities such as adequate sanitation. During 1992–93 the SDR provided shelter for 10,000 refugees at a cost of $7 million however, it comments: 'Order has collapsed. The central government did not exist any more. Economic activity was at a standstill. Political and military instability. Local authorities were often identical with command posts which had been convened by military rulers. That was where the dilemma started. Shall we begin constructing without any agreement at all? Shall we deal with people whose moral and democratic attitudes are more than doubtful? Or shall we altogether abandon shelter project activities in war areas?' Department of Foreign Affairs, Swiss Disaster Relief Unit, 'Winter Accommodation for Refugees in Ex-Yugoslavia', unpublished paper presented at the UNHCR, First International Workshop on Improved Shelter Response and Environment, Geneva, 29, 30 June/1 July 1993, p7.

13 M Douglas Stafford, statement at the UNHCR, First International Workshop on Improved Shelter Response and Environment, Geneva, 29 June 1993.

14 Mirta Demare, 'Agencies, Non-Governmental Organisations, Consultants', unpublished paper presented at the UNHCR, First International Workshop on Improved Shelter Response and Environment, Geneva, 29, 30 June/1 July 1993, p8.

15 Stafford, p2. The 2000 annual budget for the UNHCR was US$1 billion; however, deducing the actual spend on shelter is complex as money is now divided into projects rather than types.

16 Mirta Demare comments: 'The resonance of the untuned, poor collaboration is sensed continuously in the field, specially in the shelter sector.' Demare, p12.

17 See UNDRO, *Shelter After Disaster*. This report concludes that in general: 'Emergency shelter has more often than not been regarded as a product with design criteria developed by the donor. This approach has consistently failed to satisfy the needs of the surviving families.' See pp24–9.

18 UNDRO reported on such shelters in 1982: 'A summary of the success of these [imported] shelters has indicated that their use as emergency shelter or temporary housing has been extremely limited, their performance and acceptability poor, and their cost high.' Ibid, p27. Yet at the 1993 UNHCR, First International Workshop on Improved Shelter Response and Environment, the products and literature of current manufacturers in the field were exhibited. Some of these cost many thousands of dollars per unit and took the efforts of skilled operators to erect.

19 'Emergency shelters, especially those donated by the international community and imported into disaster-stricken areas, can serve to upset a delicate socio-economic balance by raising expectations, which in most cases, neither the local, nor the national, nor indeed international, authorities have the means to satisfy. The importation of shelters can furthermore play a negative role by stifling local and even national initiative, especially when they comprise prefabricated systems

20 UNDRO, *Shelter Alter Disaster*, p12.

21 See F Cuny, 'Refugee Camps and Camp Planning: the State of the Art', *Disasters*, 1:2, 1977, pp125–43, and F Cuny, 'Review of Twelve Years' Experience of Disasters and Small Dwellings', in Y Aysan and I Davies (eds), *Disasters and the Small Dwelling: Perspectives for the UN IDNDR* (London) 1992.

22 Dr Roger Zetter, 'An Overview of Shelter Provision and Settlement Policy', unpublished paper presented at the UNHCR, First International Workshop on Improved Shelter Response and Environment, Geneva, 29, 30 June/1 July 1993, p10. Zetter also states: 'In the literature on refugee camps two themes predominate; technical and field reports concerned with camp planning – logistics, site planning, operational needs – and a growing body of research based literature examining the largely negative impact and consequences of encampment on the refugees ... Unfortunately for the refugees, their hosts, and for policy makers, these two literatures have never sufficiently engaged.' p10.

23 'The affected population needs to become active participants in the process of reconstruction rather than onlookers. This is essential to maximise resources of skills and labour, but also to assist those who need work as a process of therapeutic readjustment, in order to restore their self-esteem and their place in society.' Ian Davies (ed), *Guidelines for Authorities Responsible for the Reconstruction of Towns and Cities Devastated by War*, Disaster Management Centre, Oxford and the Institute of Advanced Architectural Studies, University of York, 1989, p33. Mitchel and Bevan also comment: 'we believe that local people are the only ones who can reliably identify their own problems ... we need to work with them and to their definition of needs and priorities. We may together be able to find ways to use the existing skills base, locally-available materials and low-cost, sustainable technologies as the basis for solving their problems in a way which will not be dependent on outside help, but will be adopted and maintained locally.' *Culture Cash and Housing*, pxiii.

24 'Extensive case study experience confirms that the design and construction of shelter, even in emergencies, should be based on local materials, indigenous technologies, or the careful adaptation of imported or non-traditional methods and materials, where this does not happen, shelter provision is either too expensive (and thus meets too few needs) or is incapable of replication because required skills are not available.' Zetter, 'An Overview of Shelter Provision and Settlement Policy', p4.

25 Ian Davies paraphrases the motto used by Christian Aid: 'Buy a man a fish and you feed him for a day – train him how to fish and you feed him for life' with the suggestion: 'Give a man a safe home and you have housed his family – but train him how to build his own safe house and you have housed his family, and very probably his children's families and his relatives and friends.' Davies, *Shelter After Disaster*, p36.

26 Douglas Stafford comments on this problem of refugees that have been left without help and advice to establish themselves in a new area: 'it has often meant crowded, poorly planned and unsanitary communities, and it has often meant combing the surroundings for materials – branches, thatch, wood. Where a refugee camp is, once stood a forest; once flowed fresh water; once lay good top-soil. The environment around these communities has suffered, in part due to non-existent or poor shelter response.' However, he also states the benefits of aiding them establish their own settlement: 'let them do the work of providing for their own shelter and building their own homes. ... It has promoted self-reliance and ensured cultural appropriateness. It has been cost-effective. It has been fast.' Stafford (see note 13), p2.

27 The problems associated with the lack of an effective shelter strategy for refugees has been recognised by the UNHCR and it is attempting to mobilise agencies to address the issues in a meaningful way. The resolution of the Chateau du Penthes working group convened by the UNHCR at Geneva on 16 February 1993 states: 'The need for appropriate and cost-effective shelter for refugees and displaced persons has grown considerably in importance in the last decade. The magnitude and complexity of conflicts has placed humanitarian organisations into an exhaustive race in time and circumstance. This sequence of refugee events has so far prevented an in-depth analysis of appropriate responses ... What is needed is a comprehensive shelter strategy with appropriately developed standards, supply methods, specifications, and production capabilities related to local needs and circumstances.' UNHCR, 'Shelter Response and Environment for Refugees', p3.

28 '... there is no universally applicable emergency shelter system and attempts to invent such systems are based on the many mistaken assumptions discussed throughout the [UNDRO] study. Guidelines on post-disaster shelter for individual communities can only be formulated by qualified local personnel, in the light of the prevailing local conditions (types of hazard, climate, building traditions, economic base, social organisation, etc).' UNDRO, *Shelter After Disaster*, p62.

29 'The tent is often viewed as the most obvious form of emergency shelter, and remains an effective and flexible relief item, especially when compared to the many alternative forms that have been tested and failed.' UNDRO, *Shelter After Disaster*, p26.

30 This is true in most cases; however, some designers have noted the gap between what is offered and what is required. One example is Arthur Quarmby who wrote in 1974: 'the failure of so many ... well-meaning disaster operations lies surely not so much in the product (unless something basic like insulation or the need to sleep on the roof is involved) as in the way in which it is done. Take the inhabitants from an intimate, complex and, in planning and sociological terms, sophisticated group of little units and put them into a sterile, straight, flat and crude row of other little units and they will rebel.' Arthur Quarmby, *The Plastics Architect* (London) 1974, p120. An applied example where a European architect became involved in housing issues in a developing country with sensitivity (though not in disaster relief) is Renzo Piano and Peter Rice's design for a 'mobile constructional unit' for Senegal. In 1978, the designers were approached by UNESCO to devise a self-build housing project for Senegal villages. Rather than importing a system and letting the villagers assemble it, Piano and Rice devised a complete logistical system based on a series of vehicles that contained tools, a library and other resources. The villagers discussed with the architects their requirements, the sort of materials they were used to working with and what materials might be made from local resources. The buildings were therefore a result of collaboration and a learning process on both sides. See Jonathan Glancey, 'Piano Pieces', *Architectural Review*, May 1985, pp59–64.

CHAPTER IX

1 Greg Bear, 'Mandala', first published in Robert Silverberg (ed), *New Dimensions 8*, as reprinted in Greg Bear, *The Venging*, Legend (London) 1992, p109.

2 William Gibson, *Count Zero*, first published Gollancz (London) 1986. This edition, Grafton (London) 1987, p72.

3 Bear's description sounds remarkably like Ron Herroni's Walking City of 1965, and Gibson's like Future Systems' Wilderness Retreat projects from 1975 on.

4 Jim Burns, *Arthropods: New Design Futures* (London) 1972, p165. The arthropod is a technical term for an insect: 'articulate invertebrate animals with jointed limbs, the body divided into melameric segments'.

5 Ibid, p8.

6 Martin Pawley comments on this point: 'Architects like Yona Friedman in France, and groups like Archigram in England and the Metabolists in Japan, although acknowledging more readily the influence of the Mercury and Apollo space programmes, in effect worked on variants of Fuller's images of how a more efficient man-made world might be.' Pawley, *Theory and Design*, p106. Fuller's reputation continues to be reassessed. The recent major touring exhibition of his work and associated publications did much to bring the scope of his achievements to the notice of a wider contemporary audience.

7 Burns, p130.

8 Ant Farm, *Inflatocookbook* (Sausilito, USA) 1970.

9   Peter Cook, *Experimental Architecture*, p90. Cook also stated that they needed to: 'prop one another up against the boredom of working in London architectural offices.' Peter Cook, *Archigram* (London) 1972, p 8.

10 Cook, *Experimental Architecture*, p90.

11 Cook, *Archigram*, p36.

12 Bryan Lawson, *How Designers Think* (London) 1980, p65.

13 Ibid, p36.

14 Peter Blake, *Architectural Forum*, 1968, as quoted in Cook, *Archigram*, p48.

15 Ibid, p61.

16 Mike Webb, 'The Cushicle', in Cook, *Archigram*, p64. It is of interest that Webb refers to his work as an invention rather than a design; this is no longer an architectural object, but a science/technology object.

17 Mike Webb, 'Suitaloon', ibid, p80.

18 Probably the most famous built work by an ex-Archigram member is the Imagination headquarters in London by Herron Associates. a wonderful revitalisation of an old building in an innovative, contemporary manner, which, however, has none of the philosophical underpinning of impermanency so manifest in the theoretical work.

19 Cook, *Archigram*, p7.

20 Reyner Banham called the group: 'short on theory, long on draftsmanship and craftsmanship.' As quoted in Cook, ibid, p5.

21 David Greene, 'Gardeners Notebook', 1968, as quoted in Cook, ibid, p113. Howard Johnson is an extensive motel chain in the USA.

22 Cedric Price, 'Life-Conditioning', *Architectural Design*, October 1966 as quoted in *Cedric Price*, Architectural Association Works II (London) 1984, p18. This quote also made an appearance in *Archigram* 8, 1968.

23 Cedric Price, 'On safety pins and other magnificent designs', *Pegasus*, Spring 1972, as quoted in *Cedric Price*, p50.

24 Ibid.

25 Cedric Price, 'Fun Palace', *Link*, June–July 1965, as quoted in *Cedric Price*, p56.

26 Reyner Banham, ibid, p98. More recently, the relevance of Price's ideas has begun to be recognised by the architectural establishment. Frank Duffy, former President of the RIBA, states: 'I am convinced that his ideas about flexible accommodation are critical. Designing for flexibility is the most important issue that architects face today.' As quoted in Naomi Stungo, 'Not just puff', *RIBA Journal*, November 1994, p30.

27 David Nixon, *Constructing the Future*, as quoted in Martin Pawley, *Future Systems: The Story of Tomorrow* (London) 1993, p25.

28 Nixon was a partner from 1979, but has now established an independent practice. Amanda Levete became a partner in 1989. Kaplicky also worked with Richard Rogers and Norman Foster prior to starting his own practice which he now runs in partnership with Amanda Levete.

29 The design which was built for the Sydney Museum of Contemporary Arts in 1991, makes the most of a compact space to create a comfortable womb-like interior. Though the design is aerodynamically contoured to create a low drag coefficient, its actual shape does not appear to have taken the problems of uplift into account and the placing of the door in the rear, a feature which, though from a planning point of view is desirable, was abandoned by the caravan and trailer industry in the 1930s because of the problems of air suction pulling road dirt and dust into the interior.

30 As quoted in Pawley, *Future Systems*, p38.

31 John Welsh, 'Moving Image', *Building Design*, 15 May 1992, p18. The cataclysmic destruction of the tent by high winds funnelling between high rise blocks at its deployment for the 'Croydon – the Future' exhibition on 8 December 1993 did not overshadow the potential it showed of beautiful and efficient portable buildings.

32 Martin Pawley believes that Future Systems' work is not just predictive but a physical representation of what the architecture of the future will be: 'If these projects are so impressive that their image commands the attention of a world that remains fearful to commission them in actuality, what does this say about their status in the creative realm? Surely no more and no less than that they are being "stored up" for execution at some future time – a time when the triumphs of ignorance, prejudice and vested interests that have led to our present state of abject fear of all forms of architecture except those that slavishly imitate the past, gives place to clearer thought and a more honest acceptance of the irreducible importance of advanced technology in the structure of modern life.' Pawley, *Future Systems*, p39.

33 Lebbeus Woods, *Anarchitecture: Architecture as a Political Act*, Architectural Monograph No 22 (London) 1992, p18.

34 Ibid, p10.

35 Ibid, p31.

36 Ibid, p40.

37 For example, Neil Dinari investigated the effects resulting from the inclusion of time as a parameter in the design of a building in his project Solar Clock. This structure circumnavigated the perimeter of the walls at the Tower of London, in relation to the movement of the sun on a day by day and an annual basis. The power for its movement is derived from a photon-absorbing solar curtain wall, so the building not only describes the sun's route in relation to the city, but also uses the sun's power to carry out its task. Kenneth Frampton, concluding notes in Robert McCarter (ed), *Pamphlet Architecture No 12, Building: Machines* (New York) 1987, p61.

38 The term was initially used by a Los Angeles company, Environmental Communications. Chip Lord and Ant Farm, *Automerica* (New York) 1976, p79.

39 Dennis Turnguisy, 'Housecar', *Shelter* (California) 1973, reprinted 1990, p89.

40 Lord, *Automerica*, p123.

41 David J Neuman, 'The American Courtship of House and Car', *Popular Architecture*, Marshall Fishwick and J Meredith Neil (eds) (Ohio) c1974.

42 In fact recent confrontations between the authorities and New Age travellers in the UK show clear open hostility from many parts of conventional society. This is partly the mistrust felt for any people who have an alternative lifestyle which Romanys have felt for centuries, and partly the friction that results when a small group of individuals refuses to acknowledge some of the rules established by society at large.

43 Margaret Morton, 'The Architecture of Survival', *Progressive Architecture*, Aug 1993, p78.

44 The domes' inventor is Craig Chamberlain who worked with Buckminster Fuller between 1975 and 1980. See Frances Anderton, 'Dome Sweet Dome', *Architectural Review*, No 1161, Nov 1993, pp66–70. See also Frances Anderton, 'Domes of their own', *Building Design*, 10 Sept 1993, p2.

45 The similarity of problems between terrestrial and extraterrestrial portable architecture is manifest. Yousef Hijazi of Architectural Horizon comments: 'The first habitat and work station on the lunar surface undoubtedly has to be prefabricated, self-erecting, and self-contained. The building structure should be folded and compacted to the minimum size and made of materials of minimum weight. It must also be designed to provide maximum possible habitable and usable space on the Moon.' Yousef Hijazi, 'Prefabricated Foldable Lunar Base Modular Systems for Habitats, Offices, and Laboratories', in WW Mendell (ed), *The Second Conference on Lunar Bases and Space Activities in the 21st Century*, Vol 1, NASA (Houston, Texas) 1992, p261.

46 The work previously carried out on *Skylab* has now become part of the modular space exploration system designed around the Space Shuttle, utilising reusable orbital laboratories like the European Space Agency's *Spacelab*.

47 President Bush made a keynote speech on 20 July 1989 that outlined objectives for the Space Exploration Initiative (SEI): 'First, for the coming decade – for the 1990s – Space Station Freedom, our critical next step In all our future endeavours. And for the next century, back to the Moon. Back to the future. And this time, back to stay. And then a journey into tomorrow, a journey to another planet, a manned mission to Mars.' As quoted in Will Z Sadeh, Stein Sture, Russell J Miller, *Engineering, Construction and Operations in Space II, Space '92, Proceedings of the Third International Conference*, American Society of Civil Engineers (New York) 1992, piii.

48 See Brent Helleckson, Richard Johnson, George W Morgenthaler, 'Evaluating Lunar Base Conceptual Designs', ibid, p213.

49 Brent Sherwood, 'Lunar Architecture and Urbanism', in Mendell, p239.

50 Ibid.

51 K Miura, 'Concepts of Deployable Space Structures', in H Nooshin and ZS Makowski (eds), *International Journal of Space Structures Special Issue: Deployable Space Structures* (Essex) 1993, p3.

52 See Richard A Kaden and Leonard D Pense, 'Inflatable Form Construction in Space', in Mendell, pp564–75. Also, Robert Kronenburg, *Portable Architecture* 2nd Edition, 2001, pp144–59.

53 David Nixon, former partner in Future Systems, is partly responsible for these proposals which use a mix of components developed by ESA such as the *Ariane 5* and the *Hermes* spaceplane, and by NASA such as the Columbus Attached Pressurised Module which will form part of Space Station Freedom. See David A Nixon and Robin C Huttenbach, 'Phased Assembly of a European Space Station', in Sadeh *et al* (New York) 1992, pp850–61.

54 Gary T Moore, Kerry I Paruleski, Janis Huebner-Moths, Joseph P Fieber and Pakick J Rebholz, comment in their paper 'Lunar Base Requirements for Human Habitability': 'the temptation to trade cost or structural efficiency for habitability would be a major mistake for lunar missions'. See Sadeh *et al*, p226.

55 Kriss J Kennedy, 'A Horizontal Inflatable Habitat for SEI', ibid, pp135–45.

56 The Mars Habitat projects carried out at A&M University, Texas for NASA have produced a range of detailed designs including Lavapolis, an inflatable facility based within lava tubes on the planet's surface and Hexamars, a partially buried space frame structure. See *Mars Habitat*, Department of Architecture, Prairie View A&M University (Texas) August 1991.

57 See Larry Bell and Guillermo Trotti, 'Earth-Based Analogs of Lunar and Planetary Facilities', in Mendell, pp243–48.

58 The International Space University is a global institution that brings together a wide variety of disciplines to study the problems and opportunities of development in space. The ISU has recently established a permanent campus based in Strasbourg where it holds a Master in Space Studies degree course, however, its annual ten-week summer school which brings together experts and students from all disciplines and countries has resulted in its most innovative programmes which include the design of lunar and Mars settlements, a solar power space programme, a gravity research facility, and an international space-based global disaster network. For a report on the Mars settlement project see Marya Burgess, 'Designing at the Final Frontier', *The Architects' Journal*, Vol 194, No 11, 11 Sept, 1991, p14.

59 Hara states: 'If we contemplate the design of our current buildings and cities we can recognise that they also have a strong guiding star, intuition. Thus, also in outer space, I believe in intuition's power of creation.' Hiroshi Hara, 'Extra-Terrestrial Architecture', *SD*, Jan 1994, p9.

60 Nicholas Grimshaw recalls visiting the site in June 1989 and described it as: 'just flat mud'. Nicholas Grimshaw and Richard Haryott, 'Solar-powered Pavilion', transcription of a lecture at the RIBA, London, 16 June 1992, *RIBA Journal*, Oct 1992, p34.

61 *The Architectural Review*, Special Issue on the South Bank Exhibition, Vol 110, No 65, Aug 1951, p73.

62 There is only one significant aspect of demountability that is commented on (though it is intriguing), the beginnings of what has become known as High-Tech, described in 1951 as the 'Nautical Style' – relatively lightweight steel construction utilising cables and marine connections by architects Eric Brown and Peter Chamberlin for the Seaside Pavilion. 'The constructional techniques and characteristic finishes evolved by generations of shipwrights and dock engineers are well adapted for use in modern architecture, which takes the same delight in economy of line and structure.' Ibid, p87.

63 JM Richards, 'Expo '70', *The Architectural Review*, Vol CXLVIII, No 882, Aug 1970. p67. Richards also compares the 1970s crop of exhibition buildings with the Crystal Palace: 'An exhibition is best designed as a light all-sheltering structure (the first international exhibition, the Crystal Palace of 1851, has never been improved upon), not as a temporary town more difficult to pull down than to put up.' p70.

64 Robin Boyd, 'Expo and exhibitionism', *The Architectural Review*, Vol CXLVIII, No 882, Aug 1970, p100.

65 Ibid.

66 Subsequent large scale pneumatic buildings have favoured low pressure systems, however, in this case high pressure was particularly suitable as it allowed easy access for the thousands of visitors to the audio-visual display it contained without the need for airlocks at the entrances and exits.

67 This building was really only recognised as a precursor of a new tradition after the building of the Pompidou Centre by Piano and Rogers in 1977. Colin Davies describes it as an example of a 'highly sophisticated Italian version of High Tech.' Davies, *High Tech Architecture*, p20.

68 This was the slogan for Expo '92. Dinah Casson, 'Expo's End', *Building Design*, 9 October 1992, p23. This sounds familiar – the slogan for Osaka 70 was Harmony for Mankind.

69 The response of the USA could be related to Spain's emphasis on the discovery in 1492 of what became the Latin American countries, its major role in establishing the Latin American Confederation and the push to establish stronger links between Spanish speaking nations on both sides of the Atlantic.

70 Alan Brookes commented that the Danish Pavilion 'demonstrate(s) how good modern architecture can be harnessed to positive and subtle effect.' Alan Brookes, 'Danish Balance', *The Architectural Review*, No 1144, June 1992, p51.

71 The designers stated: 'The … initial idea was to reuse as many components as we could, … The steel was designed so that it could easily be unbolted and the building could be transported elsewhere.' Nicholas Grimshaw and Richard Haryott, 'Solar-powered Pavilion', *RIBA Journal*, 1992, p34.

72 They also have the benefit of reducing the energy use of the building by 24 per cent compared to a conventional air conditioned building.

73 Paul Finch, 'Export Special', *Building Design*, 17 April 1992, p14.

74 It would seem appropriate that this building return home to its country of origin, to find a new public role, however, though it was brought back to the UK and was sold on to a developer it now seems unlikely it will be reassembled in any recognisable form. The British contribution at Expo 2000 consisted of a dismal fit-out of a standard shed that one would surmise had been designed specifically to exclude any hint of excitement and innovation. See David Hayward and Delroy Alexander, 'Expo pavilion waits for redesign', *New Builder*, No 186, 10 Sept 1993, p3.

75 The German Pavilion in Seville 1992 incorporated a tension system similar to earlier designs by Frei Otto as part of its building envelope, though not in an innovative way, but more as a historical acknowledgement of the designer's influence on exhibition structures as a whole.

76 From the Danish exhibition handbook as quoted by Alan Brookes, 'Danish Balance', p50.

77 The internal exhibition was designed by Conran RSCG and appears to have been created around which companies were able to make a contribution, rather than which would be suitable. Catherine Slessor commented: 'Nicholas Grimshaw's British Pavilion, despite its high-tech appearance does attempt to address issues of recycling and alternative technology, but these are marginalised by the muscle of dull corporate sponsorship that would have the world believe that Britain is a nation of Marks and Spencer clad Royal Doulton collectors.' Catherine Slessor, 'Seville and Expo', *The Architectural Review*, No 1144, June 1992, p2.

78 Expo '67 Special Issue', *The Architectural Review*, Vol CXLII, No 846, Aug 1967, p87.

79 Catherine Slessor, 'Seville and Expo', p2.

CHAPTER X

1 E Relph, *Place and Placelessness* (London) 1976, p78.

2 EB White, *Harper's Monthly*, May 1941.

3 Martin Heidegger, *The Question of Being: An Ontological Consideration of Place* (New York) 1958, p19. The basis for this chapter is the author's essay 'Architectural Identity and the Portable Building', *Oz: Journal of the School of Architecture and Design*, Kansas State University (Kansas) 1994, pp46–49.

4 Christian Norberg-Schulz, *Genius Loci: Towards a Phenomenology of Architecture*, London, 1980, p. 70.

5 Susanne Langer, *Feeling and Form* (New York) 1953, p95.

6 C Lévi-Strauss, *Tristes Tropiques* (New York) 1971, p66.

7 Relph, p29.

8 Richard Rogers, as quoted in Wilkinson, piii.

9 Robin Spence, 'Building technology: master or servant?', *Scroope: Cambridge Architectural Journal*, Issue 6, 1994–95, p20.

10 This has been one of the primary aims of the Portable Buildings Research Unit at Liverpool John Moores University and since 1995 at University of Liverpool of which the author is principal investigator. The Unit's first report, *UK Database of Portable and Demountable Building Manufacturers*, was completed in 1994.

11 In history, many exciting ideas appear to have faltered at this final stage, for example the Acorn house, designed by Carl Koch in 1945. See Chapter VI.

12 An example from the vehicle manufacturing industry which verifies this point is the Austin Mini (or Morris Minor, Volkswagen Beetle, Citroen 2CV, etc.), a car that utilises manufacturing and design experience from more expensive vehicles made by the same manufacturers. These entry level vehicles are still perceived as quality, desirable objects due to the care taken in their design.

13 Reyner Banham, 'A Home is not a House', *Meaning in Architecture*, Charles Jencks and George Baird (eds) (London) 1969. p112.

14 BMW actually used an advertising campaign that implied the redundancy of buildings. Their cars, equipped with computer and telephone (therefore FAX and modem) led to the question: 'with a car like this who needs an office?'

15 Individual examples of appropriate portable buildings already exist; however, what is meant here is the lack of a coherent image for portable architecture as a genre. For example there is no question that a successful school building can be built, that a successful car can be manufactured, but the issue of the successful portable building is still confused by the lack of understanding of its nature. This is one reason why current mobile home manufacturers feel it necessary to make their products appear like conventionally constructed buildings, even using artificial brick and stone cladding panels.

CHAPTER XI

1 From the preface to *The Architecture of M. Vitruvius Pollio*, translated from the original Latin by W. Newton, architect. Published by J. Dadsley, Pall Mall (London) 1771, 2 vols, pvii.

2 Wes Jones, 'Stillness' in *Oz: Journal of the College of Architecture, Planning and Design*, Kansas State University, Vol. 23, 2001, p46.

3 Durham Cathedral (AD 1096–1290), Pantheon, Rome (AD 120–124), Temple of Ammon, Karnak, Egypt (c2000–300 BC).

4 Of course, there are many impressive historic buildings where the skill of the original designers and craftsmen have enabled them to continue (with suitable alterations) as meaningful, useful artefacts, sometimes fulfilling a similar role to that for which they were originally intended, sometimes something quite different. Nevertheless, many older buildings, now protected by well-meaning but essentially backward looking legislation, are of dubious historical worth. Buildings left over from a previous age have often survived by accident before being preserved for a mixture of confused reasoning regarding what counts as genuine heritage and what is just old.

5 Not everyone adheres to the idea of the Internet creating new communities. Though those who have taken part in user group discussions and dedicated help forums immediately recognise this description as an apt one, Neil Postman of New York University states: 'To me, e-mail is not a conversation; it is two people typing messages to each other. Likewise, "community" on the Internet has exactly the opposite of the usual meaning – a community not of people of shared interests but people with different interests who have to negotiate with each other's interests to achieve harmony.' Neil Postman, 'Stop!' in *The Guardian, The Editor*, 5 December 2000, p13.

6 John Worthington (ed), *Rethinking the Workplace*, Architectural Press (London) 1997, p7.

7 See Gary Brown, 'Freedom and Transience of Space' in *Transportable Environments 2001: Proceedings of the 2nd Conference on Portable Architecture*, pp37–49.

8 Neil Postman comments in 'Stop!': 'The transformation of a technology into a kind of product always realigns economic and political power. A new medium creates new jobs and makes old ones obsolete. A new medium gives prominence to certain skills and subordinates others.'

9 The Private Finance Initiative (PFI) set out to improve the public sector on building which accounts for 40 per cent of the UK annual expenditure. *Rethinking Construction: The Report of the Construction Task Force* (Department of the Environment, Transport and the Regions, London 1998) aims to establish critical methodology on how building procurement can be made more efficient and more competitive. The Movement for Innovation (M4I) website sets out all the Key Performance Indicators (see www.m4i.org.uk). A useful concise overview of these initiatives is the RIBA publication *Architects and the Changing Construction Industry*, RIBA Publications (London) 2000.

10 Regardless of the ever-expanding range of appraisal criteria specific to the construction industry, it is important to note that the design and operation of buildings cannot be seen as a separate issue from the inter-linked issues of transportation, manufacture and food supply. One proposal for such an appraisal technique is the Bio-Regional Group's 'eco-footprinting', an energy audit method that estimates on a global scale the effect that energy and material consumption have in comparison to the total amount of the earth's bio-productive land mass. The world average is 1.9 hectares per capita – the USA energy usage is 12.2 hectares per capita, the UK 6.29 per capita, Bangladesh 0.6 per capita. Relatively underdeveloped countries like Bangladesh are currently therefore funding the industrialised nations' overspending and polluting of our natural resources. See Jonathan Glancey, 'What Does Green Mean?' in *The Guardian Saturday Review*, 4 August 2001, p5.

11 Detailed studies describe the RSSB shelter, the AT&T Global Olympic Village, the TSB bank, HKTA pavilion, the Volvo UK pavilion and the 'Airtecture' hall can be found in Robert Kronenburg, *Portable Architecture,* 2nd Edition, 2000.

12 See 'An Itinerant Building: Temporary Exhibition Tent' in *Detail*, No 8, 1998, pp1410–13.

13 See Jennifer Siegal's Office of Mobile Design website at www.designmobile.com.

14 See 'Floating Pavilion, Groningen' in *Detail*, No 8, 1998, pp1428–31.

15 For a detailed summary of the impact of intelligent systems and materials on building design see *Construction: A 2020 Vision*, Construction Industry Board, 1999. See also Ted Krueger 'Intelligence and Autonomy' in *Oz: Journal of Architecture, Planning and Design*, Kansas State University, Vol 23, 2001, pp22–7.

16 Michael A. Fox effectively draws attention to this trend for adaptability to lead to greater economy in materials in his paper 'Sustainable Applications of Intelligent Kinetic Systems' in which he speculates on the methods and strategies available for developing more and more sophisticated and useful kinetic structures in architecture. See *Transportable Environments 2001: Proceedings of the 2nd Conference on Portable Architecture*, pp145–57. Also see Fox's website http://kdg.mit.edu/. A prototype design for an ultra-lightweight skyscraper made solely from recyclable portable components has already been designed by architect/engineers FTL Happold utilising gas-filled translucent pillows for cladding and cross-over entertainment industry erection technology.

17 Wes Jones states: 'Ultimately, though, it all comes down to this: the architecture should embrace movement because it can. For the same reason that technological progress will eventually make blobs buildable, and so they will be built, movement will become as common as stillness is today … and it will lose its capacity to sustain wonder.' Wes Jones, 'Stillness', p51.

18 Kas Oosterhuis states ' … virtual reality is in all respects more real than so-called reality. Virtual reality, including all software ever written for any platform is hyper-real. Simply because we know the stuff it is made of.

We know every bit and byte. In the Digital Revolution reality has been rewritten from ground zero. And if we look closely at commonplace reality, our so-called natural world, we really do not know much … All matter, including all material [which] architecture is made of, is being redefined as information flow.' See Kas Oosterhuis, 'Game, Set and Match' in *Oz: Journal of Architecture, Planning and Design*, Vol 23, 2001, p10. See also the website: www.oosterhuis.nl/variomatic. The US company Deckhouse creates buildings of conventional appearance though they utilise contemporary industrial prefabricated building processes. The design process is an interactive one between client designer and manufacturer. See the website at www.deckhouse.com.

19   As Heidegger states: 'We attain to dwelling, so it seems, only by means of building.' Translation by Albert Hofstadter, 1971 reprinted in David Krell (ed) Martin Heidegger, *Basic Writings*, 1978, 2nd ed, 1993, p347. Martin Heidegger, 'Building Dwelling Thinking', first published in Germany in 1954.

Select Bibliography

Historic and Vernacular Portable Architecture

Baeder, John. *Gas, Food and Lodging.* New York: Abbeville Press, 1982.

Battisti, Eugenio. *Brunelleschi, the Complete Works.* Translated by Robert Erich Wolf. London: Thames and Hudson, 1981.

Billard, Jules, B. ed. *The World of the American Indian.* Washington, DC: National Geographic Society, 1989.

Brunskill, R.W. *Timber Building in Britain.* London: Victor Gollancz, 1985.

Bogardus, James. *Cast Iron Buildings; their Construction and Advantages.* New York, 1856.

Coon, Carleton, S. *The Hunting Peoples.* Boston, MA: Little, Brown and Company, 1971.

Dillehey, T.D. 'A Late Ice Age Settlement in Southern Chile.' *Scientific American*, 251.4, 1984, pp106–13.

Dupavillon, Christian. *Architectures du Cirque.* Paris: Moniteur, 1982.

Dutton, Geffrey. *Founder of a City.* London: Chapman and Hall, 1960.

Faegre, Torvald. *Tents: Architecture of the Nomads.* London: John Murray, 1979.

Fitzgibbon, James. 'Calais 1520 The Banquet Hall and Theatre.' Mrs. Margaret Fitzgibbon, St. Louis, MI.

— 'Guisnes 1520 The Field of Cloth of Gold.' Mrs. Margaret Fitzgibbon, St. Louis, MI.

Guidoni, Enrico. *Primitive Architecture.* History of World Architecture Series, London: Faber and Faber, 1987.

Herbert, Gilbert. *Pioneers of Prefabrication: The British Contribution in the Nineteenth Century.* Baltimore, MD: John Hopkins University Press, 1978.

Laubin, Reginald and Gladys. *The Indian Tipi, its History, Construction and Use.* 2nd ed. Normal, OK: University of Oklahoma Press, 1984.

Leakey, M.D. *Olduvai Gorge: Vol. 3, Excavation in Beds I and II 1960–63.* Cambridge, 1971.

Lévi-Strauss, Claude. *Structural Anthropology.* English translation by Claire Jacobson and Brooke Grundfest Schoepf. New York: Basic Books, 1963.

— *Tristes Tropiques.* New York, 1971.

Nicolaisen, Johannes. *Ecology and Culture of the Pastoral Tuareg.* Copenhagen, 1963.

Nougier, L.R. 'Prehistoric Archaeology' in *Larousse Encyclopedia of Archaeology*, pp143–60. Edited by Gilbert Charles-Picard. Middlesex, England: Spring Books, 1987.

Oakley, Kenneth, P. *Man the Tool-maker.* 6th ed. London: British Museum, 1972.

Oliver, Paul, *Dwellings: The House across the World.* Oxford: Phaidon, 1987.

— ed. *Shelter in Africa.* London: Barrie and Jenkins, 1971.

— *Shelter and Society.* London: Barrie and Jenkins, 1969.

— *Shelter, Sign and Symbol.* London: Barrie and Jenkins, 1975.

Pevsner, Nikolaus. *A History of Building Types.* London: Thames and Hudson, 1976.

Rapoport, Amos. *House Form and Culture.* Englewood Cliffs, NJ: Prentice-Hall, 1969.

Rudofsky, Bernard. *Architecture Without Architects.* New York: Museum of Modern Art, 1965.

Stevenson, Katherine Cole and Jandl, H. Ward. *Houses by Mail; A Guide to Houses by Sears, Roebuck and Company.* Washington, DC: Preservation Press, 1986.

Vitruvius. *The Architecture of M. Vitruvius Pollio*, translated from the original Latin by W. Newton, architect. Published by J. Dadsley, London: Pall Mall, 1771, 2 vols.

Windsor, John. 'Relics of a Lost Theme Park'. *The Independent*, 16 October 1993, p32.

Wodehouse, L. *Indigenous Architecture Worldwide: A Guide to Information Sources.* Detroit: Gale Research Company, 1980.

'Wonder of Jena, The.' In *Shelter*, pp110–11. Bolinas, CA: Shelter Publications, 1973.

Zuelebil, M. 'The Rise of the Nomads in Central Asia'. In *Cambridge Encyclopaedia of Archaeology*, pp252–6. Edited by A.G. Sherret, Cambridge, 1980.

Vehicles and Non-Architecture

Brino, Giovanni. 'Nomadic Truchitecture.' *Casabella*, No 412, April 1976, pp24–36.

Burgess, Marya. 'Designing at the Final Frontier.' *The Architect's Journal*, Vol 194, No 11, 11 September, 1991, p14.

Chesnau, Rojer. *Aircraft Carriers of the World, 1914 to Present.* London: Arms and Armour Press, 1984.

Cianchi, Marco. *Leonardo's Machines.* Florence: Becocci Editore, n.d.

Gibbs-Smith, Charles. *Early Flying Machines 1799–1909.* London: Eyre Methuen, 1975.

Hancocks, David. *Animals and Architecture.* London: Hugh Evelyn, 1971.

Hanson, Harry. *The Canal Boatmen 1760–1914.* Manchester: Manchester University Press, 1975.

Hara, Hiroshi. 'Extra-Terrestrial Architecture.' *SD*, January 1994, pp7–37.

Lord, Chip and Ant Farm. *Automerica.* New York: E.P. Dutton and Co. Inc., 1976.

Mars I labitat. Prairie View, Texas: Department of Architecture, Prairie View A&M University, August 1991.

Mendell, W.W., ed. *The Second Conference on Lunar Bases and Space Activities in the 21st Century.* 2 vols. Houston, TX: NASA, 1992.

Molinari, Cesare. *Theatre Through the Ages.* Translated by Colin Hamar. London: Cassell, 1975.

Morton, Margaret. 'The Architecture of Survival.' *Progressive Architecture*, August 1993.

Mondey, David, ed. *The International Encyclopedia of Aviation.* London: Octopus, 1977.

Nooshin, H. and Makowski, Z.S., eds. *International Journal of Space Structures Special Issue: Deployable Space Structures.* Brentwood, Essex: Multi Science Publishing Co., 1993.

Sadeh, Will Z., Sture, Stein, and Miller, Russell J. *Engineering, Construction and Operations in Space II, Space '92, Proceedings of the Third International Conference.* New York: American Society of Civil Engineers, 1992.

'Space, Openhouse' in *Popular Science*, p33.

Thornburg, David. A. *Galloping Bungalows: The Rise and Demise of the American House Trailer.* Hamden, CT: Archon, 1991.

Turnguisy, Dennis. 'Housecar.' In *Shelter.* Bolinas, CA: Shelter Publications Inc., 1973; reprint ed., 1990.

Whiteman, W.M. *The History of the Caravan.* London: Blandford Press, 1973.

Worcester, G.R.G. *Sail and Sweep in China.* London: HMSO, 1966.

Military Engineering

Churchill, Winston S. *The Second World War.* London: Cassell, 1949.Vol. II, *Their Finest Hour.* Institute of Civil Engineers. *The Civil Engineer in War: a symposium of papers on War-Time Engineering Problems.* London: ICE, 1948.

Mallory, Keith and Ottar, Arvid. *Architecture of Aggression.* London: Architectural Press, 1973.

Neumann, G.P. *The German Airforce in the Great War.* London: Hodder and Stoughton, 1921; reprinted in London: Chivers, 1969.

Rei, Stephen A. *Projected Performance Characteristics for Large Quickly Erectable Maintenance Shelters.* Natick, MA: US Army, 1993.

'The Nissen Hut on the Western Front.' *The Architects and Builders Journal*, 14 February 1917, p92.

'These War Buildings were Significant.' *Engineering News Record*, 19 October, 1944, p111.

Tytler, I.F.B., Thompson, N.H., Jones, B.E., Wormell, P.J.H., Riley, C.E.S. *Vehicles and Bridging*. London: Royal Military College of Science, 1985.

US Army, *Survey of Buildings of Prefabricated, Expandable, Inflatable, or Chemically Rigidised Types Suitable for Military Use*. US Army, August 1968.

'War-Time Buildings. The Stancon System.' *The Architect and Building News*, 3 May 1940, p.92.

Winney, Mike. 'On Active Service.' *New Civil Engineer*, 10 March 1994, pp20–1.

The Construction Industries

'Antarctic Survey Rapped Over Budget Overruns on Research Station and Airstrip.' *Building*, 8 April 1993, p6.

BRE documents (selected): BRE Report BR 215. 1991, *Investigation into the structural adequacy of relocatable buildings under wind loading*, BRE Leaflet XL2. 1990, *Resistance of relocatable buildings to wind loads*, BRE Digest 374. 1992, *Relocatable buildings: structural design, construction and maintenance*.

British Standards (selected): BS 3632: 1981 *Specification for Mobile Homes*, BS 6661: 1986 *Guide for design, construction and maintenance of single-skin air supported structures*, BS 6765: 1991 *Leisure Accommodation Vehicles – Caravans*, BS 6767: Part 1 1992 *Transportable Accommodation Units*.

Construction: A 2020 Vision. London: Construction Industry Board, 1999.

Department of the Environment, Transport and the Regions. *Rethinking Construction: The Report of the Construction Task Force*. London: Department of the Environment, Transport and the Regions, 1998.

'First City Heliport.' *Building Design*, 12 February 1993, p6.

Fisher, Frederick H. 'Flip II.' *IEEE Journal of Oceanic Engineering*. Vol 13, No 4, October 1988, pp174–85.

Harrison, D. Dex. 'An Outline of Prefabrication'. In *Tomorrow's Houses*. Edited by John Madge. London: Pilot Press, 1946.

Harris, Peter. 'Air-Supported Structures.' *The Structural Engineer*, Vol 71, No 18, 21 September 1993, p2.

Hutton, David. 'Barrier Reef Floating Hotel.' *Process: Architecture*, 96, June 1991, pp82–7.

Illingworth, J.R. *Temporary Works; their role in the Construction Industry*. London: Thomas Telford, 1987.

Kaufmann, Edgar Jr. 'Design, Sans Peur and Sans Ressources.' *Architectural Forum*, September 1966.

McConville, Daniel J. 'When Winter Comes: Coping With Cold Weather Construction.' *The Construction Specifier*, October 1988, pp42–9.

Okada, Hajime. 'Polycastle and Polyconfidence.' *Process: Architecture*, No 96, June 1991, pp106–7.

'Prefab Building Unfolds at Site', *Engineering News Record*, 5 June 1980, p32.

'Prefab Powerplant Floats into Place.' *Engineering News Record*, 10 September 1981, p14.

Ratay, Robert T. 'Building Around a Building.' *Civil Engineering*, Vol 57, No 4, April 1987, pp58–61.

Rawson, John. 'Buying Buildings off the Shelf.' *Architects' Journal*, Vol 198, No 9, 8 September 1993, pp25–7.

Royal Institute of British Architects. *Architects and the Changing Construction Industry*, RIBA Publications, London, 2000.

Russell, Helena. 'Dome Base.' *New Builder*, No 196, 19 November 1993, pp18–9.

'State Gets into Portable Cells', *Engineering News Record*, 26 April 1990, p20.

Vernes, Michael. 'Jean Prouvé, Architect-Mechanic', translated by Judith Landry, *Architectural Review*, July 1983.

White, R.B. *Prefabrication*, National Building Joint Special Study Report 36. London: HMSO, 1965.

Yanagida, Eiichi. 'Floating Island.' *Process: Architecture*, No 96, June 1991, pp88–93.

Mobile Homes and Manufactured Housing

Bernhardt, Arthur D. *Building Tomorrow: The Mobile/Manufactured Building Industry*. Cambridge, MA: MIT Press, 1980.

Brino, Giovanni. 'The Myth of the Mobile Home.' *Casabella*, No 403, 1975, pp20–37.

Burn, Grant. *Affordable Housing*. Jefferson, NC: Mc.Farland and Co., 1989.

Carreiro, Joseph. *The New Building Block: A Report on the Factory-Produced Dwelling Module*. Ithaca, New York: Cornell University, 1968.

Drury, Margaret J. *Mobile Homes: The Unrecognized Revolution in American Housing*. New York: Praeger, 1972.

Fisher, Thomas. 'Industrialized Housing: Changing a Commodity.' *Progressive Architecture*, December 1991, p47.

Herbert, Gilbert. *The Dream of the Factory Made House: Walter Gropius and Konrad Wachsmann*. Cambridge, MA: MIT Press, 1984.

'Instant Housing Feeds Japanese Needs.' *New Civil Engineer*, 14 October 1993, pp32–3.

Irwin, Bryan, Pollak, David and Tate, Anne. 'The P/A House.' *Progressive Architecture*, August 1992, pp44–51.

Jackson, J.B. 'The Mobile Home and how it came to America.' In *Discovering the Vernacular Landscape*. New Haven, CT: Yale University Press, 1984.

Jandl, H. Ward. *Yesterday's House of Tomorrow*. Washington, DC: Preservation Press, 1991.

Latina, Corrado. *Sistemi abitativi per insediamenti provvisori*. Serie Progettazione in Architettura. Milano: BE-MA Editrice, 1988.

McCoy, Esther. '17 Miles Between Mesa and Apache Junction.' *Lotus International*, No 8, September 1974, pp176–212.

Neuman, David J. 'The American Courtship of House and Car.' In *Popular Architecture*. Edited by Marshall Fishwick and J. Meredith Neil. Bowling Green, OH: Bowling Green Popular Press, c1974.

Rabb, Judith and Bernard. *Good Shelter*. New York: Quadrangle/New York Times Book Company, 1975.

Smithson, Alison and Peter. *Ordinariness and Light*. Cambridge, MA: MIT Press, 1970.

Thornburg, David, A. *Galloping Bungalows, The Rise and Demise of the American House Trailer*. Hamden, CT: Archon, 1991.

'Toyota Goes on Sale: the Western-Style House as Cars.' *Business Japan*, 31 May 1986, p.18.

Wachsmann, Konrad. *Turning Point of Building*. New York: Reinhold, 1960.

Wallis, Allan D. *Wheel Estate*. New York: Oxford University Press, 1991.

Willson, Corwin. 'Mobile House.' *Architectural Record*, July 1936, pp64–5.

Shelter After Disaster

Abeles, Schwartz Associates and Beyer-Blinder-Belle. *Cost Effective Housing Systems for Disaster Relief*. US Department of Housing and Urban Development, September 1974.

Bronson, William. *The San Francisco Earthquake: the Earth Shook the Sky Burned*. New York: Doubleday, 1959.

Cuny, F. 'Refugee Camps and Camp Planning: the State of the Art.' *Disasters*, 1:2, 1977, pp125–43.

— 'Review of Twelve Years' Experience of Disasters and Small Dwellings.' In *Disasters and the Small Dwelling: Perspectives for the UN IDNDR*. Edited by Y. Aysan and I. Davies. London: James and James, 1992.

Davis, Ian, ed. *Guidelines for Authorities Responsible for the Reconstruction of Towns and Cities Devastated by War*. Disaster Management Centre, Oxford and the Institute of Advanced Architectural Studies, University of York. York, 1989.

— *Shelter After Disaster*. Oxford: Oxford Polytechnic Press, 1978.

Demare, Mirta. 'Agencies, Non-Governmental Organisations, Consultants.' Paper presented at the First International Workshop on Improved Shelter Response and Environment. Geneva: UNHCR, 29/30 June/1 July 1993.

Kreimer, Alcira. 'Emergency, Temporary and Permanent Housing after Disasters in Developing Countries.' *Ekistics*, No 279, November/December 1979, p362.

Mitchel, Maurice and Bevan, Andy. *Culture Cash and Housing*. London: VSO/IT Publications,1992.

Office of the United Nations Disaster Relief Coordinator (UNDRO). *Shelter After Disaster*. Geneva: UN, 1982.

Swiss Disaster Relief Unit, Department of Foreign Affairs. 'Winter Accommodation for Refugees in Ex-Yugoslavia.' Paper presented at the First International Workshop on Improved Shelter Response and Environment. Geneva: UNHCR, 29, 30 June/1 July 1993.

Zetter, Roger. 'An Overview of Shelter Provision and Settlement Policy.' Paper presented at the First International Workshop on Improved Shelter Response and Environment. Geneva: UNCHR, 29/30 June/1 July 1993.

Twentieth Century Architecture and Theories

'Airtecture Exhibition Hall' in *Detail*, December 1996, pp1204, 1274.

'Airtecture' in *Design News*, January 1999, pp44–7.

'Airtecture' in *Space*, December 1998, pp163–5.

'Airtecture: The Festo Exhibition Hall' in *The International Design Magazine*, July/August 1997, pp142–3.

Anderton, Frances. 'Domes of their Own.' *Building Design*, 10 September 1993, p2.

— 'Dome Sweet Dome.' *Architectural Review*, No 1161, November 1993, pp66–70.

Ando, Tadao. 'Karaza Theatre.' *Japan Architect*, No 372, April 1988, pp35–39.

'An Itinerant Building: Temporary Exhibition Tent' in *Detail*, No 8, 1998, pp1410–13.

Ant Farm. *Inflatocookbook*. Sausilito: Rip Off Press, 1970.

Appleyard, B. *Richard Rogers*. London: 1986.

Ballast, David, Kent. *The Architecture of Temporary Structures*. Monticello, IL: Vance Bibliographies, 1987.

Balmori, Diana and Morton, Margaret. *Transitory Gardens, Uprooted Lives*. New Haven, CT: Yale University Press, 1993.

Banham, Reyner. 'A Home is not a House.' In *Meaning in Architecture*, pp109–18. Edited by Charles Jencks and George Baird. London: Cresset Press, 1969.

— *Theory and Design in the First Machine Age*. London: Architectural Press, 1960.

— *The Visions of Ron Herron*. Architecture Monographs No 38. London: Academy, 1994.

'Beating the Big Blue Drum for Britain' in *Evening Standard*, 17 February 1998, p18.

Boyd, Robin. 'Expo and Exhibitionism.' *The Architectural Review*, No 882, August 1970, pp99–100.

— 'Germany.' *The Architectural Review*, No 846, August 1967, pp129–35.

Brawne, Michael. 'The Wit of Technology.' *Architectural Design*, September, 1966, pp449–57.

Brookes, Alan J. and Grech, Chris. *Connections*. Oxford: Butterworth-Heinemann, 1992.

Brookes, Alan J. and Grech, Chris. *The Building Envelope*. Oxford: Butterworth Architecture, 1990.

Brown, Gary. 'Freedom and Transience of Space' in *Transportable Environments 2001: Proceedings of the 2nd Conference on Portable Architecture*, Singapore: National University of Singapore, 2001, pp37–49.

Buchanan, Peter. 'Barely There.' *Architectural Review*, No 1087, September 1987, pp81–4.

— 'Big Top Down Under.' *Architectural Review*, May 1987, pp64–7.

Burns, Jim. *Arthropods: New Design Futures*. London: Academy, 1972.

Cable, Carole. *Contemporary Temporary Structures: a Selected Bibliography of Recent Articles*. Monticello, IL: Vance Bibliographies, 1983.

Cargill Thompson, Jessica. 'Moving Images' in *Design Week*, 7 November 1997, p24.

Casson, Dinah. 'Expo's End.' *Building Design*, 9 October 1992, p23.

Chaslin, François. 'Jean Prouvé: His Own House.' *Global Architecture Houses 21*, 1987, pp8–25.

Cook, Peter. *Archigram*. London: Studio Vista, 1972.

— *Experimental Architecture*. London: Studio Vista, 1970.

Covault, C. 'Mars Initiative Leads Station Course Change' in *Aviation Week and Space Technology*, December 1997, pp39–40.

Davies, Colin. *High Tech Architecture*. London: Thames and Hudson, 1988.

Dawson, Layla. 'Invitation to the World'. *Building Design*, 24 February 1995, p12.

Dawson, Susan. 'All the World's a Stage', *The Architects' Journal*, 10 July 1997, pp37-39.

Dent, Roger, N. *Principles of Pneumatic Architecture*. London: Architectural Press, 1971.

'Dramatic Arts – From *Avante Garde* to Old Guard, Two Recent Projects Profiled' in *Light*, July 1998, pp36–7.

Drew, Philip. *Frei Otto*. London: Crosby Lockwood Stopes, 1976.

'Expo '67 Special Issue.' *The Architectural Review*, No 846, August 1967.

'Festo's Exhibition Hall' in *World Interior Design (WIND)*, Spring 1997, pp34–6.

Finch, Paul. 'Export Special.' *Building Design*, 17 April 1992, p14.

'Floating Pavilion, Groningen' in *Detail*, No 8, 1998, pp1428–31.

Fuller, Buckminster. *The Buckminster Fuller Reader*. Edited by James Meller. London: Cape, 1970.

— *Utopia or Oblivion*. London: Penguin, 1970.

Gazzaniga, Luca. 'Mario Botta: Tenda per il 700°b della Confederazione Elvetica.' *Domus*, No 725, March 1991, p3.

Gibson, Grant. 'Designers Power Up', *FX*, April 1998, p15.

Glancey, Johnathan. *New British Architecture*. London: Thames and Hudson, 1990.

— 'Piano Pieces.' *Architectural Review*, May 1985, pp59–64.

— and Sammartini, Tudi. 'Piano+Novo, Temporary Auditorium, Venice.' *Architectural Review*, December 1984, pp53–7.

Goetz, Joachim. 'Architektur mit Muskelspiel' in *Design Report*, January 1997, pp52–5.

Goldberger, Paul. *Renzo Piano and Building Workshop Buildings and Projects 1971–1989*. New York: Rizzoli, 1989.

Goldsmith, Nicholas. 'The Peripatetic Pavilion.' *Design Quarterly*, No 15, Summer 1992, pp30–2.

Grimshaw, Nicholas and Haryott, Richard. 'Solar-Powered Pavilion', Transcription of a lecture at the RIBA, London, 16 June 1992 by Nicholas Grimshaw and Richard Haryott. *RIBA Journal*, October 1992, p34,

Heidegger, Martin. *Poetry, Language, Thought*. English translation by Albert Hofstadter. New York: Harper, 1971.

'Houses and Aircraft Built with Air' in *Monthly Design*, January 1999, pp122–5.

'Hot Air' in *Metropolis*, December 1998, pp45–7.

Horden, Richard. *Light Tech: Towards a Light Tech*. Berlin: Birkhäuser Verlag, 1995.

Jackson, A. *The Politics of Architecture*. London: Architectural Press, 1970.

Jencks, Charles. *Architecture 2000; Predictions and Methods*. New York: Praeger, 1971.

— and Baird, George, eds. *Meaning in Architecture*. London: Cresset Press, 1969.

Jennings, Humphrey. *Pandaemonium*. Edited by Mary-Lou Jennings and Charles Madge. London Picador, 1987.

Jones, Wes. 'Stillness' in *Oz: Journal of the College of Architecture, Planning and Design*, Kansas State University, Kansas, Vol 23, 2001, pp46–51.

Kleine, Holger. 'Hanover Expo 2000', in *Architecture Today*, No 111, September 2000, pp12–33.

Krell, David, ed. *Martin Heidegger, Basic Writings*, London: Routledge, 1978 2nd ed. 1993.

Krueger, Ted. 'Intelligence and Autonomy' in *Oz: Journal of Architecture, Planning and Design*, Kansas State University, Kansas, Vol 23, 2001, pp22–7.

Kronenburg, Robert. 'Architectural Identity and the Portable Building'. *Oz: Journal of the School of Architecture and Design*, Kansas State University, Kansas, 1994, pp46–9.

— ed. Ephemeral/Portable Architecture, themed edition of *Architectural Design*, Sept/Oct 1998.

— *Houses in Motion: The Genesis, History and Development of the Portable Building*. London: Academy, 1995.

— *FTL: Softness, Movement and Light*, Academy Monograph No 41, London: Academy, 1997.

— 'Livingpool'. *BOX III*. Liverpool: John Moores University, 1993, pp104–9.

— 'Memory of the City'. *BOX III*. Liverpool: John Moores University, 1993, pp110–17.

— *Portable Architecture*, 2nd Edition, Oxford: Architectural Press, 2000.

— *Spirit of the Machine: Technology as an Inspiration in Architectural Design*. London: John Wiley & Sons, 2001.

— ed. *Transportable Environments*, London: E&FN Spon, 1998.

— and Hornsby, Joanna. *The Application of Portable and Demountable Building Systems, Part I: Survey of United Kingdom Manufacturers*. Liverpool: Liverpool John Moores University, 1994.

Langer, Susanne. *Feeling and Form*. New York: 1953.

Lyall, Sutherland. *Rock Sets*. London: Thames and Hudson, 1992.

Le Corbusier, *Vers une Architecture*. Paris: Vincent Fréal, 1923. English translation by Frederick Etchells. *Towards a New Architecture*. London: Rodker, 1927.

Maki and Associates, eds. *Fumihiko Maki: Buildings and Projects*, London: Thames and Hudson, 1997.

McCallum, Ian. *Architecture USA*. London: Architectural Press, 1959.

McCarter, Robert, ed. *Pamphlet Architecture No 12, Building; Machines*. New York: Princeton Architectural Press, 1987.

Melhuish, Clare. 'Go to Work on a Silvery Egg', in *Building Design*, 27 May 1997.

Moore, Rowan, ed. *Structure, Space and Skin: The Work of Nicholas Grimshaw and Partners*. London: Phaidon, 1993.

Murray, Callum. 'Visitors' Centre.' *The Architects' Journal*, 24 April 1991, p42.

Norberg-Schulz, Christian. *Existence Space and Architecture*, London: Allen and Unwin, 1971.

— *Genius Loci: Towards a Phenomenology of Architecture*. London: London, 1980.

Oosterhuis, Kas. 'Game, Set and Match' in *Oz: Journal of Architecture, Planning and Design*, Kansas State University, Kansas, Vol 23, 2001, pp10–15.

Otto, Frei. 'Das Hangende Dach.' Doctoral Thesis, Berlin University of Technology, 1954.

— and Stromeyer, Peter. 'Tents.' *AIA Journal*, February 1961, pp77–86.

Pawley, Martin. *Buckminster Fuller*. Design Heroes Series. London: Grafton, 1990.

— *Future Systems: The Story of Tomorrow*. London: Phaidon, 1993.

— *Theory and Design in the Second Machine Age*. Oxford: Blackwell, 1990.

Price, Cedric. *Cedric Price*. Architectural Association Works II, London: Architectural Association, 1984.

— 'Fun Palace.' *Link*, June–July 1965.

— 'Life-Conditioning.' *Architectural Design*, October 1966.

— 'On Safety Pins and Other Magnificent Designs.' *Pegasus*, Spring 1972.

Quarmby, Arthur. *The Plastics Architect*. London: The Pall Mall Press, 1974.

Relph, E. *Place and Placelessness*. London: Pion Ltd., 1976.

Rice, Peter. *An Engineer Imagines*. London: Artemis, 1994.

— *Exploring Materials: The Work of Peter Rice*. Exhibition Catalogue, RIBA London, 30 June to 25 August, 1992. London: RIBA Publications, 1992.

Richards, J.M. 'Expo '67.' *The Architectural Review*, No 846, August 1967, pp87–8.

— 'Expo '70.', *The Architectural Review*, No 882, August 1970, pp67–70.

— 'The Exhibition Buildings.' *The Architectural Review*, No 656, August 1951, pp123–32.

Rogers, Richard. *Architecture: A Modern View*. London: Thames and Hudson, 1990.

Slessor, Catherine. 'Seville and Expo.' *The Architectural Review*. June 1992, p2.

Singmaster, Deborah. 'Horden's Infinitely Flexible, Lightweight Ideas Frame.' *The Architects' Journal*, Vol 198, No 18, 10 November 1993, p15.

— 'Summer Themes Welcome Visitors to the Palace.' *The Architects' Journal*, 8 September, 1994, pp26–7.

Spence, Robin. 'Building Technology: Master or Servant?' *Scroope: Cambridge Architectural Journal*, Issue 6, 1994, pp19–20.

Stamp, Gavin. 'Exhibitionistic Architecture.' *The Architectural Review*, June 1992, p75.

Stephens, Stanton. *Charles and Ray Eames: Furniture, Architecture, Interior Design, Film, and Photography*. Leicester Polytechnic: PhD Thesis, 1991.

Stungo, Naomi. 'Not Just Puff.' *RIBA Journal*, November 1994, p30.

'Tent's Moment.' *The Architect's Journal*, Vol 193, No 7, 13 February 1991, p13.

van Zalingen, Marieke. 'Een opzienbarende doos van Glas, Staal en Beton.' *Eigenhuis and Interieur*, February 1995, pp38–44.

Vernes, Michel. 'Prouve: Architect-Mechanic'. Translated by Judith Landry. *The Architectural Review*, July 1983, pp39–42.

Visconti, Marco. 'Jean Prouvé: il Progetto della facciata.' *Domus*, June 1989, pp80–8.

Waddington, C.H. *The Man-Made Future*. London: Croom Helm, 1978, p173.

Walker, Derek. 'Eames House, Pacific Palisades, 1949, Charles and Ray Eames', pp76–77. In *Architectural Design Profile: Los Angeles*. London: Academy, 1981.

Welsh, John. 'Moving Image.' *Building Design*, 15 May, 1992.

Wilkinson, Chris. *Supersheds*. Oxford: Butterworth Architecture, 1991.

Winter, John. 'Ship to Shore.' *The Architects' Journal*, Vol 182, No 30, 24 July 1985, pp36–, 49.

Woods, Lebbeus. *Anarchitecture: Architecture as a Political Act*. Architectural Monograph No 22. London: Academy, 1992.

Worthington, John, ed. *Rethinking the Workplace*, London: Architectural Press, 1997.

Yamamoto, Riken. 'Takashima-cho Gate Area.' *Japan Architect*, No 388, August 1989, pp64–7.

Zuk, William and Clark, Roger H. *Kinetic Architecture*. New York: Van Nostrand Reinhold, 1970.

Index